Wounded Prophet

Wounded Prophet

A Portrait of
Henri J. M. Nouwen

MICHAEL FORD

DARTON·LONGMAN + TODD

First published in 1999 by
Darton, Longman and Todd Ltd
1 Spencer Court
140–142 Wandsworth High Street
London SW18 4JJ

ISBN 0–232–52274–X

A catalogue record for this book is available from the British Library.

Designed by Sandie Boccacci
Phototypeset in 10½/14pt Raleigh by Intype London Ltd
Printed and bound in Great Britain by Page Bros, Norwich, Norfolk

'Often we praise prophets after they are dead. Are we willing to be prophets while we are alive?'

(Henri J. M. Nouwen, August 1996,
three weeks before his death)

For my mother, Margaret, my brother, Nigel, and to the memory of my father, Kenneth Ford

Contents

III Body

Acknowledgements

THIS BOOK would not have been possible without the insights and observations of many friends and colleagues of Henri Nouwen whose recollections helped me paint the portrait. I should like to thank them, not only for the candid way in which they shared their memories, but for the generous hospitality they showed as I made my journey across the world in the tracks of the great spiritual writer. I am particularly grateful to all members of Henri's family, especially to Laurent Nouwen, and to Henri's other family in Canada, the L'Arche Community at Daybreak, Richmond Hill, Ontario, among them Sister Sue Mosteller CSJ, Kathy Christie and Carl MacMillan. Sharing meals, liturgies and leisure time with core members, both at Daybreak and at Trosly in France, was a particular joy.

My thanks go also to Martha Smalley and Joan Duffy at the Yale Divinity School archives for their help with research; to Robert Durback for his correspondence about Henri's writings over several years; to those who attended the Henri Nouwen Conference in the spectacular setting of Ghost Ranch, New Mexico, in October 1997; and to Father John Dear SJ, the Reverend Ainsley Griffiths, Dr Valerie Lesniak and Dr David Torevell for their support.

The BBC granted me an extended period of leave, so I should like to express gratitude to Ernest Rea, head of religious broadcasting, and to David Coomes, executive producer of religious factual programmes, for making that possible. Sylvia Reeves, research librarian at BBC North, efficiently helped me check references. I have also appreciated a number of enjoyable conversations about Henri with Janis Knox and Sophie Rolfe.

Morag Reeve at Darton, Longman and Todd has been an excellent editor whose perceptive analysis of the text and personal encouragement have always been welcome. My appreciation in the publishing field is extended to Helen Porter, Pauline Shelton, Nicola Smith and Allison Ward.

I should also like to acknowledge the friendship of Father John Squire and Sister Teresa Malone SHCJ whose wisdom and guidance over the years have enabled me to connect more fruitfully with the spirituality of Henri J. M. Nouwen.

List of Illustrations

Henri Nouwen's Life – A Summary

1932   Born in Nijkerk, Holland (24 January).

1957   Ordained to the Roman Catholic priesthood in the archdio-
            cese of Utrecht, Holland.

1957–64   Student in psychology at the Catholic University of
            Nijmegen, Holland.

1964–66   Fellow in the programme for religion and psychiatry at the
            Menninger Foundation, Topeka, Kansas, USA.

1966–68   Visiting professor in the psychology department, University
            of Notre Dame, Indiana, USA.

1968–70   Staff member of the Pastoral Institute, Amsterdam,
            Holland, and faculty member of the Catholic Theological
            Institute, Utrecht, Holland.

1970–71   Theological studies, University of Nijmegen, Holland.

1971–77   Associate professor of pastoral theology, Yale Divinity
            School, New Haven, Connecticut, USA:
            1974 Received tenure;
            1974 Six-month stay, Abbey of the Genesee, Piffard,
            upstate New York;
            1976 Fellow at the Ecumenical Institute, Collegeville, Min-
            nesota.

1977–81   Professor of pastoral theology, Yale Divinity School, New
            Haven, Connecticut, USA:

        1978 Scholar-in-residence, North American College, Rome;
        1979 Six-month stay at the Abbey of the Genesee.

1981–82 Family brother, Abbey of the Genesee;
         Six-month stay in Bolivia and Peru.

1983–85 Professor and lecturer, Harvard Divinity School, Cambridge,
         Massachusetts, USA.

1985–86 Nine-month stay, L'Arche, Trosly-Breuil, France.

1986–96 Pastor, L'Arche Daybreak, Richmond Hill, Ontario, Canada.

1996   Died in Hilversum, Holland aged 64 (21 September).

Prologue

THE WRITINGS of Henri J. M. Nouwen, like the paintings of fellow Dutchman Vincent van Gogh, emerged from an intense vision which captured the imagination of people the world over. Much of his genius was shaped by an ongoing loneliness and anguish which also afflicted van Gogh whose paintings he greatly admired. Constantly fearing solitude and rejection, especially by those they loved, both men sank at times into deep depression yet, at their lowest ebb, managed to create some of their most inspiring and memorable work.

Strangely, perhaps, Nouwen never wrote a book about van Gogh, but he did write a foreword to one called *Van Gogh and God* which considered the painter's art to have been of deep theological and spiritual significance. Here, Nouwen talked about the impact which van Gogh's pictures, and the published letters to his brother Theo, had made on his own life:

> I experienced connections between Vincent's struggle and my own, and realized more and more that Vincent was becoming my wounded healer. He painted what I had not before dared to look at; he questioned what I had not before dared to speak about; and he entered into the spaces of my heart that I had not dared to come close to. By so doing he brought me in touch with many of my fears and gave me the courage to go further and deeper in my search for a God who loves.[1]

Wherever Nouwen settled, the spirit of van Gogh rested too. While on the faculty of Yale Divinity School, he taught seminars entitled 'The Ministry of Vincent van Gogh', which, he concluded, had made a more profound impression on his students than any of his other courses:

> I still remember how we would spend long hours together in silence, simply gazing at the slides of Vincent's work. I did not try to explain much or analyze much. I simply wanted the students to have a direct experience of the ecstasy and the agony of this painter who shared his desperate search for meaning . . . A similar effect resulted from the readings of Vincent's letters. Their haunting, passionate expression of longing for a God who is tangible and alive, who truly comforts and consoles, and who truly cares for the poor and the suffering brought us in touch with the deepest yearnings of our soul. Vincent's God, so real, so direct, so visible in nature and people, so intensely compassionate, so weak and vulnerable, and so radically loving, was a God we all wanted to come close to.[2]

Within van Gogh, then, Nouwen engaged with something of his own mystery and with the divine mystery too. Both artists loved sunflowers – strong and radiant images of joy and hope after their own experiences of sorrow and despair. Just as they had been surrounded by them in life, so too were they in death. Today wooden sunflowers stand on Nouwen's grave in an isolated Canadian cemetery near Richmond Hill, Ontario, 15 miles or so from the community for the mentally and physically disabled – L'Arche Daybreak – which he transformed while serving as pastor there for the last ten years of his life, often using images of art as illustrations in his preaching and teaching. Visual arts enabled Nouwen to get in touch with the transcendent: paintings were like windows on to heaven, glimpses of the beyond. Van Gogh, like an iconographer, painted in such a way that Nouwen was put in touch with more than what he could see, a presence which was uplifting and beyond words. In his office, Nouwen had three of van Gogh's paintings mounted in a frame: vases of sunflowers on either side of the artist's self-portrait. He would point to a bloom and remark: 'If you look at every flower individually, they look quite miserable. Put them together in a vase and they become a bouquet and that's quite attractive. I think about our community often in that way.'[3]

When Henri Nouwen died in Holland of a heart attack on 21 September 1996, the Christian Church lost one of its most dynamic and compassionate priests, and the world of contemporary spirituality mourned one of its most prolific and influential commentators. Nouwen reached an unparalleled cross-section of people and gathered around him an international network of friends. Whether they had met him, worked with him or simply absorbed his words in print, each one thought they knew him personally, whether they were Eastern Orthodox monks, evangelical Protestants, radical Catholics or secular Jews. His books were read in a variety of locations: one edition, which had been translated into Croatian, was plucked from the debris of a desecrated presbytery in Bosnia; another found its way to the White House and into the hands of an avid new fan, Hillary Rodham Clinton – indeed, at the time of Nouwen's death, the First Lady's office was in the process of arranging for her to meet Nouwen, though he was always concerned about the political inferences which might be read into such encounters. He had friends in high places, including senators, but he rarely talked about them.

He himself came from a background of wealth and privilege, the son of a loving warm-hearted mother and a more distant, success-driven father. He became a priest in his twenties, and left his native Holland to train as a clinical psychologist in America, an experience which, though lonely and bewildering at times, gave the young Dutchman with limited English invaluable insights into the workings of the human mind, and a linguistic framework through which to interpret them. In his writings, he was able to integrate this knowledge with his own spiritual tradition in the Roman Catholic Church. As his lecture notes were gradually turned into books, he realised that he was around at the right time with the right words, speaking directly to people's deepest needs in a style which was accessible and unjudgemental and with a message that was profoundly hopeful in a culture more attracted to therapy than religion. His words spoke with a specific sensitivity to people who had suffered psychologically in their lives. He discovered that it was from the wounded places in himself that he could reach the wounded places in others.

But it was as a teacher and preacher, too, that he made his name – sometimes on three different continents in one week. No matter how tired he was, every lecture incorporated every limb of his body. Nouwen wouldn't dream of perching himself on a podium, shielded by a lectern and carefully prepared notes: he moved around the auditorium like a circus performer, with penetrating eyes, electrifying expressions and contorted postures, waving his giant hands and flowing arms, his fingers outstretched to choreograph a point. A natural actor, he knew the art of perfect timing, and audiences would go home inspired and enthralled not only by what they had heard but by what they had seen as well: an audience of Henri Nouwen's engaged with the life of the spirit through a performance of the body.

There were, however, times when, after entertaining people in their thousands, the much-loved spiritual mentor would go back alone to his hotel room and become the sad clown. And fans who had booked the world-famous writer for their special night had no hint of the private despair into which he could suddenly dive, especially if nobody had thought of inviting him for a meal or a drink afterwards. For the preacher who loved to be the focus of everyone's attention found life out of the spotlight hard to embrace. The man who could hold a multitude for hours desperately needed to be held himself. Oblivious of international time zones, he sometimes phoned friends around the world at all hours of the night to share the desolation he felt and, more especially, to talk through his need for special friendships and intimacy which the celibate priesthood would not allow and which seminary training in pre-Vatican II days had done its utmost to exorcise. Exasperated by the absence of close companionship – and even what seemed like the absence of God at times – he knew sleeplessness in the terrors of the night. Frantic phone calls – either to receive counsel or offer it himself – were a lifeline to him.

In his fifties, Nouwen took the surprising and courageous step of leaving academia to become a pastor for people with developmental disabilities; he was at the height of his fame as a spiritual guide – but still as lonely as ever. In the context of a community which knew nothing of his prestige, he discovered more and more of his own handicaps, but at the same time experienced a security he had not known anywhere else. But during his first year at the L'Arche community in Toronto, a close friendship broke up and triggered a complete emotional breakdown. Nouwen later left to undergo therapy which included hours of being physically held. The treatment eventually brought him to a place of healing within himself, and at the same time opened up many dimensions of his being which he would never seal off again. Through all this brooding time, he never lost the capacity to write. He returned to the community and the friendship was restored, but he continued to want more from it than he could possibly hope to receive. He made no secret of his infatuation in some of his writings, but friends and editors toned down the original texts because they felt that he was describing his needs and longings too explicitly. As one of them put it: 'Henri liked the idea that what was most personal was most universal. We had to remind him that what was most personal was sometimes best kept private.'

While this advice was given with the best intentions, it sometimes produced books which failed to tell the whole story and left readers to draw their own conclusions. Many accurately deduced that Nouwen was a priest who was also gay. It is impossible to begin to understand the complexity and anguish of the man without considering this aspect of his life. It was something he was aware of from a very early age, but which he only started coming to terms with in his last years.

It is also difficult to explain the author without acknowledging a certain disconnection between his writing and his living, not because of any scandalous gap between the two, but because he always managed to write way beyond what he himself could actually live. This was especially true in terms of what he said about solitude and community. Nouwen's spirit, mind and body all ran ahead of him; his books were often reminders to himself of how he ought to be. As Carolyn Whitney-Brown, a former member of the L'Arche Daybreak community, explained:

> When I think of Henri, I think of two 'books': one is the book that Henri wrote 40 times, yet couldn't quite live; the other is the book that Henri lived for almost 65 years, yet couldn't quite write. The second book waits to be written, as the meaning of Henri's life and wisdom reveal themselves now, after his death.[4]

Encounter

I WELL REMEMBER my very first Henri Nouwen paperback, given to me by a friend. The book was called *Reaching Out*. It was well thumbed, with waves of pencil underlining significant sentences and occasional scribblings in the margins. Initially I was not so much entranced by the words or the comments as by the cover photograph of a sunlit forest: it was a meditation just to stare at the trees and the hopeful horizon beyond.

The preface was written by an English Catholic priest, Father Michael Hollings, who likened Nouwen's spirituality to the work of Michelangelo, 'a good example of the combination of feelings, desires, tensions and joys which go on in a man'.[1] Although his contemporaries had almost made him a god, Michelangelo was all the time aware of the struggle within his own nature, a wrestling which seemed to Hollings necessary for the development of the artist's character and work. His creative genius illustrated Nouwen's insight that 'the spiritual life is a reaching out to our innermost self, to our fellow human beings and to our God'.[2] So right from the beginning I saw Nouwen as a highly sensitive artist, helping people become attuned to their spiritual lives through the graces of their own difficulties. For me, trying to integrate my own spiritual life with my career as a newspaper reporter, Nouwen also seemed to have all the curiosity of mind, tenderness of heart and clarity of style to be called a spiritual journalist. The book and its author became faithful companions.

When, a few years later, I temporarily left full-time journalism to study theology, I had the opportunity to take options which seemed to have a distinctly Nouwenesque ring: Christian mystical writings (such as those by St Teresa of Avila and St John of the Cross), the work of Thomas Merton and the history of medieval religious art. As Nouwen too had been shaped by these influences (among others), and had become a prolific author, I felt compelled to buy his books.

By then I was working for the BBC and, every time I went away on an assignment, Nouwen would come too in the form of a paperback tucked in between the socks, shirts and sound equipment in the over-night bag. Here was someone I could journey with, the spiritual guide to whom I felt closest when the institutional Church in particular seemed at its most unspiritual. One day in 1992, I learned that Nouwen was in Britain speaking at the Greenbelt Arts Festival. His book, *The Return of the Prodigal Son*, a meditation on the seventeenth-century painting by Rembrandt, had just been published. I decided to approach him about the possibility of recording an interview for *Seeds of Faith*, a late-night Sunday slot on BBC Radio 4. I didn't know for certain whether Nouwen, with his strong Dutch accent, would be easy to understand or even whether he would merit a half-hour broadcast: he was much more famous in the United States than he was in Britain. In any event, it was a chance to meet Nouwen at last, so I went ahead. I tracked him down to a retreat centre in Surrey, and left a message on the answering machine there, waiting for a call back from one of his PR people. Within the hour, the phone rang. It was the man himself, pronouncing his name as 'Henry Now-un', and telling me how pleased he would be 'to connect'. In personal terms at least, it was a scoop.

A week later, I found myself driving to Northampton to meet him face to face. For an encounter with someone who had written so extensively about restlessness, the date could not have been more appropriate: 28 August, feast day of St Augustine of Hippo who had prayed, 'Thou madest me for thyself and my heart is restless until it repose in thee'. I was punctual but what I didn't realise then was that Nouwen expected people to turn up at least a quarter of an hour before their appointments. As I walked into the hotel with my tape recorder, I noticed a tall, gaunt figure with a flat cap, plaid scarf and bright red shoulder-bag standing by the reception desk – about to leave. A large, firm hand reached out to greet me, the same expressive hand which was to give the microphone a clout or two during the interview. The conversation covered many areas of the priest's life and was the only interview Nouwen ever gave to the BBC. (For the broadcast 11 months later, the interview was interspersed with the jazz violin playing of Yehudi Menuhin and Stéphane Grappelli to symbolise Nouwen's restless soul.)[3]

After the recording, Nouwen invited me to Greenbelt to hear him lecture, so I drove him and his assistant, film-maker Bart Gavigan, to the camp site. But in the car on the way over, I noticed Nouwen's change of mood. After our lively discussion at the hotel, he sat pensively beside me saying little. The passion and energy had evaporated, and he seemed preoccupied, possibly thinking about the talk he was to give.

Once inside the hospitality tent, Nouwen began to take great interest in the other speakers who were arriving. Catching sight of a grey-haired figure in a purple shirt, he blurted: 'Who's he?' Informed that it was one of the senior bishops in the Church of England, Nouwen abruptly left his seat and darted over to introduce himself. But he returned to his seat crestfallen: 'He wouldn't come and join us', he lamented. Then he spotted somebody else who looked intriguing: 'Who's that?' And he vanished. But he was back before lunch, joining hands with those around the table. As I had to wait a little longer for my meal than the others, he insisted on breaking off a piece of his Red Leicester cheese so I didn't get hungry. After lunch, he charged to the back of the tent to thank the kitchen staff, brushing off gentle pleas from Bart Gavigan to move towards the Odyssey Tent where he was due to give the first of three talks. Although he clearly had a mind of his own, he soon returned, saying nervously, 'Now what am I going to talk to them about?' Reassured, he made his way to the tent for his opening lecture, 'Being the Beloved of God', a central theme in all his preaching and writing. I sat on the grass and watched him in action for the first time, his animated hands and elastic body preaching the Good News to over 100 young people whom he excited with his words but could quieten to silent prayer with equal command.

After the seminar, he came up and quietly thanked me for staying. He told me to keep in touch and we did over the next couple of years, writing occasionally and sending books. But, more than anything else, it was his presence that day which remained with me. I remember my shock and sorrow one Friday morning at the BBC when I caught sight of a front-page headline in an Anglican religious newspaper – 'Nouwen dies at 64'. It felt like the death of a close friend, even though I hardly knew him. 'Henri Nouwen's dead', I exclaimed to colleagues as they walked into the office – but one by one they replied, 'Who?'

Who indeed was Henri Nouwen? He was not a name on everyone's lips in Britain, even in the religious world, whereas in America his death was announced on National Public Radio and the *National Catholic Reporter* published pages of memories, many of which were relayed to the Internet which became a global mourning ground. As I surfed the Nouwen net, it was apparent just how many people he had touched, directly or indirectly. The best-selling author seemed to have a following second to none. The tributes revealed a world of friendships and concerns. I recollect especially the words of a nun who shared her memory of praying with Nouwen prostrate on the floor: 'I heard the intensity in his voice as he begged God to protect the people he knew in South America. I opened my eyes and saw his massive hands tensed with the depths of his words, dug deeply into the carpet', she wrote. I also liked the story of an artist, about to be ordained, who had been given by a friend one of Nouwen's books. He took the present with him on a private retreat and was struck by one particular sentence. He decided to walk through woods near the retreat house and look for a stone on which to paint the phrase which meant so much. As he walked about, looking pensively at the ground, another man on retreat passed by and asked if he had lost anything. The artist explained about the book and the words which had spoken to him. Smiling, the stranger replied, 'Well, I'm Henri Nouwen. Let's look together.'

Such stories set me thinking about the person behind the books, the tapes and the videos. A year after his death, I took a sabbatical and set off on several trips to Europe and North America to meet over 100 people who had known him. I was surprised to discover many conflicting perspectives on him, pointing to a paradoxical and somewhat mysterious figure, much loved but never completely fathomed. My travels began in the music room of an Anglican theologian's Oxford home and ended in the kitchen of a Catholic Worker house in Liverpool. In between, there was a variety of locations, from New York to New

Mexico, Berlin to Boston, Toronto to Trosly in France, all of which had a connection with Henri Nouwen. But the places were less significant than the people who had known him and were prepared to talk frankly about him. Their recollections form the brush-strokes of this portrait – there are dashes of colour too from Nouwen himself in the form of articles from his archives at Yale, extracts from his books and the BBC interview.

This is not intended to be a full-scale biography, an assessment of his literary output or a systematic theology of his thinking but an exploration of the person of Henri Nouwen as a wounded prophet for our time. Henri tended to write his books in three sections. This one follows a similar pattern. The first section, 'Heart', outlines some of the important themes of his life. It explores his inner and outer worlds, examining his character, the main roles he played and the difficulties he faced. It is presented as a kaleidoscopic introduction to the many and varied strands of Nouwen's life and personality. It does not follow any chronological sequence.

In the subsequent sections, the sequence of Nouwen's story unfolds in a more explicitly chronological format. Part II, 'Mind', follows Nouwen from his early days in Holland, through his psychological and theological development as a student, teacher and professor, up until the time he left the academic world to join L'Arche. Part III, 'Body', covers the last and perhaps most significant decade of his life, through periods of doubt and anguish, resurrection and joy, to a deeper understanding of himself, of God and of how, in his words, the body could tell a spiritual story. The Epilogue offers some conclusions and reflections.

I
HEART

1. Mystical Path

HENRI NOUWEN was a priest whose identity was rooted in what he always referred to as 'God's first love'. Praying before the Blessed Sacrament every day, sometimes lying prostrate, he believed in theology's original meaning – union with God in prayer – and nothing would keep him from this encounter. Even if he had been awake all night, as he often was, compulsively telephoning friends around the world, offering as well as receiving support, he would still get up at 6 a.m. to say the divine office. When staying with his family in Holland, his brother would hear him pacing around the attic bedroom at dawn, following the Liturgy of the Hours before going off to Mass in a local church. But wherever his reveille with the Lord, it was rarely without its own chaotic chorus.

His primary need for prayer meant he was completely oblivious to more mundane things. He would dash to the bathroom wherever he was staying and shower without closing the curtain, soaking the whole place in water. Then, without looking in the mirror, he would shave as quickly as possible so he could get downstairs and be with God. As a result, he often ended up with a one-inch patch of old whiskers on his neck and fresh soap in his ear.

Nouwen was, in fact, a sensuous man whose massive hands, alive with nerve endings, were drawn to the smooth contours of aromatic soap as intensely as they were to the shiny grey rosary beads which he always carried around in his pocket. During prayer he could become transfixed by the size and weight of the stones as well as by the distinctive sounds they made. In his room, often aglow with candles and icons, he would rub the beads over the surface of his hands as if they were Braille and, with the same sensory touch when celebrating Mass, he would sometimes lift the glass chalice with one hand and caress its curvature with the other. Although rarely seen in his Roman collar, he loved to wear long, coarsely woven stoles, made of soft pastel fabrics. As he walked around, the big, weighty tassels hit his legs and back reminding him of his responsibility to the priesthood into which he had been ordained in Utrecht Cathedral in 1957 and to whose archdiocese he was ultimately answerable.

Contemplation was at the heart of everything for Henri Nouwen. It was a discipline of dwelling in the presence of God. Through fidelity in prayer, he could awaken himself to the God within him and let God enter into his heartbeat and his breathing, into his thoughts and emotions, into his hearing, seeing, touching and tasting. Nouwen was convinced that Christian leaders need to reclaim the mystical so that every word they speak, each suggestion they make and every strategy they develop, will emerge from a heart which knows God intimately. He wrote:

> I have the impression that many of the debates within the Church around such issues as the papacy, the ordination of women, the marriage of priests, homosexuality, birth control, abortion and euthanasia take place on a primarily moral level. On that level, different parties battle about right or wrong. But that battle is often removed from the experience of God's first love which lies at the base of all human relationships. Words like right-wing, reactionary, conservative, liberal, and left-wing are used to describe people's opinions, and many discussions then seem more like political battles for power than spiritual searches for the truth.[1]

Through acts of devotion and adoration Christian ministers had to learn to keep listening to the divine voice of love and find within it the wisdom and courage to address contemporary issues. Only then would it be possible for them to remain flexible without being relativistic, convinced without being rigid, willing to confront without being offensive, gentle and forgiving without being soft, true witnesses without being manipulators.

Such thinking underpinned the whole of Nouwen's theology and was never more evident than in his relationships with other people, especially in a sacramental context. Every Mass at the L'Arche Daybreak community in Toronto, where he spent the last ten years of his life, was an artistic event. He would involve children and adults, handicapped and able-bodied, asking them to act out what he was saying. No one was excluded and it had to be alive. 'There was a kind of living artistic sensibility in Henri's way of being, in his way of structuring worship and in his way of celebrating', said his friend, Carolyn Whitney-Brown, herself an artist. 'L'Arche celebrates diversity and eccentricity, and that was one of Henri's fundamental beauties: his absolute delight in eccentricity, peculiarities and the uniqueness of people. He had very good eyes to see that, and for me that was a profoundly artistic sensibility.'

But for Nouwen the practice of prayer was never easy. While many readers might imagine their favourite author to be a serene guru-figure, praying in a contemplative posture, they could not be more mistaken: he could rarely sit still for long. When he was in prayer, he fidgeted, coughed and moved but seemed to have no awareness he was doing it. His apparently restless and distracted prayer nurtured him. While his body was twitching, his spirit could be deeply present to God.

It was all the more surprising, then, that a man of such distracted temperament should have decided to accept an invitation to join the still world of the Quakers. The writer Parker Palmer has never forgotten the first time Nouwen turned up at a retreat centre where the traditional gathering in silence was practised for 45 minutes every morning:

> I was conscious of being in the company of a world-class contemplative and I was expecting to have an extraordinary experience sitting next to him during worship. But as we sat in this plain, unadorned room and settled into the silence, I realised that the bench was jiggling. I opened my eyes, glanced to my left and saw Henri's leg working furiously. He was anxiously trying to settle but without much success. As time went on, the fidgeting got worse. I opened my eyes again only to find him checking his watch to see what time it was.

This incident introduced Parker Palmer to a person of paradox who indeed had a profoundly contemplative heart but who needed to be constantly on the move, a man filled with immense energies which were difficult to harness. But did such tensions collaborate to form a certain kind of genius? As a spiritual author himself, Palmer believes that Nouwen's books were deeply engrossing and engaging precisely because they came out of this ongoing wrestling match between the paradoxes in his own life. He practised what he preached – and he preached the struggles, sometimes the anguish, sometimes the joy, which he himself was living.

Wherever he was in the world, Nouwen celebrated Mass every day, in churches, chapels or hotel suites. If he was staying with friends, he would ask them to join him for a celebration around the dining-room table, usually at 5 p.m. He welcomed anyone, Catholic and non-Catholic alike, to receive the sacrament. He was sufficiently secure in his belief that the Eucharist was a gift to humanity to be able to sit loosely to the official Roman position that only Catholics in full communion with the Church should be allowed to receive. Nouwen was even prepared to give the sacrament to non-baptised members of his own family – although, if they received regularly from him, he would suggest that they might like to think about joining the Church officially; but he would never insist.

In the setting of L'Arche, where community members came from many traditions, Henri Nouwen was sensitive to the difficulties surrounding intercommunion. But in the context of small community gatherings, he was pastorally concerned for non-Catholics, who always found him welcoming if they wished to receive Holy Communion: people and their relationship with God mattered much more than strict adherence to ecclesiastical law. What was harder for him was getting to Mass on time. The congregation at Daybreak grew accustomed to their pastor rushing in at the eleventh hour – the art of genuflecting on the run became a liturgical gesture in itself – yet the impact of his eucharistic services was always profound and was remembered long afterwards.

His Masses were never divorced from the immediate needs and concerns of the particular community he was serving and were celebrated with reverence, passion and joy. For Father Nouwen the

Eucharist, or thanksgiving, came from above. It was freely offered and therefore could be freely received. A eucharistic life was one lived with gratitude, and the celebration itself prompted 'a crying out to God for mercy, to listen to the words of Jesus, to invite him into our home, to enter into communion with him and proclaim good news to the world; it opens the possibility of gradually letting go of our many resentments and choosing to be grateful'.[2]

At the Protestant-founded Yale Divinity School in the 1970s and early 1980s, the Catholic professor's daily Masses were packed every evening, seminarians squeezing into the octagonal basement chapel where the grey stone walls, wicker chairs and icons gave a sense of prayer and intimacy. Michael Christensen, now assistant professor of spirituality at Drew University, New Jersey, was one of the many who attended. This evangelical student soon found himself entering a bewildering new liturgical world with Father Nouwen as a mentor:

> Every day I would go to his Mass with the Catholics and the Protestants in that cave-of-the-heart room. On Monday nights I would join the group in his house where we talked and chanted psalms, and I took one of his courses on contemplative spirituality every semester. When I graduated, Henri advised me to take a retreat in a Trappist monastery, so I went for 30 days as a monastic associate. I emerged from that month-long experience of spiritual direction with new and profound insights into my vocation. From that day, I have gone on a retreat once a year.

But whatever their religious backgrounds, Nouwen sensed that there was always a danger of Christian leaders becoming tempted by individual heroism and forgetting that ministry should always be a communal and mutual experience. Just as ministers should be steeped in contemplative prayer, so he believed they should always be willing to confess their own brokenness and ask for forgiveness from those to whom they ministered. He believed that the sacrament of confession should be a real encounter 'in which the reconciling and healing presence of Jesus can be experienced'.[3]

Nouwen himself regularly made and heard confessions. Once, when staying at his father's house in Holland, Henri decided to go to a neighbouring village to make his confession to a priest who had

(Nouwen believed) a particular gift as a confessor. When he came out Nouwen expressed not only relief and joy, but also distress because he had apparently been the first priest in seven years to go to that man for confession. Here was somebody with a rare charism for helping people experience the mercy of God, and no one wanted it.

As a confessor himself, Nouwen had a special gift. Brother Christian, of the Abbey of the Genesee in upstate New York, whom Nouwen got to know during his stays there, has vivid memories of making his confession to Father Nouwen on Holy Saturday 1979:

> I'll never forget it. His voice was low and he embraced my feelings. I walked out of there as if it was really something. It lasted 45 minutes and it wasn't easy, but it was one of the greatest times that I ever made use of the sacrament of penance. He didn't do a lot of talking but it was a beautiful experience because he had the ability to put you at rest.

But what was so special about Nouwen's approach to spirituality, and how presumptuous is it to call him a mystic? Nouwen clearly had a great gift for articulating what was in his heart, and felt that it would profit his fellow Christians if he shared his insights, much in the way that Julian of Norwich felt compelled to share her mystical experiences so as to edify and give pleasure to her fellow Christians. Henri was perhaps a mystic in the making. But in his monastic experiences at the Abbey of the Genesee he embraced the mystical dimension, and spirituality became his theology and psychology.

Nouwen saw the human heart as the centre of being, a sacred space within all people 'where God dwells and where we are invited to dwell with God'.[4] As the mind descended into the heart, through contemplative meditation (for example, by using the Jesus Prayer), so a person's core identity could progressively conform to the image of Christ. Through spiritual practice, that person could enter into the heart of God. For Nouwen, the heart was that place where humanity and divinity touched, the intersection of heaven and earth, where the finite heart of humanity was mystically unified with the infinite heart of God. Henri Nouwen tried to look at people and the world with the eyes of God, speaking and writing from the place of divine–human encounter. He called it speaking 'from eternity into time'.[5] But to stay close to God meant being near to the person of Jesus, to whom he was utterly devoted and whose spirit he saw most strikingly at work in the poor, the disadvantaged and the marginalised. Real theological thinking was thinking with the mind of Christ, not engaging in what he termed pseudo-psychology, pseudo-sociology and pseudo-social work. Psychology, sociology and much theology, he argued, asked questions 'from below', shedding light only in one realm of reality. Real theology was *theo-logia*, the personal and prayerful study of God, which could access answers 'from above', of the higher, deeper eternal realm. These positions were not literal, but were symbols of divine and human sources of wisdom and understanding.

When Nouwen was in Rome, experiencing many complicated issues as a priest, he sought advice from Mother Teresa of Calcutta who was also visiting the city. After he had shared his anxieties with her for ten minutes, Mother Teresa said simply but profoundly, 'Well, when you spend one hour a day adoring your Lord, and never do anything which you know is wrong . . . you will be fine!'[6] Nouwen later explained that Mother Teresa had 'punctured my big balloon of complex self-complaints and pointed me far beyond myself to the place of real healing'.[7] He had raised a question 'from below' and she had given him an answer 'from above'. At first, the response had not seemed to fit his question, but then he had begun to see that her answer had come from 'God's place and not from the place of my complaints'.[8] This convinced Nouwen that most of the time people responded to questions from below with answers from below. The result was more questions and more answers, and often more confusion.

He liked to meditate on the words of Mother Teresa, as he did on the writings of Thérèse of Lisieux and Charles de Foucauld. But Nouwen's chief theological source was always the Bible, and in particular the Gospel of St John where he found the most intimate connections with his own prayer life. Among his other influences were John Henry Newman whose sermons preached at St Mary's, Oxford, before Newman's conversion to Roman Catholicism, had impressed Nouwen as a seminarian. Newman's *Apologia pro vita sua* and his *Idea of a University* also made their mark, as did *A Grammar of Assent* in which Newman defended theology. While theology could be regarded as a mere intellectual exercise, separate from the life of faith, its formulas nevertheless clarified for worshippers the object of their imaginations and affections – God. But while theology dealt in intellectual truths, the practice of faith embraced, with the imagination and the heart, the living truths about the nature of God. Nouwen said it was this distinction between personal experience and intellectual abstraction (between 'real' and 'notional' assent to God's truths) which had set him on the mystical path and underlain much of his spiritual theology.[9]

The writings of Thomas Merton and his skilful harnessing of concrete issues of the day with the spiritual life were also significant, especially the books *Seeds of Contemplation, Conjectures of a Guilty Bystander, The Sign of Jonas* and *Zen and the Birds of Appetite*. For Merton the contemplative life had been one of constant movement from opaqueness to transparency, and for Nouwen too it was a life with a vision – just as ministry was a life in which that vision was revealed to others. The great mystery was not that people saw God in the world but that God, within each person, recognised God in the world. Ultimately it was about divine self-recognition. Vincent van Gogh's letters to his brother, Theo, increasingly affected Nouwen's deeper emotional life:

> Although Vincent van Gogh is certainly not a religious writer in the traditional sense of the word, for me he was a man whose spirit touched my spirit very deeply, and who brought me in touch with some aspects of the spiritual life that no formal spiritual writer ever did.[10]

Another influence on Nouwen's spirituality was the Hesychastic tradition of the Eastern Orthodox Church – the writings of the Desert Fathers, the early monks of Mount Sinai, the tenth-century monks on Mount Athos and the brothers who wrote in nineteenth-century Russia. For him, the *Philokalia* and *The Art of Prayer* were its most important expressions. Nouwen said that he had probably learned more about the spiritual life from that tradition than from any Western spiritual writers. He was particularly struck by the writings of one Desert Father, Evagrius Ponticus, who saw the contemplative life as one which began to see the world as transparent, pointing beyond itself to its true nature. The contemplative was someone who saw things for what they

really were, who saw the real connections, who knew, as Merton used
to say, 'what the scoop' is.[11]

Henri Nouwen felt a natural affinity for Russian Orthodox spirituality
and culture. He always remembered a conversation with an Orthodox
priest who had said to him that Western Christianity's problem was
that its theology was not done on the knees. He naturally identified,
then, with the Orthodox insight that the true theologian was the person
who prayed – and the person who really prayed was the theologian.
However, the strong influence of Eastern Christian spirituality on his
own life really did not really strike home until 1993 when he visited
Ukraine, a country in which he took a keen interest and for whose
suffering people he felt deep compassion. One morning there it dawned
on him just how much his love of prayer, the liturgical life and sacred
art, especially icons, had been nurtured by the Christian East. The trip
became a pilgrimage to the source of his spiritual life. He realised why
the famous book about the Jesus Prayer, *The Way of the Pilgrim*, had
had such a deep effect on him: it recounted the story of a peasant who
walked through the country visiting holy places in Ukraine saying
nothing but 'Lord Jesus Christ, have mercy on me'. The prayer gradually
moved from his lips to his heart until it had become one with his
breathing. Wherever the peasant went, he radiated love and goodness
and saw how people's lives changed through meeting him. Nouwen
admitted that his own prayer life had many highs and lows, but
somehow the Jesus Prayer had never abandoned him even during his
driest periods. It had kept him connected with Jesus, especially during
times when little else seemed to.[12]

Although he worshipped in the West and was nurtured daily by the
Eucharist of the Latin rite, he had occasional contact with the liturgy
of St John Chrysostom which had given him a deep understanding of
being in the world without being of it, a sense of being in heaven before
leaving earth. There too he had discovered icons, not as illustrations,
decorations or ornaments, but as windows on the eternal. At first they
had seemed forbidding but as he had started to pray before them
they gradually revealed their secrets and drew him away from his daily
preoccupations and, as he discerned it, into the kingdom of God.

One of Nouwen's Orthodox friends, John Garvey, a priest in New
York, was a convert from Catholicism. He explained that, after

Vatican II, Nouwen was disturbed and discouraged by the move away from the transcendent – the sudden decline of interest in the Church, and the politicisation of Christianity in the form of a struggle between the forces of the left and the right. Part of Nouwen's attraction to Orthodoxy, he suggested, was the idea of an alternative approach to Christianity in which one could have a deep sense of freedom and at the same time a deep sense of fidelity to tradition:

> Both of these things appealed to him greatly and he understood that they did not need to be contradictory. He found something of that in Orthodoxy which appealed to him, especially when he looked at the clarity of the Desert Fathers or the Fathers of the Church. He saw that it understood the psychology of spirituality at that incarnate level, without needing the jargon of contemporary psychology. At the same time, unlike any psychology, it was capable of looking at the cross and the hope of resurrection. Henri was a curious, questing soul. Once he began to be interested in Orthodoxy, he came to see how integral icons were to its worship. I think he saw in icons something profoundly helpful to prayer, especially in the way they could become the focus of an interior stillness.

Nouwen did not draw extensively on non-Christian spirituality, although he valued the writings of Rabbi Abraham Joshua Heschel and liked to quote Jewish stories when illustrating points about the spiritual life. The same was true with tales of Zen Buddhist enlightenment. During the early 1970s he had marched alongside Buddhist monks in anti-Vietnam War protests but this never led him to take much of an interest in the East, as van Gogh had done, or to explore Oriental spirituality with anything like the vigour of Merton, although he did have a genuine respect for the Dalai Lama. In later years, though, he visited the Hindu meditation master, Eknath Easwaran, in California, taking some of his contemplative insights into his own prayer life, and quoted Ramakrishna as an important spiritual figure.

While he drew on rich spiritual resources, his own contemplation was born of much inner conflict. Colleagues and friends did not regard him as a mystic in the modern sense of being gifted with extraordinary graces: he was not a man of easy prayer, but he wasn't a person of illusions either. He wasn't mystical in the sense of 'ecstasies'; he was, however, a mystic in the traditional sense of being deeply spiritual.

Nouwen was a priest who tried to follow the mystical path through earnest prayer and a disciplined sacramental life focused on the Eucharist. He read Scripture carefully, studied many of the spiritual classics and was drawn to God through icons and other forms of art. His was fundamentally a theology from the knees but, in spite of his faithfulness, the practice of prayer did not come easily to a man of such distracted temperament. His deepest contemplative moments often came when he was writing: these were times of solitude and centring for him.

2. Deep Wells

WRITING WAS, for Henri Nouwen, a spiritual discipline.* It helped him to concentrate, get in touch with the deeper stirrings of his heart, clarify his mind, process confusing emotions, reflect on his experiences and give artistic expression to what he was trying to live – which could then be integrated more fully into his spiritual journey. As he writes in *Bread for the Journey*:

> As we simply sit down in front of a sheet of paper and start to express in words what is in our minds or in our hearts, new ideas emerge, ideas that can surprise us and lead us to inner places we hardly knew were there. One of the most satisfying aspects of writing is that it can open in us deep wells of hidden treasures that are beautiful for us as well as for others to see.[1]

Through words, he believed, people appropriated and internalised what they were living. Mother Teresa had told him to write 'very simply', because people needed simple words – but his thinking was never simplistic. It succeeded in converting complex concepts into phrases which connected with the spirit of the age. In a postmodern culture which is uncomfortable with absolutes and certitudes, Nouwen communicated that sense of disquiet and uncertainty, but detected within it a thirst for spiritual meaning.

His highly personal style was powerful because he explored so much

* A full list of Henri Nouwen's books is given in the Bibliography (pp. 236–7).

in himself. Although often autobiographical in content, his writing was organised and controlled. People felt they knew more about him than they actually did. Canadian writer Michael Higgins, a professor of English and religious studies, feels that Nouwen's genius lies in his remarkable ability to communicate at a level of transpersonal intimacy which many spiritual writers fail to achieve comfortably:

> He could operate outside the narrow confines of theological discourse and could resonate with the disturbing dimensions of twentieth-century culture – its technological frenzy, its wild eclecticism, its obsession for efficiency. He acted as a counterpoint to all that, but at the same time fully understood its implications. He constantly looked at his culture and currents of change, less as threats and more as probes.

Nouwen enabled readers to join him on a spiritual journey which went against the tide of contemporary culture. His guidance encouraged them to confront their fears, to let go of their false securities and enter the stillness of God's presence where the possibility of hope could be discovered. To live a Christian life meant living in the world without being of it. The personal struggle of faith often included periods of darkness and doubt.

Writing for him was usually connected with an intense experience. When his mother died, he felt compelled to write. He showed the resulting work to friends who found strength in it, so he went on to publish it: 'I hadn't even thought whether it was good for others. My primary concern was to be honest with myself and to know what I was living, to get in touch with it and to trust that somewhere, if it would be good for others, I would find out.'

Nouwen was a hypersensitive man who needed to integrate his personal experiences in his writings initially for himself. It was a naked style which opened him to the criticism that he had never had an unpublished thought. He undoubtedly wrote too many books, and some of them were seen as sentimental and naive, but he was convinced that the language of the heart is universal, that whatever he experienced could somehow touch another person's experience. He wasn't concerned with the theories of subjectivity or objectivity – it was the personal and interpersonal which mattered: 'Writing can be a creative and invigorating way to make our lives available to ourselves and to others. We have to trust that our stories deserve to be told – we may discover that the better we tell our stories, the better we will want to live them.'[2]

Trained in psychology and steeped in the riches of Christian spirituality, Nouwen managed to balance his awareness of the dynamics of the human psyche with his openness to the workings of the Spirit. As a theologian, he articulated the process whereby faith seeks understanding, in language that appealed especially to North American Christians. He allowed the Spirit to shed light on his mistakes and empower him to speak and to write. For many readers he became a prophetic figure, and in the sense that he conveyed to them the life of the Spirit this is surely an accurate description of him.

It has to be said, though, that the actual ideas in his books were not always Nouwen's own – he tended to popularise concepts which had previously been worked out more systematically in the many psychological and theological tomes he kept on his shelves. His originality lay in reinterpreting the texts in an accessible style, and harnessing them to illustrations from his own experiences, observations and personal encounters – no small achievement for a man whose mother-tongue was Dutch.

In 1979 Henri Nouwen won the Catholic Press Association's journalism award for the 'Best Treatment on Prayer' – for an article he had written in the magazine *America*. It was one of many honours he received over the years. In 1980 he was awarded an honorary doctorate of divinity from Virginia Theological Seminary. The citation bore witness to his prophetic style of communication:

> Through your books and essays, your published meditations and reflections, you have become one of the most widely read interpreters of the Christian way for seekers and followers in our time. And when you preach and teach the Gospel of God's renewing love in Christ, your hearers know the power of prophecy, evangelism, and priestly cure of souls.

The Henri Nouwen collection at Yale Divinity School, and the papers found at Daybreak after his death, comprise a phenomenal library of spiritual thinking. They include hundreds of articles written for an extraordinary range of publications across the world, from *Monastic Studies* to *Acupuncture*. He was always in demand by magazine and newspaper editors but it was as an author of spiritual books that he made his name across the world, some 40 titles being translated into many different languages. He had, though, never planned on becoming an author. When he was a child, his father had joked that the one profession Henri would not go into would be writing because he did not seem to have more than 300 words in his vocabulary. Nouwen started by contributing articles to Catholic newspapers in Holland – but his potential as a writer was only discovered in the late 1960s when, as a visiting professor in pastoral psychology at the University of Notre Dame in Indiana, he was asked to give a lecture to a conference of priests. A stringer for the *National Catholic Reporter* sent the text of his speech to the paper, where it was printed in full. The response from readers was more than encouraging. Nouwen once recounted how it all happened:

> I came to Notre Dame to give a summer course but, after I arrived, I found that the programme had been cancelled for lack of response. So, because they now had nothing for me to do, they asked me to give five lectures over the course of five weeks. I had nothing prepared but had a whole week to work on each lecture. So I would chose a topic and then begin to talk with everyone about it. I decided not to go to the library to do research on the topic but instead just kept asking myself what I knew about it. What did I have available from my own experience? What did *I* know about it? Did I have some experience with this topic that I could articulate so that other people could recognise it as a real experience?
>
> And ever since then I have felt it crucial to think and write about things in such a way that people who listen will be able to recognise the experience and say, 'You articulate something for me that I know but still need to hear. It is just over the threshold of my consciousness'.
>
> So I have always used as my prime resource some of my own observations and my own personal struggles with whatever I am writing about. This is because I have always believed that one of

the main objectives of ministry is to make your own faith struggles available to others, to articulate for others your own doubts and to say, in effect, 'I don't know the answers either. I am simply a catalyst, simply somebody who wants to articulate for you the things that you already know but might get a better grip on if there are some words for them.'[3]

Nouwen was unquestionably prolific, even by the standards of a full-time author. His output is all the more staggering because, effectively, he produced it in his spare time (though he was often reminded that he frequently wrote the same book again and again). There was never a stage in his life when he worked wholly as a writer – he was a priest who was always fully committed as a professor, preacher and minister, and who was always searching for ways of encountering God in new and exciting situations. His whole life was a divine adventure. So how did he manage it – and what was he like to work with as a creative artist, a writer?

His own bustling world provided no haven for writing, so he often had to travel to find the solitude he needed. Friends around the world offered him rooms in their homes where he could be left alone in peace and comfort. He sometimes wrote in beautiful hardback note-books bought in museums and art galleries and, using a roller-ball pen, would fill one side of a page in his elegant handwriting so he could return later and make corrections on the other side.

Nouwen's secretary at L'Arche Daybreak in the later years was Kathy Christie, who recalls that he kept in touch with her almost daily when he was abroad writing: 'When he was working on a manuscript he would write a few pages, fax them through, write a few more, then fax those through too. They were all written in long-hand and in English. He liked to get up early and spend the morning writing.'

Henri Nouwen always acknowledged that, from his earliest publishing achievements, friends and colleagues had played a pivotal part in his success. John Mogabgab, Nouwen's research and teaching assistant at Yale between 1975 and 1980, edited everything he wrote around that period, including *The Genesee Diary*: 'The manuscripts would take a fair amount of rewriting. Henri's ego wasn't involved in what he had written – he was really only concerned that his words were expressing fully and clearly what he was trying to say.'

Mogabgab was one of a circle of friends to whom Nouwen sent his manuscripts which often appeared first in the form of articles in such magazines as *Sojourners*, *America* and, later, *Weavings*. Nouwen's greatest gift, according to Mogabgab, was his ability to write about intimate, hidden things in his own life and make them accessible for others, helping them to make a real connection with the spiritual life:

> His writing was at times more personal than some people would be comfortable with. I had to point out to him that what was most personal was not always the most universal, and should be kept private. I was amazed sometimes at how well he took my editing which sometimes turned things upside down and inside out, but he was never offended by the liberties I took with his text.

Some people, though, found his style egotistic, even mawkish, lacking any systematic theological approach – and they told him so. While these may have been justifiable criticisms, they were ones Nouwen sometimes found hard to take. Nouwen wrote for several publishers and, while their opinions of their relationships varied, he seems always to have been intent on friendship as well as business.

Robert Ellsberg had known Nouwen as a friend and adviser for many years before working with him professionally, when Ellsberg became editor-in-chief of Orbis Books (the publishing arm of the Catholic Foreign Mission Society of America, the Maryknoll Fathers and Brothers). Ellsberg noticed how Nouwen changed over the years as their personal and professional relationship grew and developed:

> I came to recognise how important it was for Henri to feel he had a relationship with his publishers based on commitment to him as a person. I only felt I had truly won his trust after I rejected a manuscript he sent me – a journal account of a fairly uneventful trip to Ukraine. I told him bluntly that I didn't think it amounted to a book; he ought to publish it as a series of articles. I remember swallowing hard before mailing that letter, knowing how badly

he could take criticism. In fact, he called to say how much he appreciated my honesty.

Frank Cunningham of Ave Maria Press (at the University of Notre Dame, Indiana) knew Nouwen for almost 20 years: 'Henri was a good author to work with, even though he didn't take direction that well'. Reflecting on the quality of Nouwen's writing, Cunningham commented: 'I don't think he will have the impact that Merton had – but only time will tell. His books are selling better now than they ever did. He speaks to the frustrations of modern times and, until there is a major cultural shift, I think he will be relevant.'

His publishers were aware that Nouwen was one of the first contemporary Catholic writers to cross over to the readers in the evangelical market who, for many years, looked at Catholicism as something other than Christian. At the far extreme of fundamental Protestantism his Catholicism still put people off – but in a book like *In the Name of Jesus*, where he focused on the fundamentals of the Christian faith (as C. S. Lewis had done in *Mere Christianity*), the differences were put aside and people who weren't of his background were very at home in his language.

William G. Barry, of Bantam Doubleday Dell, worked with Nouwen on several titles, including *The Return of the Prodigal Son* and *The Inner Voice of Love*, and found him to be a person of great passion, attempting to disseminate his spirit of enthusiasm among all members of the production team. He was concerned about the physical specifications of each book – the paper, the typeface and the quality of colour reproduction on the jacket:

> He showed a healthy sense of vanity about the author picture, which always got more than passing attention. He always wanted input from friends before submitting the final manuscript. He also insisted on seeing the catalogue copy to make sure it accurately described the point and nature of a book. But as a businessman he was almost naive. I do not think he had the language or experience to articulate some of the things he desired in terms of advancing or widening his career as an author. He was a genuinely spiritual person who lived and contended with the issues he wrote about. He spoke to the questions which surged up from people's

souls and hearts. Because his world-view was as wide, as open and as liberal as it was, he was never dissuaded from speaking from his heart and resonating with the hearts of others. He rarely, if ever, got hung up in terms of denominational issues.

Many people who read Henri Nouwen's books and then got to know him discovered that he was not like the person who had come across to them in his writings. Carolyn Whitney-Brown always believed there was much more to Henri than ever got into his books, more to the gospel of his life than he ever had words for:

> To love Henri, in part you had to love the fact that he couldn't live up to his books. His vision of what was possible and his horizons were always bigger than his ability to live them out. His books sometimes left me cold – but his life never did. The word that summed up Henri for me was abundance. There was always more of Henri and more to Henri than ever emerged in his writings.

Nouwen wrote compellingly about the ability to discern between loneliness and solitude, but he did not like his own company, and retreats proved testing experiences for him. Yet, in his books, he seemed to have understood precisely why solitude might be helpful to people. Because of what he wrote, many people were able to gain a much clearer sense of what it meant to be alone and how God's Spirit could speak to them in solitude. The paradox was that, while he wrote so convincingly about the need to be alone with God, it was not something he ever resolved for himself. The same was true about community. He wrote elaborately about the concept, but needed to have long spells away from L'Arche and found monastic community life difficult. His desire for prayer and for God, for community and for ministry, seems to have been greater than he could manage to integrate psychologically for himself, although he always hoped he might live up to it.

Nouwen was always seeking more imaginative ways of 'catching the mystery' in words. Towards the end of his life he told friends that he wished he could write in a very different way, a way that was more poetic, more dramatic, or perhaps he could even write a children's book. He felt he wrote too literally and failed to express what he wanted to say because a different style of writing eluded him. He wanted to find a model which wasn't so personal. This might have been one reason why he never managed to write a book on the theology of the flying trapeze, the subject which absorbed him most in his later years. It was the circus which gave birth to some his most original spiritual insights.

3. High Wires

IN A CARAVAN just west of Frankfurt, a video film is playing. On the screen are the slow-motion images of a tall, gangly figure climbing a steel ladder and getting into harness for his second flight on the swinging trapeze. It is not perhaps where you would have expected to find a tired-looking 64-year-old priest just two months before his death – but Henri Nouwen had so relished his first experience on the bar three years before, he'd come back to try it again.

When Nouwen had eventually got out of the net on that first occasion, he said it was the most exciting experience of his life. He'd asked to go up again, and again – each time trying to swing higher. What is striking about the film is Nouwen's unashamed childlike delight in flying. Could this really be a one-time Yale and Harvard professor swinging through the air and jumping around in the net?

It had all begun when the German circus, Simoneit-Barum, had rigged up in Freiburg one day while Nouwen was visiting his publisher friends there. He went along out of curiosity and became so fascinated by the technique that he continued going to see the troupe in action, later even hiring a camper and touring with them. He planned to write a new style of book – but the more he outwardly observed the doubles and triples, the more he inwardly found himself formulating a whole new theology. The art of the trapeze was much more than an exhilarating showpiece: it was a whole picture of life. He wanted to learn everything he possibly could about the artistes' professional lives, and came to realise that, behind every ten-minute thrill, lay a strict discipline which he 'just wanted to grab from the inside'.

When he encountered the Flying Rodleighs, a trapeze troupe from South Africa, he had been working at L'Arche Daybreak for a number of years. There he had seen how assistants from 21 different nations managed to create community around people with weak bodies who weren't able easily to express themselves. As he watched the Rodleighs flying through the air, he detected something similar about them. Here was a group of performers who didn't speak during their act, who did something with their bodies and who formed community, first of all among themselves and then among the wider audience who had come to see them. As Nouwen perceived it, they brought people together and, through their bodies, their beauty and interaction, invited others to create community in the form of friendship, belonging, togetherness, laughter, applause, freedom and discipline. 'It's all there in one act', he would say. 'It's what life is all about and what the world badly needs.'

So the Flying Rodleighs became for Nouwen not trainers in acrobatics but tutors in theology. Just as the handicapped members of L'Arche had become his teachers of the heart, convincing him through their silence that being was more important than doing, so the trapeze artists revealed to him 'the incredible message which the body can give', not least in their ability to be 'totally present to the present'. It was a symbol of the concentrated meditative life which offered, in the same instant, both a sense of temporal freedom and a glimpse of eternity.

Nouwen also came to understand that the star is not the flyer – the figure who soars through the air and trusts – but the catcher whose hands are always there to receive and welcome home. Out of that insight came a new way of seeing and experiencing the divine: 'I can only fly freely when I know there is a catcher to catch me', commented Nouwen in *Angels over the Net*, a film about his trapeze theology: 'If we are to take risks, to be free, in the air, in life, we have to know there's a catcher. We have to know that, when we come down from it all, we're going to be caught, we're going to be safe. The great hero is the least visible. Trust the catcher.'[1]

Although his fixation with the trapeze emerged relatively late in life, Henri Nouwen's love of the circus went back to childhood. The world of risk and celebration appealed to him immensely; he may have recognised within it something of the chances and excitements of his own life. The circus is often related to a clutter or pandemonium, an organised chaos – which might also have been a description of Henri's own life. His attraction to circus life was also related to the fact that audiences were at liberty to respond to the many silent acts in whatever way they wished. Nouwen liked freedom of interpretation.

Although he loved many of the performers – jugglers, sword-swallowers, exotic dancers – it was always the flying trapeze troupes which drew him back every time. To him, they were not just the most elegant and exciting of acts but they brought him closest to flight, to his secret longing of being able to move in ways which his unco-ordinated body had never allowed. He liked clowns too, because Nouwen could laugh at himself just as much as others sometimes laughed at his real-life clownishness. Whether he was boiling away a kettle of water before he had managed to make tea, dipping the sleeve of his white woolly jumper in a jar of marmalade as he intently quizzed someone about their prayer life over breakfast or crashing into the car in front as he drove with gesticulating arms and a rear-view glance, he accepted his physical gaucherie with a smile.

When Nouwen celebrated his sixtieth birthday, his friends devised a party with a circus theme and arranged for him to be reborn as a clown in front of 100 guests including a professional clown. He had to climb into a bag as himself, and then emerge as a clown. He responded with childlike delight and, once inside the bag, he loved it so much that the whole episode lasted 45 minutes.

Nouwen could also see the serious side of clownishness. The cover of one of his books, *Clowning in Rome*, shows a costumed jester looking over the eternal city. The book, written while he was on the staff of the North American College for five months, emerged from lectures he gave to the English-speaking community on solitude, celibacy, prayer and contemplation – 'four clownlike elements in the spiritual life':

> Clowns are not in the centre of the events. They appear between the great acts, fumble and fall, and make us smile again after the tensions created by the heroes we came to admire. The clowns don't have it all together, they do not succeed in what they try,

they are awkward, out of balance and left-handed, but . . . they
are on our side.[2]

Nouwen recognised that people respond to clowns not with admiration,
amazement and tension but with sympathy, understanding and a smile.
Of the virtuosi, people might exclaim, 'How can they do it?' but from
the clowns comes the realisation, 'They are like us'. Tearfully and
joyfully the clowns – in reality, peripheral people who 'evoke a smile
and awaken hope' through their humble, saintly lives – share the same
human weaknesses as everyone else.[3] It was significant (Nouwen noted)
that pastoral psychologists such as Heije Faber and Seward Hiltner had
used the image of the clown to understand the role of the minister in
contemporary society. In one sermon, written for seminarians, he said
that the circus would be depressing if people only looked up to the
artistes whose breathtaking heroics were hard to emulate:

> But the clown saves us: he is our man, because he fails, like we
> do, he makes mistakes like we do, he says to us, non-virtuosity
> is OK too. And in his white face we recognise ourselves in our
> daily tasks of which so many fail . . . Christ is the clown who came
> into our circus and made us laugh because he came to tell us that
> we are not what we perform. He came for the crying, the per-
> secuted, the weak, the hungry, the poor. He who is called to be a
> minister is called to be a clown.[4]

Nouwen sensed that within the very vulnerability of a clown lay secrets
about discipleship. Ministers were not only the healers, the reconcilers,
the givers of life, but were also broken people who needed as much
care as anyone they cared for – and this was especially true of him.
Just as the clown could not operate without the laughs and smiles of
the audience, so an apostle could not be sent out without the love and
support of a community. When he was sent out to preach with
members of the Daybreak community, he found the imagery of a circus
act appropriate in describing how L'Arche had changed his perspective:

> Living in a community with very wounded people, I came to see
> that I had lived most of my life as a tightrope artist trying to walk
> on a high, thin cable from one tower to the other, always waiting
> for the applause when I had not fallen off and broken my leg.[5]

Throughout his adult life he never lost the capacity to be stunned by something which most people would overlook. He never felt he had to hide behind his own sophistication, which was not inconsiderable. It was also part of his savouring an experience in the present moment. Nouwen's former teaching assistant at Yale, John Mogabgab, witnessed the wonder on many occasions:

> When he went to a circus at New Haven, Connecticut, to watch the renowned tightrope walker Philippe Petit, he got restless with excitement, just like a child. Petit was doing extraordinary things on the tightrope. Still holding his balance pole, he came down one of the guide wires which was at a 45-degree angle then, when he got to the ground, he continued walking as though he were still on the tightrope. It was totally exaggerated walking because he was now on the flat ground. What Henri saw there was a circus performer showing us what a miracle it was to be able to walk.

Nouwen could make a connection between the antics of a circus ring and the practice of spiritual living. He also knew how to use hyperbole to best advantage, to reveal to others the missed and hidden miracles of their lives. He dramatised to great effect so that people could see the extraordinary in the ordinary, and the ordinary in the extraordinary. The artist in Nouwen sculpted people's sensibilities to see the world in a way which others might not. It could happen with art as much as it could with music. An accomplished pianist himself, he always discovered in the blend of keys and strings in a Mozart piano concerto something about the harmonious way in which God supported people in their lives.

Nouwen even pondered on the meaning of his own ministry and whether it literally fell into the category of 'entertainment'. Examining the word's Latin roots – *inter* (between) and *tenere* (to hold) – he questioned his own capacity for holding people up in between the fragmented moments of their lives. Did he succeed in giving them a glimpse of the beyond? He knew his own life was not so far removed from that of a nomadic entertainer, moving from place to place, trying to make people feel safe or excited, helping them come to terms with their feelings of loss and failure, as well as with their moments of growth and success. He also made a direct connection between the circus tent and the Church: weren't they both trying to lift up the human spirit and help people look beyond the boundaries of their daily lives? Yet, at the same time, weren't they also in danger of becoming places for lifeless routines which had lost their vitality and transcending power? He wrote:

> There is no reason to idealise the circus. Much that goes on there is quite unspectacular, inside as well as outside the tent. Nor is there any reason to romanticise the church. Much that goes on there is quite unspiritual. And still, the human heart searches for something larger, something greater than its own pettiness, and everyone who enters the circus or the church is looking for something that reaches out to the stars, or beyond! Shouldn't there be something of the trapeze artist in every priest and something of the priest in every trapeze artist?[6]

These were original questions which were leading him into new territory in terms of the way in which he wanted to write, and the less cerebral, more body-centred message he wanted to impart. The circus contained many of the elements of Henri's *modus vivendi* and he wanted to live it in an even bigger way, extending his arms with total faith so that God could hold him, embrace him and bring him to a place of safety. Like the Flying Rodleighs, he knew that there could only be true celebration after the risks had been taken. It was all wonderful material for a book – but for some reason he procrastinated, despite doing phenomenal amounts of research. In his personal notes from the period, when he was also devouring books about creative writing, he scribbled with the excitement of a journalist uncovering a hidden truth:

> I now see how they are connected. I love the circus, but I love it so much because it gives me so much to write about. I love to write, but I love it so much because I have the circus to write about. As I read these books on writing, I see how much there is to write about. At first it seemed that the spectacular trapeze act was the main subject, but as I entered more deeply into the circus world while reading these books, I can see little stories everywhere and can be away from my camper scarcely more than 10 minutes

without wanting to run back and report what I have just heard or seen. So my life here is a strange running to and from the little writing desk in my camper; a strange tension between action and contemplation, between observing and reporting, between listening and writing, between walking around and sitting down.[7]

Nouwen became convinced that he had been sent to the Rodleighs to discover something fresh about life and death, love and fear, peace and conflict, heaven and hell, which he could not have got to know or write about in any other way. While the clowns, magicians, animal trainers and musicians remained on the periphery of his vision, the flying trapeze act was his primary focus, leading him towards an inner revelation. But despite his extensive research, he never managed to write the book. Some reflections from 1993 show he was searching for a new kind of storytelling:

Many of my books no longer express my spiritual vision and, although I am not dismissing my earlier writing as no longer valid, I feel that something different is being asked of me. My many encounters with people who have no contact with the church, my contact with AIDS patients, my experience in the circus, and the many socio-political events of the past few years all ask for a new way to speak about God. This new way includes not only content but form. Not only what I say, but also how I say it should be different. What mostly comes to mind is stories. I know I have to write stories. Not essays with arguments, quotes and analyses, but stories which are short and simple and give us a glimpse of God in the midst of our multifaceted lives. But writing stories, real stories, human stories, God-given stories, will ask the most of me.[8]

During his sabbatical year in 1996, which was also to be his last, Nouwen carried around his notes and cassette interviews from his circus days and planned to get the new book under way, but he wrote several others instead. He left, however, a few hints as to what it might have been about:

The body tells a spiritual story. The body is not just body, it's an expression of the spirit of the human person and the real spiritual life is an enfleshed life. That's why I believe in the incarnation. There is no divine life outside the body because God decided to dress himself in a body, to become body.[9]

It was as a celebrity speaker that Henri Nouwen most used his body to communicate deep truths about the spirit. An audience would watch spellbound as he brought every limb and facial muscle into play in what was described by one friend as 'the whole vibrating system of Henri'. His command performances became the talking points of cathedrals, colleges and convents – though some of them got more than they bargained for.

4. The Dance

DURING HIS career as a university professor in the United States, Henri Nouwen became something of a phenomenon for his stage presentations on the life of Vincent van Gogh. The audience would sit in a darkened hall – then, gradually, the lights would reveal the curtains and Nouwen would enter with one ear bandaged up. The performance, along with a sideshow, would use tales and insights from van Gogh's life and art to make some profoundly spiritual points. When Nouwen received a letter from an order of nuns inviting him to speak about Vincent as the keynote address at their anniversary celebrations, he took his show on the road again. The hall was packed with sisters from dozens of convents, thrilled to have Nouwen as their main speaker on their day of commemoration. The exuberant show included all of Vincent's insanity and, while Henri's eyesight was never that good, he nevertheless noticed that the nuns had some strange expressions on their faces. There were looks of surprise, delight and even joy – but there were also enough frowns of incomprehension and nervous giggles to make him suspect that he was not creating his usual runaway success. After a two-hour presentation and a more hesitant applause than usual, he was thanked by the Mother Superior who went on to add, 'But, Father, when we asked you to come and give our keynote address about Vincent, we were actually referring to our founder, St Vincent de Paul'.

Such was the demand for Nouwen as a public speaker and preacher that, every week, he had to turn down 50 invitations from many different countries. He would have agreed to everything were it not for friends who had his best interests at heart. Whether preaching to wedding guests in an overflowing church, to an assembly of clergy, to a crowd of peace-workers on the eve of the Gulf War or to an international television audience via satellite, he gave himself completely. Sometimes he prepared a few carefully connected notes for a special occasion – but at other times he didn't work out his homilies until perhaps an hour before the service. One friend recollected watching Nouwen opening his missal to the appointed readings and just needing a few minutes to connect with the message. He then nodded his head, closed the book and said that he was ready to speak from the heart.

If he had to fly across the USA to address a gathering of thousands of people, he might not start to think about his words until the air steward was twisting open a small bottle of red wine at 30,000 feet. Then he often got so engrossed in conversations with fellow passengers that there wasn't much time to work on a speech. Living the present moment with people was always a priority. There were times, though, when he felt the pangs of inner panic at the thought of addressing so many people – but he usually found himself trusting in Julian of Norwich's dictum that 'all shall be well'.

To the conference hosts, eager to see their renowned speaker walking in with a bound manuscript, the absence of papers could come as a shock. Professor Michael Higgins, who had invited Nouwen to give a lecture at St Jerome's College, Waterloo, Ontario, before an audience of 500, was experienced in welcoming high-profile names from around the world. But he found himself disarmed by Professor Nouwen, who was indifferent to the celebrity status being conferred on him:

> It was a little disconcerting for a co-ordinator to realise that his lecturer had arrived but didn't seem to have prepared a full-bodied, cogently argued text. But what made him stand out from other spiritual people who had been speakers here was that, before starting, he insisted on finding a space outside the foyer in order to pray. He retired from the fray and wanted quiet time. Although we'd had others at the college speaking about prayer and theological matters, he was the only one to integrate into his evening

a moment of deliberate quiet time. At the beginning and near the end of his speech, he involved the audience in a Taizé mantra which achieved an element of quietness and serenity which was important for his presentation. But he also needed it himself. The lack of prepared text and the importance of recollected time struck me as unusual – but perhaps it spoke directly to the personality of the man.

Whatever the public occasion, Nouwen's angular, ascetic appearance concealed an intense, focused and animated energy which burst forth as he moved around the auditorium like a dancer. It was pure theatre. One of his closest friends, Father Don McNeill, a priest of the Congregation of the Holy Cross, compared him to a conductor who could bring all the different musical instruments together in a crescendo, using his hands, eyes, gestures, his passion and his impeccable timing. The orchestral analogy is fitting because whenever Nouwen went to a concert he would hang over the balcony or lurch forward engrossed by the conductor's relationship to the musicians, a mirror image, perhaps, of his own zealous style. 'When giving a talk, Henri put so much of his heart into every word and gesture, you felt he would go up in flames!' said Don McNeill. 'He stretched with every pore of his body. He stood on tiptoe, his arms and fingers reaching out and drawing us in. The difference between Henri and Laurence Olivier was that Henri spoke his own lines which erupted from his inner heart, soul, passion and integrity.'

But although there was spiritual grace in his theatricality, there was not always physical co-ordination. Just as he would sometimes send chairs flying when he was moving around a room teaching so, when he was giving a public talk, obstacles could get in the way. Once, when leading a retreat for members of the Church of the Savior, Washington, he was so intent on leading people into a deeper relationship with Jesus, that with an upward flourish of his hand, he stuck a finger in the whirring ceiling fan. Fortunately a doctor who was on the retreat bandaged it up – and Henri carried straight on. He showed no signs of pain because he was so intently focused on his commitment to be with those people, helping them to grasp the truth which he was trying to communicate.

It was not unusual for Nouwen to speak for two hours without a break, and often so many people would turn up to hear him that another public address system would have to be rigged up in a neighbouring hall. But, like a Chinese whisper, the message received was not always the one which had been sent. In his last year at Yale, Nouwen was invited to give one of the prestigious Convocation lectures. As usual the chapel was full, so an ageing audio system crackled his words to the overflow audience in another room. Nouwen had a minor speech impediment ('faith' would sound like 'face') and this, combined with his distinctive Dutch accent and the university's dysfunctional relay equipment, led to a situation worthy of the circus. He spoke about Christ's temptations in the wilderness – the temptations to be relevant, spectacular and powerful; but when he came to the section about relevance, the listeners in the overflow hall thought he was talking about the 'temptation to be an elephant'. They weren't so much amused as intrigued – many came up to him afterwards to point out that, although they had never thought about temptation in elephantine terms before, now that he had mentioned it, they could see how it would involve a spiritual inflation of the ego. They complimented him on his colourful originality. Nouwen had no idea what they were talking about but, once the confusion was unravelled, he found the episode hilarious.

When listening to Nouwen, many people found themselves silently connecting with a Quaker expression, 'It speaks to my condition'. Nouwen had a gift for that kind of honesty and he accomplished it primarily by talking about Jesus, 'who lived his life with an increasing willingness to face his own condition and the condition of the world in which he found himself'.[1] In this way, he believed people could be encouraged to follow and to live with that same authenticity even if it lead to 'tears, sweat and, possibly, a violent death'.[2] It was about a growing willingness to stretch out one's hands and be guided by others.

Preaching was not about trying to convert. It meant developing a spirituality, a way of living, through which people could be brought to a liberating insight to make them free to follow Christ. To achieve that, preachers had to take the views and experiences of the congregation as seriously as their own, so that people could respond to what was being said from their own life experience. What mattered was that preachers made themselves 'totally and most personally involved'[3] and did not remain untouchable and invulnerable. Nouwen did not suggest that preachers should self-indulgently share their own personal idiosyncrasies, worries and hang-ups, but he did expect them to have the courage to offer their own understandings and experiences of doubt and faith, anxiety and hope, fear and joy, as a source of recognition for others if the word of God were to bear fruit. Preachers could not be available to others until they put the full range of their own life experiences – including prayer, conversations and lonely hours of suffering – at the disposal of those who had come to listen to them. In effect, preachers had to be willing to give their lives for the people. 'Every time real preaching occurs the crucifixion is realised again: for no preacher can bring anyone to the light without having entered the darkness of the cross himself.'[4]

Nouwen's sense of his vocation as a preacher emerged in his book of prayers, *A Cry for Mercy*:

> Dear Lord, you have sent me into this world to preach your word. So often the problems of the world seem so complex and intricate that your word strikes me as embarrassingly simple. Many times I feel tongue-tied in the company of people who are dealing with the world's social and economic problems.
>
> But you, O Lord, said, 'Be clever as serpents and innocent as doves.' Let me retain innocence and simplicity in the midst of this complex world. I realise that I have to be informed, that I have to study the many problems facing the world, and that I have to try to understand as well as possible the dynamics of our contemporary society. But what really counts is that all this information, knowledge, and insight allow me to speak more clearly and unambiguously your truthful word. Do not allow evil powers to seduce me with the complexities of the world's problems, but give me the strength to think clearly, speak freely, and act boldly in your service. Give me the courage to show the dove in a world so full of serpents. Amen.[5]

One of Nouwen's weaknesses, though, was his need to be centre-stage, not because he was vain but because he was insecure. He expected rapt attention and did not like people moving from their seats. If someone had to leave for the best of reasons, he tended to become extremely tense, fearing they might have objected to what he had said. Any indication, however misread, that someone might be rejecting him could be dramatised within his own mind. The positive side of this was that, unlike superstars who steer clear of crowds the more famous they become, he spoke to everyone who came up to him afterwards, making them feel important. If, for some reason, people did not approach him, he looked uncomfortable, standing on his own at the front of the hall like a lost child looking for his family. The down side was that he preferred the company of people with whom he was not in any kind of competition – the attention had to be on him. It was rare to find him sharing the platform with fellow Roman Catholic priests. Yet in later years he was happy to share the stage with people who had developmental disabilities. He said that audiences would remember their presence long after they had forgotten his words.

As a preacher, Nouwen not only drew people from his own tradition but from Anglicanism and most of the Protestant denominations, including evangelicals who particularly liked his Jesus-centred approach to spirituality. That he could appeal to such a range was a hallmark of his evangelism – and of his ability to walk the tightrope. It was possible for him to speak in the morning to a group of left-wing Catholic liberation theologians, lead a lunchtime seminar with Nonconformists, and in the afternoon exhort members of the Religious Right. He invited listeners into his interior journey and identified himself as a pilgrim permanently *en route*, and people liked that. In postmodern culture people feel very uncomfortable with absolutes, fixity and the easy certitude which comes with the older school. Nouwen successfully communicated that disquiet and ill-at-easeness, but at the same time he presented an integrated search for spiritual meaning. He disclosed things about himself, but was calculated enough to ensure it was reasonably organised self-disclosure. He allowed people to see his wounds and his struggles and to feel his anxieties so they sensed that they were accompanying somebody as a companion.

Robert Schuller, one of America's most celebrated tele-evangelists, was one of many leading Protestants in America who held Nouwen in high esteem. Schuller invited Nouwen to preach for three consecutive Sundays on his one-hour televised church service, *The Hour of Power*, beamed to 20 million people in 150 countries from the glass-structured Crystal Cathedral in California, the first church designed as a television 'super studio' for congregational Christian worship. Nouwen's theme was belovedness and, according to Schuller, people have never forgotten it. In his interdenominational preaching school for ministers at the Crystal Cathedral, Schuller now uses the videotape of Nouwen's guest appearances as a model of preaching:

> All of our students have to watch and listen to Henri Nouwen. I keep interrupting and stopping the video machine, telling them to notice how he uses his hands, to look at the twinkle in his eye, to see how he connects his eye with the eye of the listener, to be aware of the words he uses – all positives, no negatives.

He saw Nouwen essentially, though, as a witness to the incarnation rather than a preacher of sermons: 'He witnessed to the reality of what happens when the love of God is embraced in human life. He was an incredibly gifted person. The same spirit that was in Mother Teresa – love, laughter, humour, twinkle – was also in Henri Nouwen.'

Nouwen was already popular among Protestant evangelicals, but after his television homilies his reputation increased. In a 1994 survey of 3400 US Protestant church leaders, he was named as their second greatest influence, ahead of Billy Graham. He appealed to evangelicals because he honoured the historic essence of the Christian faith and was never into revisionism. He was able to combine this successfully with contemporary analogies from the world of psychology and anthropology. Nouwen himself had always felt that evangelicals, while fervent, committed and word-centred, lacked the mystical dimension to spiritual living – a balance he attempted to redress.

Though Nouwen was often illuminating, some found his talks baffling. New York lawyer Jay Greer, an Episcopalian, listened respectfully to what he had to say on one of his weekend retreats but did not rave like everyone else:

> I told him that I wasn't sure I had got any of what he was saying. He was very patient but also very persistent. At the end of the third reflection I could see he was beginning to get very impatient with me – he said that he wished he could anaesthetise me from

the neck up. At the end he said, 'Do you understand, Jay, that God is at work in your life?' I'm not sure I knew what to make of it all, but the thing that struck me as I looked back on it was that he had indeed opened me up to that possibility.

Unlike some of the American evangelists, Henri clearly did not have all the answers. He was struggling with a lot of the things I was struggling with, at a much greater depth and much more intensely than I had ever dreamed of. Henri approached his faith with a tremendous intellect and a tremendous heart, which was thoroughly compelling. I don't think he understood it fully but, whatever his doubts, I am sure he believed it.

Whether it was in the form of spiritual dance, theological theatre, televised church evangelism or an intimate retreat, Nouwen held his audience, not so much in the palm of his hand but in the glare of his eye. He felt compelled to preach, and vocation, for him, was always 'something you feel you have to do'. His was a powerful communication of the Gospel truths which stayed with people long after the event. It left many of them spellbound – though it often left Nouwen in disarray.

5. Backstage

IT WAS 11 p.m., and Parker Palmer was waiting in Nouwen's apartment to greet Henri when he arrived home after giving a talk. When the door eventually opened, Palmer saw a dishevelled figure in a thick overcoat, looking awful. Sensing that something was seriously wrong, he asked what had happened: 'I really can't talk right now', Nouwen replied. 'Would you please just hold me?' So Palmer stood in the middle of the living room holding his friend, who did not seem to have the energy even to take off his coat or his hat:

> He just clung to me fiercely, and I hugged him tight in return. Finally, after several minutes, his grip relaxed and I asked him if he wanted to talk. He explained that he had been up in front of a couple of thousand people, as he often was, being terribly charismatic and outreaching with all these energies. He then said, 'In the middle of this talk, I suddenly had the feeling that my body was exploding into a million atoms and merging with the audience; that my sense of self was disappearing, my body itself was disappearing. It was one of the most terrifying experiences I have ever had.'

Nouwen lived constantly with the excruciating tension between giving himself to others and maintaining the boundaries of his own identity and integrity. On that occasion he seemed to have had some premonition or a psycho-spiritual experience of losing his identity in the crowd. It was not the only time he was to suffer a sense of disintegration. Once,

Yushi Nomura, a Japanese student and friend of Nouwen's, became concerned when he answered the phone one night. He lifted the receiver to hear only the noise of someone crying. Eventually he realised that it was Henri. Nouwen – who had just resigned from Yale, given up his apartment and was living in an attic flat – asked Nomura if he would drive over to be with him:

> He was alone when I got there. He hugged me and really thanked me. He settled down, we prayed together and he became very calm, almost like a different person. He explained that he had needed to call because he felt he was alone and just vanishing from the earth. He was scared that he was being taken away somehow. He had been to a party in his honour and he was disappointed that I couldn't be there. He said that everybody had been very kind, and there had been lots of noise and music but, when the dust had settled, nobody had been there, not even me. He wept a bit, we prayed a little again and then we parted. He was saddened by the fact that most of the close friendships he had developed at Yale seemed to have gone into dust and they might all have been in vain. There had been pleasant gestures at the party, but then he had been dropped back at his flat in the middle of nowhere.

These two stories underline the complexities of Nouwen's personality. His spiritual force and physical energy could be creative – but could also be destructive, making him feel that he was losing his self-identity. Being held by a friend was the means of getting over it. Throughout his life, Nouwen seemed to desire intimacy more than adulation. Often, after addressing the masses and earning the plaudits, he felt completely alone. There were many occasions when the organisers of an event simply forgot to invite him for a meal or a drink after his talk; he took this as a personal affront. They might have booked him into some elegant suite at a top hotel, but sometimes they overlooked the friendship and hospitality for which he silently longed and was so faithful in offering. So, after the applause, Nouwen would often walk back alone to his hotel room, unlock the door, close it with a sigh and stare at the telephone beside the bed.

It was not unusual for his friends to receive long, desperate phone-

calls from him in the middle of the night, often after he had been at
a particularly prestigious event. He knew all too well the dangers of
gaining the whole world but losing his own soul, the poverty of being
at the top. At the L'Arche Daybreak community, where his phone bills
were higher than his rent, he had to limit his public appearances away
from the community. In later years, whenever he was invited to speak
at a function, he would take a member of the community with him,
which diverted the spotlight away from him a little and gave him a
sense of companionship. He also sensed the spirit of the first apostles
who were sent out to proclaim the Gospel in pairs.

While Nouwen had a natural zest for life and people, the stimulation
of being the star seemed to feed a darker place of belonging in him.
On the stage or up and down the aisle, he was an open and gregarious
mentor with a genuine and immediate warmth for others in whom he
took intense interest. Backstage, there hovered a nervous and less
confident individual who knew that he couldn't take the public affirmation home with him – so he would start to fret, feeling desperately
lonely and tired. There was clearly a paradox in all of this because he
was always worried that his public image would get in the way of the
Gospel message he was trying to proclaim. Any ambivalent feelings he
had towards his international renown emerged most strongly when
he found people focusing on him and not on the God to whom he was
pointing. It was as though his followers got so preoccupied with him
as a John-the-Baptist-figure that they failed to look at the Christ-figure
for whom he was preparing a way.

Daybreak's director of development, Carl MacMillan, experienced
Nouwen's struggle at first hand:

> There was a gap between what he spoke about and what he was
> actually able to live, and I found that a bit maddening at times.
> When I travelled with him he would give stunning lectures about
> the spiritual life, then get off stage, and collapse from exhaustion
> or be snarly and irritable. I found that quite difficult to take.
> Eventually I recognised that my own expectation of Henri being
> able to live absolutely all of what he talked about so compellingly
> was quite unfair and unrealistic. Once, when I was preparing to
> give a reflection on the Gospel, I talked to Henri about my own

difficulty in preaching something that I myself could not live very well. Henri encouraged me to do what the Desert Fathers had done, 'to keep preaching that I might be converted by my own word'. The fact that Henri could not live every moment of life in the spirit of his preaching did not take away from the fundamental truth of his message. And in the end, his own humanity was part of what made his spirituality so accessible and real.

Nouwen knew that he didn't manage to live up to all the high standards he set himself – which is why his writings were, in the first instance, spiritual memos to himself. This is not to say that he was living hypocritically, because he was articulating in print the real feelings which he thought should be found in every preacher. Yet in spite of talking honestly and often eloquently in his books about his failings, many readers still tended to spiritualise or deny the reality of what he was, in fact, expressing. Even though they sympathetically related to his references to his inadequacies, they sometimes preferred to overlook the truth. In this sense, Nouwen did not like being put on a pedestal, because he knew that he was not a perfect spiritual leader who could live harmoniously. As he pointed out in *The Inner Voice of Love*, a series of meditations where he is initially speaking to himself, the spiritual life is about searching for that balance:

> There is within you a lamb and a lion. Spiritual maturity is the ability to let lamb and lion lie down together. Your lion is your adult, aggressive self. It is your initiative-taking and decision-making self. But there is also your fearful, vulnerable lamb, the part of you that needs affection, support, affirmation, and nurturing.
> When you heed only your lion, you will find yourself over-extended and exhausted. When you take notice only of your lamb, you will easily become a victim of your need for other people's attention. The art of spiritual living is to fully claim both your lion and your lamb. Then you can act assertively without denying your own needs. And you can ask for affection and care without betraying your talent to offer leadership.[1]

Living with his own contradictions, though, troubled Nouwen greatly: he needed constant reassurance, even from people he did not know.

Once, while he was in England, Nouwen decided to call on Donald Reeves, then rector of St James', Piccadilly, whom he had never met but had heard about. Reeves had been helped by Nouwen's writings in his own ministry and was surprised that the distinguished author wanted to meet him. When Nouwen arrived at the rectory next to the church in central London, it was clear to Reeves that any initial small talk was out of the question:

> He came into my study and opened the conversation by saying, 'Now what do you do about your prayers?' – and so we spoke for an hour and a half about the spiritual life, the difficulties I had in praying and the difficulties he had.
>
> He was a very vulnerable man, searching for something, somebody, somewhere, somehow, which would give him the peace he was looking for. He didn't say too much about himself and I felt ever so slightly overawed by him. He was quite a formidable person, and it took a bit of time for both of us to unwind. I still don't know why he came. He was rather different from the person I had imagined him to be from his writings. He came across as a much more complicated person – more human, gruff, edgy and understanding than I'd expected from the rather apostolic and systematic way in which he wrote about things.

Nouwen knew that the search for intimacy was fraught for celibate Roman Catholic priests whose seminary training had underlined the dangers of special relationships and of getting too close to people. But he was not a person to keep up his clerical guard all the time, and friends talk about his readiness to admit to his needs: 'You may think I'm the famous one and that you need me to help you understand your spiritual life', he would say. 'But actually I need you more.'

As a spiritual guide, he was intuitive enough to speak to the hidden places in people's lives where they felt most vulnerable and least capable – but the vulnerability in him went much deeper and he needed physical places where he could prize it open. One such haven was the Holy Redeemer Center, an old Spanish mission-style retreat in Oakland, California, where he went for peace, prayer and writing. He loved the tranquillity and anonymity – yet would often blow his own cover by introducing himself to the other guests, longing to share with them who he was and getting to know who they were. Fame was both a blessing and a curse but, especially in his later years, he yearned for a space where he could be accepted as a human being and not as an author.

Although in pastoral situations he could display an intensity of concern for the other person, making them feel special and understood, there were friends such as Michael Harank who found that Nouwen was not always a good listener:

> There was a profound desperation and neediness on the part of Henri to be loved and to love. For some people that can be a way of deepening the love of God in their lives; for others it can be an endless cycle of distraction and busyness, trying to find the pearl of great price. There were times when Henri would not listen to the advice of his friends, especially about the implications for his health of his relentless, driven lifestyle. He did not even heed the warnings of his own doctor.
>
> I think it was very difficult for Henri to be with people who did not share his background in terms of wealth, privilege, words and speaking skills. This began to change when he went to L'Arche towards the end of his life, and the community members became his primary teachers. It was much harder for him to sustain a presence with them in a way that he did with people who shared the same background as him in terms of class, values and experience.

Even though Nouwen's affluent background enabled him to feel at ease with, and have access to, powerful figures in the United States and Europe, he never flaunted his privileged status. As to the distribution of his own personal wealth, he spent little on himself and was abundant in his generosity: he would often arrive with presents, kept his local florist in business, frequently wrote personal cheques for colleagues and students who could not afford to fly home to visit sick relatives, and willingly made donations to a range of charitable causes (expecting the money to be spent appropriately). Friends talk about Nouwen's generosity as keenly as they discuss his intensity. His father once became so concerned that Henri was giving away all his money that he decided to open a bank account for him in Holland, so that he would have some savings for his retirement. Although Nouwen was almost always the first to get out his credit card in a restaurant, there were times when he would wait to see if the friend offered to pay. This was one of the ways in which he tested the friendship, the deprived part of Henri needing to know that he was loved unconditionally.

Nouwen relied on his friendships and expected much from them. If friends did not respond to his letters as quickly as he hoped, or didn't ring him to thank him for a gift as soon as they received it, he could become resentful and hurt, sometimes to dramatic degrees. He would call his friends to account and make his feelings known. The explanations were often straightforward and understandable, and Nouwen would quickly apologise if he had been out of order (which he often was). But there were also occasions when a slow response sparked irrational doubts in his mind about the validity of a particular friendship and bad feeling started to fester. It was, however, from this inflamed wound of love that a gift to heal emerged.

6. Wounded Healer

ALTHOUGH SOME members of the royal houses of Europe were occasionally in touch with Henri Nouwen to seek his advice, it was only after his death that his name became linked to the House of Windsor with whom he had had no dealings whatsoever. When Diana, Princess of Wales, died a year later, she was described in one magazine as having been 'like Henri Nouwen's Wounded Healer', a woman who had not disguised her own struggles but, by living through them, had managed to give hope to others – especially those who suffered and those who were marginalised. Both shared an admiration for the work of Mother Teresa.

Nouwen's name became synonymous with the phrase, 'The Wounded Healer' (the title of one of his best-known books) – and few words sum him up more accurately. He did not, however, invent the concept, but came across it in his psychological training, and popularised it. In the autobiographical *Memories, Dreams and Reflections*, published in the 1960s, Carl Jung had written:

> As a doctor I constantly have to ask myself what kind of message the patient is bringing me. What does he mean to me? If he means nothing, I have no point of attack. The doctor is effective only when he himself is affected. 'Only the wounded physician heals.' But when the doctor wears his personality like a coat of armour, he has no effect. I take my patients seriously. Perhaps I am confronted with a problem just as much as they are. It often happens

that the patient is exactly the right plaster for the doctor's sore spot.[1]

The phrase 'wounded physician' is not referenced in the autobiography but its origins lie in the Hebrew Scriptures. Nouwen was also fond of an old legend in the Talmud, taken from the tractate Sanhedrin, which made the same point:

> Rabbi Yoshua ben Levi came upon Elijah the prophet while he was standing at the entrance of Rabbi Simeron ben Yohai's cave . . . He asked Elijah, 'When will the Messiah come?' Elijah replied,
> 'Go and ask him yourself.'
> 'Where is he?'
> 'Sitting at the gates of the city.'
> 'How shall I know him?'
> 'He is sitting among the poor covered with wounds. The others unbind all their wounds at the same time and then bind them up again. But he unbinds one at a time and binds it up again, saying to himself, "Perhaps I shall be needed: if so I must always be ready so as not to delay for a moment".'[2]

Nouwen explained that Christ had given this story a fuller interpretation and significance by making his own broken body the means to liberation and new life. Likewise, ministers who proclaimed liberation were called not only to care for other people's wounds but to make their own wounds into an important source of healing. They were called to be wounded healers. The wounds he often spoke of were those of alienation, separation, isolation and loneliness – ones he shared himself.

He formulated his thinking in *The Wounded Healer*, first published in 1972 and in print ever since. Here, he compares the wound of loneliness to the Grand Canyon – 'a deep incision in the surface of our existence which has become an inexhaustible source of beauty and understanding'.[3] The Christian way of life (he states) does not take loneliness away but protects and cherishes it as a precious gift. The painful awareness of loneliness could be an invitation to 'transcend our limitations and look beyond the boundaries of our existence'.[4] Then, with words which must have reverberated in his own mind and heart for the rest of his life, he spoke about the greatest void:

> We ignore what we already know with a deep-seated intuitive knowledge – that no love or friendship, no intimate embrace or tender kiss, no community, commune or collective, no man or woman, will ever be able to satisfy our desire to be released from our lonely condition. This truth is so disconcerting and painful that we are more prone to play games with our fantasies than to face the truth of our existence. Thus we keep hoping that one day we will find the man who really understands our experiences, the woman who will bring peace to our restless life, the job where we can fulfil our potentials, the book which will explain everything, and the place where we can feel at home. Such false hope leads us to make exhausting demands and prepares us for bitterness and dangerous hostility when we start discovering that nobody, and nothing, can live up to our absolutistic expectations.[5]

Nouwen argues that the wound of loneliness in ministers hurts all the more because they not only share in the human condition of isolation but find that professionally they do not necessarily bring benefit to those they seek to help. A deep understanding of their own pains, however, makes it possible for them to convert their weakness into strength and to offer their own experience as a source of healing to those 'who are often lost in the darkness of their own misunderstood sufferings'.[6] But in so doing, he writes, ministers have to walk the tightrope: they should neither conceal their own experiences from those they wanted to help, nor be tempted by any form of spiritual exhibitionism – 'open wounds stink and do not heal'.[7]

To help ministers achieve a right balance, Nouwen develops the Judaeo-Christian concept of hospitality, seeing it as a virtue which allows people to break through their own fears and open their houses to strangers: a jaded traveller can be the very person to bring salvation to a house. Hospitality makes anxious disciples into powerful witnesses, suspicious owners into generous givers, closed-minded sectarians into recipients of new ideas and insights. Hosts have to feel at home in their own houses, creating free and fearless places for unexpected visitors. Hospitality is the ability to pay attention to guests (concentration) and create an empty space where the guests can find their own souls (community). For Nouwen this is real healing ministry because it takes away the illusion that wholeness can simply be given by one to another. It does not remove the loneliness and pain of the other person, but invites them to recognise their loneliness on a level where it can be shared.

The Wounded Healer is one of Nouwen's most influential books, but it was not received with open hands by everyone. One critic commented:

> Many people see the Nouwen minister as a weakling and either turn away in disgust, suspect they are being used by the minister, or treat the pastor like a bumbling grandchild. The wounded-healer pastor may become an inward-looking chaplain of the emotions who forgets her or his function as a prophet of God and servant of those in need.[8]

Nevertheless, the book continues to be recommended in many seminaries, Protestant and Catholic. One Anglican bishop observed that when he visited the clergy offices in his diocese, he always saw a number of Nouwen's books, including *The Wounded Healer*. He reflected on the importance of the concept of the wounded healer, citing clergy who had suffered from alcoholism or had gone through painful divorces – and what empathy and understanding they were then able to bring to their ministry: 'I think the Church ought to take a leaf from Henri Nouwen's book and allow wounded healers to have a place in the life of the community; and to recognise that, in our heart of hearts, everybody is wounded and everybody is healing out of some wound that they've had in the course of their life.'

Nouwen's own gift as a wounded healer is attested by many. In 1996 he received a message from an old friend, Thomas Day, pastor of the Huguenot Church in Berlin, that his son Lars, a 20-year-old student at Oxford University, had died in tragic circumstances. Nouwen wrote back, saying that he hoped to visit the family. And just two months before his own death, Nouwen made a seven-hour train journey from Holland to meet them. Wearing one of his favourite Central American stoles, he said Mass around their dining-room table every day at about

5 p.m. As always, he carried his own unconsecrated hosts in an envelope and asked the Days to provide the wine. Thomas Day recalls the occasion:

> He made it live. He always commented, the way a good rabbi does at the Seder meal at Passover. He talked and prayed about Lars and our situation so we could identify with the whole thing, despite all sorts of theological issues which would have been unhelpful to discuss. He didn't solve any problems, but he didn't have to. He was just with us in a very special way. There are only three people who have been with us in that way since Lars died, and the other two were rabbis. There was a trust there, and it was a trust which held.
>
> The first thing Henri did was to try to soak in our situation, just to listen and talk to us, to get us to describe our feelings about what had happened. He didn't know our boy so he wanted to learn as much as possible about him. He read everything we had that Lars had written, and what had been written about him. I can't remember Henri giving us advice – but he was one of the few Christians who realised that he helped most by being there and listening. He didn't feel he had to teach us anything particularly – although he taught us a great deal.

Although Nouwen did not always find it easy to be at the bedside of a sick person for long periods, he gave considerable spiritual support to a young man called John Lucey who was dying of AIDS and who had become disillusioned with the Church over the years. Through his friendship with John's parents, Henri became close to him and gained his trust. It was the first time John had ever trusted one of his parents' friends – 'And a priest at that', said Rose Lucey. 'John opened his heart to Henri and felt free to tell him things that Henri had never dreamed of. Henri also opened his heart to John and was absolutely honest with him.'

Nouwen stayed close to John Lucey, especially during his last months. He writes about his suffering in *The Road to Daybreak*: 'Like a wild animal caught in a cage, he could find no rest, and his whole body moved in pain. To see his agony and not to be able to do anything, to know that he would only get worse, was nearly intolerable.'⁹ John welcomed Henri's presence to the end – he had never wanted to turn his back on his baptism or the Church but could not bear the hypocrisy that seemed to exist sometimes in ecclesiastical institutions. John then asked Henri to give him the Sacrament of the Sick and Holy Communion – the last rites. They sat at the kitchen table and prayed Psalm 23. Henri blessed him, made the sign of the cross with sacred oil on his forehead and hands, then prayed for healing and also the grace to die with Christ. Together they prayed the Our Father. 'Johnny became more peaceful when Henri was with him', said Rose Lucey. 'Henri sensed that John was aching for a kindred spirit in the Church and, as John was getting sicker and sicker, they just sat together and talked while they could.'

Every person who was suffering was important to Nouwen. During one retreat in Connecticut, a woman in the front row told him that her husband was dying of cancer. Henri walked over to her, knelt at her feet, looked in her eyes and held her hands. Like many priests, he shared the pain of other people and, from that well of loneliness deep inside him, could talk movingly about the inexhaustible mystery of human suffering and human love.

His training in psychiatric hospitals and his own bouts of depression brought him particularly close to those who suffered from psychological afflictions. Friends who suffered from extreme depression discovered the lengths to which Nouwen would go to be alongside them – transatlantic phone-calls, hospitality, intercontinental air-tickets – and, above all, companionship, and open, honest sharing. He was a man through whom people could experience God's mercy, and that's not something that can be said of many men and women.

Nouwen's words gave hope and encouragement to thousands of people the world over who suffered from depression. In her apartment overlooking Central Park in New York, Wendy Greer had battled with a deep depression for two years. Although she had read Nouwen for years, it was a copy of his *Heart Speaks to Heart* which inspired her to write a 14-page letter to Nouwen from which a friendship evolved:

> I realised he knew a lot of what I was going through. I had felt abandoned by God and didn't realise that God was actually closer than ever. It was a devastating depression. I'd always thought I

was very successful, that I did everything well. I ran this and was president of that, I was a successful wife and mother – but Henri made me realise that being a child of God was the most important thing, to appreciate that and to really claim it. I had always thought that success was measured in terms of awards or promotions; then when I met Henri I realised it was the heart which really mattered, it was how much you could give to people that was important – and I realised that my depression could become a gift.

So, encouraged by Nouwen, Wendy Greer started to be open about her depression – and now people in similar situations contact her frequently: 'My whole outlook changed. Suddenly the poor, the handi-capped and the homeless were all God's children and that has been a great blessing.'

It was Wendy Greer who encouraged Nouwen to publish the journal he had written during his own emotional breakdown. Although he had written the highly personal manuscript, he had never had any convic-tion about sending it to a publisher so it remained in the archives at Yale. She persuaded him to blow off the dust and re-work it for a wider audience. *The Inner Voice of Love* was distributed to bookshops on the day of his funeral in Canada. The book contains a gripping series of spiritual imperatives to himself, one of which is entitled 'Live Your Wounds Through':

> You have been wounded in many ways. The more you open yourself to being healed, the more you will discover how deep your wounds are . . . The great challenge is *living* your wounds through instead of *thinking* them through. It is better to cry than to worry, better to feel your wounds deeply than to understand them, better to let them enter into your silence than to talk about them. The choice you face constantly is whether you are taking your wounds to your head or your heart. In your head you can analyse them, find their causes and consequences, and coin words to speak and write about them. But no final healing is likely to come from that source. You need to let your wounds go down to your heart. Then you can live through them and discover

that they will not destroy you. Your heart is greater than your wounds.[10]

Nouwen believed then that, in a mysterious way, wounds could become a means towards both hope and healing, just as 1 Peter describes the transforming power of the bruises of Christ: 'He himself bore our sins in his body on the cross, so that, free from sins, we might live for righteousness; by his wounds you have been healed.'[11] If this aspect of his pastoral theology was not exactly original, his popular presentation of it certainly was, and Nouwen successfully built a reputation on it. His thinking was not unlike that of the Anglican monk, Harry Williams, who also suffered from depression but was able to write helpfully about it.

There was also a strong similarity between Nouwen and the British biblical translator, writer and pastor, J. B. Phillips, another victim of depression whose publishing successes caused him huge spiritual problems. Like Nouwen, Phillips had a father who pushed him too much and had created in him a fear of criticism and a longing for praise. In Phillips's case the father fixation was projected on to a demanding God and there was always the striving for uniqueness. A biography, published after his death, was entitled *The Wounded Healer*, and reads in places like a study of Nouwen: 'His ministry was worldwide. He guided many through the dark places of doubt and loss of faith. While he was doing this for others he was himself powerfully afflicted by dark thoughts and mental pains. He knew anxiety and depression, from which there was only temporary release.'[12]

The book also includes a letter Phillips received from Leslie Weatherhead, the famous Methodist preacher at the London City Temple, who had coined the phrase 'a prescription for anxiety'. Weatherhead himself won acclaim for uniting the insights of psychology with the truths of religion. His experiences, as he describes them in the letter, are not unlike Nouwen's:

I was crushed between the super-ego and the id. I think success wrought my downfall . . . I was a popular preacher, packing the City Temple, people queuing to get in, selling my books, etc., etc., when all the time I knew myself inwardly to be a lover of applause. The conflict between what I pretended to be in the pulpit or at any rate was thought to be, and what I really was, was too much and broke me in half. Could part of your trouble be the feeling that you don't deserve the praise of the whole world for your translations? You know they are jolly good. So were my sermons!! But human praise blows up the super-ego and makes bigger the contrast with the id, the gap widens when mental health demands they should be drawn together.[13]

Nouwen, then, was not alone in the world of great preachers and ministers as a person who was highly effective and compassionate but who was also psychologically scarred. Over the course of more than 20 years, he was responsible for popularising the concept of the wounded healer which he traced back to its biblical foundations. His work transformed pastoral teaching in the Church by showing that priests and ministers need not be afraid to own their own wounds and use them to heal others. But the struggles had to be lived through in the heart, not merely discussed in the mind. The healing had to come from the sacred centre, that place of divine encounter which resourced so much of his theology and teaching.

7. Visions of Peace and Justice

WHILE RARELY at peace in his own heart, Henri Nouwen took a passionate interest in issues of peace and social justice, endeavouring to bridge the gap between prayer and peacemaking, spirituality and politics, contemplation and action. He led retreats for Nicaragua's Sandinista leaders, and for US senators and military personnel, and also spoke out against the Gulf War, led worship with protesters at nuclear test-sites in Nevada and visited activists in jail. For him the prerequisites for peacemaking were a life of prayer, daily meditation on Christ the Peacemaker, and liturgical intercession for an end to war; he also believed in ongoing resistance to the forces of violence, including non-violent direct action against militarism and public calls for nuclear disarmament; forming, joining or living in communities of active non-violence such as Sojourners, The Catholic Worker or Pax Christi; and living and working among the poor and broken. In a short book, *The Path of Peace*, he wrote that the gift of peace came from those who are marginalised and crushed by society, from the powerless and vulnerable. Above all, he insisted that all work for peace and justice be grounded not in fear or anger, but in love – especially love for the enemy. Although Nouwen refused to see himself as a political priest, sometimes his actions spoke louder than his words.

In 1965, he forsook the comfort of student life in Kansas to join the historic Civil Rights march from Selma to Montgomery in Alabama. A demonstration a few weeks before had been blocked. Police had used tear gas while beating the unarmed marchers with clubs, injuring 140 people. In response, Martin Luther King Jr called on church leaders and people of faith from around the United States to come immediately to Selma for a second march. Nouwen, who usually took little interest in demos, drove nearly 1000 miles to show solidarity (the local Catholic bishop had banned every priest in Alabama from taking part). Nobody knew him or had heard of him, but as the marchers put their arms round one another's shoulders and sang 'We shall overcome one day', he experienced joy in a way he had never done before. From the 'deep, deep south' Nouwen recorded his observations and emotions:

> The road was a four-lane highway, and everyone was welcome. More than 1000 of us had left the camp that morning, and 8000 had arrived in Montgomery the night before. Buses with new participants stopped along the way, cars brought people from every corner of the United States, and the procession stretched itself out like a miraculous rubber band.
>
> It was a non-violent group, but helicopters hovered over our heads; jeeps with military police were parked on the shoulders, giving orders on their walkie-talkies; in the bushes stood the National Guard, barely hidden, with their weapons at the ready; and the state troopers patrolled the route.
>
> Defenders and enemies at the same time. Everyone knew it. The entire National Guard consisted of men from Alabama who permitted no blacks within their ranks and who wore the flag of the Confederacy on their uniforms with defiant pride. The state troopers, who had broken up the demonstration a week earlier with rubber bullets and tear-gas canisters, had become defenders by order of Washington. With growing fear the marchers watched the police officers film the whole column with movie cameras. Everyone knew what that meant. The film would become evidence that would later be used to prove charges of incitement to riot, and countless people realized that if they were identified they would lose their jobs. Protected by the enemy, that was the paradox of this march . . .
>
> The City of St Jude became like an army camp outside the ramparts of a city that had to be taken. Spirits were tense and the urge to get on with it created wild restlessness. Cutting straight

through the camp came a group of young men, clapping their hands, stamping their feet, performing together in an ecstatic choir. They sang, they shrieked, they cried.

Martin Luther King stood up, and with his heavy, dark voice he cried, 'What do you want?' And the people's answer thundered back, 'FREEEEEDOM!' And he cried out again, 'When do you want it?' And the people answered, 'NOOOOW!' And he asked 'How much of it do you want?' And the furious response, 'ALL OF IT!' 'Then let's go to the Capitol, everyone. Don't be afraid. God is with us. Come back tomorrow and gather behind the flags. No one can hold us back.'[1]

The next day Nouwen was there in front of the Capitol steps to capture the atmosphere and listen to this modern-day Moses:

He spoke differently than the others, who could no longer control their seething rage. He spoke slowly with conviction, and with enormous, penetrating power. His phrases were like explanations that went beyond the realm of doubt . . . King's voice rose to the level of holy wrath, and with accelerated rhythm he repeated the words, 'We are on the move. We won't get any further than these steps today, but let it be known: we are on the move. We will go back and we will continue to suffer, but now we know: we are on the move. Others will be killed, tears will flow, the people will bow down, but we are on the move. We can't vote, we can't govern, we can't determine our own fate, but we are on the move.'

And then the people took over. The repeated cry sounded like the blast of trumpets at the walls of Jericho: 'We are on the move'. What began as their leader's cry quickly became the cry of thousands, striking the Capitol walls with sledgehammer blows.[2]

Three years later Nouwen flew to Atlanta for Martin Luther King's funeral but was unable to get into the church because of the volume of mourners. He wrote down that experience too. It became clear to him that when he showed compassion, words flowed naturally. During the 1970s and 1980s he was to witness and write about issues of justice in Latin America as wholeheartedly as he was to support peace protesters in the United States.

A similar instinct impelled him, in 1983, to join a Witness for Peace delegation on the border of Honduras, shortly after a month's stay in Nicaragua. He felt compelled to return to the United States and call Christians to oppose the Reagan administration's war. With the backing of peace groups and the bishops' conference, he embarked on a six-week national speaking tour calling on the churches to speak out against the US-backed Contra war against the poor in Nicaragua. He spoke in packed churches in different cities every day, describing his experience among the faithful and forgiving Nicaraguan *campesinos* (the rural poor) and calling for public opposition to the Reagan government's threat of full-scale invasion. His extensive newspaper interviews and printed talks engendered much debate. His was a prophetic voice and people listened to him. At the end of his tour, just before he was to speak to a crowded congregation in Miami, an anonymous caller left a message that a bomb had been planted in the church and would go off during his speech. Right-wing Nicaraguans, opposed to Witness for Peace, were behind the deliberately planned false alarm to prevent the meeting from going ahead.

Although he never wanted to be identified in any sense as a political priest, Nouwen was undoubtedly being political through his involvement in Witness for Peace. For Nouwen, the contemplative priest, speaking out against US policy in Nicaragua was a public commitment. It was not an easy place for a contemplative to be and yet he chose to be there, tension-filled but deeply involved. Nouwen wasn't a naturally political person: he had no strategic idea about how to run a campaign or how to articulate an issue – but he would sense the theological import and the spiritual dimension.

One of Nouwen's students at Yale was a young Jew called Dean Hammer who became a Ploughshares activist in 1980, twice going into first-strike weapons facilities with hammers, enacting the biblical mandate from Isaiah, 'They beat their swords into ploughshares' – actions for which he received long jail sentences. After leaving the Divinity School, Hammer had helped develop the Covenant Peace Community in New Haven, which Nouwen supported in various ways,

including celebrating the Eucharist on Friday mornings, having breakfast with them and leading spiritual reflections.

Nouwen's theology and practice of the Eucharist became a centre-
piece in Hammer's life:

> I was raised in the synagogue and in the Jewish tradition – but it
> was through Henri and participating in his Eucharists that I came
> to believe that, even as a Jew, I belonged round the table. I also
> think Henri's theology of compassion was a linchpin of the min-
> istry of peace and justice activism. In this ministry of compassion
> there was a radical intersection of the lowest of the low meeting
> the outcasts, as well as the highest of high meeting presidents of
> state and highest leaders of all denominations. I was always
> impressed with how he spanned the spectrum.

Nouwen went to Electric Boat at Groton, Connecticut, where the
Trident nuclear submarine was being built; he spent one Holy Week
there as a witness to peace. He fully supported the campaign to end
nuclear weapons-testing, and in 1985, on the fortieth anniversary of
the US atomic bombings of Hiroshima and Nagasaki, he joined a non-
violent four-day vigil at the US nuclear test-site north of Las Vegas.
About 120 people were arrested in peaceful acts of non-violent civil
disobedience – but because he was a Dutch citizen and feared deport-
ation, he did not risk arrest. However, he cultivated a whole new
ministry among prisoners of civil disobedience whom he visited in jail
and for whom he conducted retreats. In his talks he would stress the
difference between *chronos* and *kairos* time – between killing time in
prison and believing that God could intervene to transform that time
into miracle and grace. This was active compassion on Nouwen's part:
he made no judgement about damaging government property, and
appeared to give unequivocal support to the spiritual journey the activists were following in the footsteps of the Suffering Servant.

Nouwen also shared a long correspondence with Father John Dear,
a Jesuit peace activist. In 1989, Dear was arrested at a demonstration
protesting about the lack of funding for the homeless, and was put
into a cell in Washington DC's central police station. He discovered, in
his coat-pocket, a copy of Nouwen's *In the Name of Jesus* which he
was to review for the *Cistercian Studies* journal. The book reflected on

the need for Christian leaders to be completely vulnerable, with nothing to offer but their own selves, entering powerlessly into solidarity with the anguish which underlay the glittering veneer of success. Dear was personally moved by the book and spent the day meditating on that message; then, with a pencil and paper borrowed from his cell-mates, he started writing notes. A few days after he was released, he sent a copy of the review, along with a letter, to Nouwen who replied immediately, offering support and enclosing autographed copies of his books.

John Dear was among those who had heard Nouwen speak at the Sojourners' Peace Pentecost gathering at the Catholic University, Washington DC, in 1985, where he talked for more than an hour and a half, holding over 1000 people mesmerised. He reflected on the Pentecost story, the image of Jesus washing the disciples' feet and the risen Jesus' question to Peter, 'Do you love me? Do you love me? Do you truly love me?' Nouwen said that was the most important question for those concerned about justice and peace – and it was one which was to console John Dear during his subsequent months in El Salvador where he lived in a church-run refugee camp and worked with six Jesuits who were later assassinated because of their work for peace. This was another example of Nouwen's words taking root in the heart of a fellow pilgrim, and sustaining him in his work, long after they were uttered.

For the next seven years until the week Nouwen died, he and Dear corresponded with each other regularly. Sometimes Dear became frustrated at the limited extent of Nouwen's involvement in peace and justice work. He particularly wanted Nouwen's help in developing a spirituality of non-violence. But while Nouwen offered limited political support, his personal support was unstinting. In 1993, when Dear was serving a nine-month jail sentence for his part in a Ploughshares anti-nuclear action in North Carolina, Henri was very solicitous and wrote to him regularly, sending letters, cards, books and manuscripts. Dear was personally very encouraged by his support.

On the eve of the Gulf War, Nouwen flew to Washington to pray with 10,000 people in the National Cathedral, process to the White House and walk on to the Metropolitan AME (African Methodist Episcopal) Church where he led prayers and spoke during an all-night vigil. He did not find it easy – but the fact that he wanted to take part and show solidarity was characteristic of his commitment. For a person who had a reputation as a great man of prayer, Nouwen was a very turbulent soul on so many issues – and this was evident in his social activism. He would be drawn to an issue because the Gospel would compel him, despite the personal pressures it would bring (such as the pace of being on a speaking tour).

There were many causes on which people wanted their man for all seasons to take a stand. He felt under constant pressure to please people – having Henri Nouwen as an ally gave many causes a higher profile than they would otherwise have had. For several years, for example, his friends working in the field of HIV/AIDS exhorted him to back their work publicly, but Nouwen was hesitant. At a personal level, he offered friendship and support to those who were suffering or caring, but he was less confident about making a public and national stand for this form of social justice. The fact that he was insecure about his own sexuality as a Catholic priest must have intensified his fears.

When he finally attended a conference of the National Catholic AIDS Network in 1994, Nouwen referred to the pandemic as neither God's curse nor God's grace, but 'a privileged time', going on to employ his customary trinitarian motif:

> I have just three words for what really touched me here: community, body and death. So we'll talk about the movement in community from exclusiveness to inclusiveness, the movement in the body from metaphor to reality, and the movement that our mortality helps us to realise, from a successful life to a fruitful life. That's what I've been hearing here; that's what has felt connected with my own experience.

The following year, he again attended the conference, making a much more powerful speech about befriending death. It was clear that Nouwen had become more audacious in his approach. He spoke movingly of a lay Catholic high-school chaplain called Peter who was dying of AIDS and cancer, a young man who had dedicated his life to God but now felt angry and abandoned. He also mentioned his admiration for Peter's gay partner who 'had spoken as the warrior who looked death in the face saying, "I'm going to win the struggle. I am going to win the battle." '

A few months later Nouwen preached at Peter's funeral in front of an entire school grieving for their chaplain. He dealt honestly with the situation by making sure that Peter's partner, who was Jewish, sat in the front row with the bereaved parents. A friend who attended commented:

> Henri affirmed that the funeral was for everyone who was grieving. During the homily he went up to each grieving grouping – first to Peter's parents mourning the loss of a son; then he went right over to the partner and said in front of the whole student body that this was the person who had shared Peter's life most intimately; then to the students themselves to tell them how Peter had been like a brother but would become more like a father now he was with God the Father; then he affirmed all of Peter's wider circle of friends, teachers and colleagues. The local bishop never challenged Henri over that – though I have the feeling he would have liked to.

The event marked a turning-point in many ways for Henri Nouwen, and showed him in another prophetic light. Although its motivation was pastoral and not political, it was nevertheless a very public statement by a famous Catholic priest who wanted to affirm the integrity of a homosexual relationship to a congregation of young students from a Catholic high school. Like his speeches against US policy in Nicaragua, this was no neutral action. It illustrated the deep changes which he was undergoing towards the end of his life, and indicated something about the maturing of his own sexual identity. His increasing friendships with gay people, his private support to homosexuals in relationships and his work for the National Catholic AIDS Network – all paralleled by his ministry at L'Arche – suggest that Henri Nouwen was gradually finding his own peace as a priest to the marginalised.

8. The Gift of Friendship

A GREAT MANY people loved Henri Nouwen and were moved by their friendship with him. Such was the extraordinary affection in which he was held around the world that he counted around 1500 friends in his own circle. A man with connections, he felt he had a vocation to 'talk to the world'. He remained a priest of the archdiocese of Utrecht all his life and returned to see his bishop regularly. While the world was his parish, he was always working out what his commitment should be to the Church in Holland. There were huge questions to consider about what the Church there wanted or could tolerate. It seemed to be highly conservative or radically liberal – and Nouwen was neither.

Henri Nouwen always had an ambivalent relationship with his homeland. He made his name in America and became an internationally famous Dutch priest. Not only were his writings translated into numerous languages, but he could find himself preaching in three different continents in one week. He was a world-class wanderer. For him, a DC 10 was like a number 19 bus – he even had his own travel agent who, like the local florist, was unlikely to go bankrupt with Nouwen around.

Holiness and restlessness are not uncommon partners in the spiritual life and Nouwen had large quantities of both. They often worked in tandem when he was on a long-haul flight, chatting to someone in the window seat about their life. It was not unusual for the passenger to end up both on Nouwen's mailing list and in his prayers. He was the proverbial Flying Dutchman who was on and off planes until the last few days of his life. Whether it was a flying trapeze or flying jumbo, he loved to be in the air, *en route*, going places.

For all his travelling, he was never really one for holidays. He loved beautiful landscapes and fine architecture, but it was people he was looking for more than places. Nouwen saw friends as gifts from God, but knew they could not replace God. They had limitations and weaknesses, like everyone else, and their love was never complete. But through their limitations they could be signposts on the journey towards the unlimited and unconditional love of God. He recognised that different friends brought different gifts, and that they could be reminders of one's own truth, even though that might be hard to hear at times. As he explains in *Bread for the Journey*:

> There is a twilight zone in our own hearts that we ourselves cannot see. Even when we know quite a lot about ourselves – our gifts and weaknesses, our ambitions and aspirations, our motives and drives – large parts of ourselves remain in the shadow of consciousness.
>
> This is a very good thing. We will always remain partially hidden to ourselves. Other people, especially those who love us, can often see our twilight zones better than we ourselves can. The way we are seen and understood by others is different from the way we see and understand ourselves. We will never fully know the significance of our presence in the lives of our friends.[1]

Henri Nouwen's presence in the lives of his friends will long be remembered. It seemed they could share anything with him. Though when he turned up one day on the doorstep of Kathy Bruner's home at L'Arche with a bottle of red wine, she was not in the mood for celebrating. Henri called round regularly and they shared much together. But on this occasion Kathy, a young single assistant living at Daybreak, had just learned that she was pregnant and was nervous about telling him. But when she broke the news, Henri could not have been more thrilled and insisted that they open the bottle. He was amazed and delighted at the new person growing, developing and becoming. Characteristically he expressed excitement and intense joy at creation, transcending the pain of the situation by reaching and grasping for the joy in the moment.

For Kathy Bruner, Nouwen was prophetic because he could express what was true. However, because he came from a place of truth and authenticity, it meant that he was also vulnerable in his own suffering: 'Somehow, through the suffering he lived, came an intense authenticity that enabled him to jump into people's hearts and lives. Out of all his inner pain, he was always able to ask where God was in it all, where truth was located and where the joy could be found.'

Kathy's first child, Timmy, came to look on Henri as a father-figure. Kathy recollected Henri exploding through the front door with the latest story about his adventures, joyfully disrupting whatever was happening in the house. Henri also joined Kathy and Timmy for a holiday at Cape Cod, the sort of break by the sea he often yearned for. Kathy cherishes fond memories of that time:

> There was a great desire in his heart to know children and be creative, just to play in the sand or run in the waves where there would be no judgement. I saw a great longing in him to be simple, to be loved for who he was, to be carefree (which didn't come easily to him). Yet at the same time he could also be incredibly wise. Timmy's father killed himself, and it was terribly anguishing for us as a family. Right away, Henri could move in with great wisdom and say, 'Let's live this, talk about the Dad you never knew and what that means; let's have a service and celebrate this father you never knew'. He just wasn't at all afraid of the taboos of suicide, loss or death. That was the beauty of Henri. He could move from playing like a child to being a wise man who said, 'Now is the moment'. Sometimes his two lives could be within seconds of each other. I think they were both always there.

Nouwen did not just become friends with individuals – he wanted to connect with families and build up lasting relationships. This was particularly true in the case of his 30-year friendship with Father Don McNeill whom he met at the University of Notre Dame. Henri loved all the family, including Don's father (also called Don), his mother Katherine, and his aunt Agnes. The McNeills became a second family to him, at least in the Chicago area, and their 40-acre home beside a lake in Barrington Hills, Illinois, became an oasis from the pressures of work – not that he was ever able to relax for long. Don recalled:

> Henri gave retreats to us out at the lake. We would always share the Eucharist around the table. When we broke the bread and shared the cup with Henri, we deeply believed we were with the communion of saints – the Nouwen and McNeill families were present, both the living and the dead. It was always a deep and unforgettable experience for all of us in friendship.
>
> When my mother died of Alzheimer's disease, Henri could not have been more supportive. He came to stay afterwards and, with great gestures, mesmerised all of us with stories of his encounters with the Flying Rodleighs. When he dramatised this in our living room, we actually thought that he was flying and we were catching. I remembered how I had held Dad when Mum was near the end of her life, and when Henri had become the catcher for me, holding me when I needed to trust that I would get through an illness.
>
> Henri had abundant gifts of joy, contagious laughter and spontaneous humour. His joyful expansive smiles evoked a response in all age-groups. Henri's life was one of passion, excitement and *alegría* [joy]. He was deeply in love with God and deeply loved by God.

Another important friendship in his life, which lasted 20 years, was with a freelance journalist who was on an assignment from the *New York Times* when they first met. Fred Bratman had been sent to interview him at Yale. Bratman was then 23, Jewish, and a child of Holocaust survivors – a background with which Nouwen was familiar in view of the Nazi occupation of Holland during his early years. A week after the interview, Nouwen phoned to arrange a meeting with Bratman, who by this time had moved on to other stories and had almost forgotten about their conversation, during which he had talked about his fantasy of becoming a novelist. Nouwen came prepared to invite Bratman to spend a year at Yale, and offering to fund him. Bratman eventually accepted – and though the resulting novel has never seen light of day, far more important was the bond that grew between them.

And so the Catholic writer and the Jewish writer began a friendship in which they supported each other in good times and bad, including Bratman's divorce and Nouwen's breakdown. Bratman, the secular Jew, challenged Nouwen, the devoted Christian, to write a book about how he and his colleagues could live a spiritual life within a Western materialistic culture. The result was *Life of the Beloved*. While not seeking to convert his friend to Catholicism (never an agenda for Nouwen), he did try to bring Bratman back to his religious roots:

> He really sought to make me a better Jew. That was his mission, his *raison d'être*, to encourage me to learn more about my own faith. I had grown up with some knowledge of Judaism, I was Bar Mitzvahed, I did go to synagogue on the high holy days and I'd read many books on Judaism but I didn't really practise the faith in any regular way. But virtually every time he called me he would ask, 'So what's going on in your spiritual life?' And when he came to New York we'd go the theatre or a concert, but he'd also cleverly manoeuvre to get us to a synagogue, often on Shabbat.

It was at one of these services that Henri felt touched in a powerful way. At a Bar Mitzvah, which he was attending with Fred, he watched and listened intensely as a Jewish father, in an eloquent and moving speech, told his son how proud he was of him and how much he loved him. Both Fred and Henri were in tears – but it was particularly meaningful to Henri for personal reasons. He so longed for the affirmation and affection of others that the poignancy of the moment struck a deep chord of yearning within him, for these were the very words and gestures which he had so wanted to hear from his own father.

Through his own needs and insecurities, Nouwen made demands on some of his friends in attempts to gain their attention. He sometimes contrived situations and manipulated friendships. But he was his own worst enemy. He accused people of having agendas for him – and many did; but he sometimes set people up to have those agendas in the first place, in his own complex need to be needed. The mistake some made was not to challenge Nouwen about his behaviour because they were frightened of upsetting him.

He appreciated honesty, as Michael Harank – his part-time assistant at Harvard, and later his friend – realised. Harank had finally come to the truth of accepting himself as a gay man. He was deeply conscious of the freedom of self-acceptance, and the knowledge of being able to accept the unconditional love of God:

> Because of the generation Henri was a part of, because of the Catholic Church which he grew up in, was formed by and, in my opinion, deformed by, the area of sexuality was repressed by him for many years. What the AIDS epidemic did for him, and for a lot of people like him, was somehow provide him with a way of connecting with his sexuality and his compassion.
>
> It was very clear to me from the very beginning of our relationship that Henri was a gay man, but he was not able to say those words for a very long time. However, he was eventually able to share with a small circle of friends that he was gay. That he could share this truth gave him an enormous sense of relief. The coming-out process enables you to build a sense of solidarity and community with others who have shared the hellish journey that gay people have to go through in order to come to a new sense of freedom about who we are.

Because of the Western lack of a healthy theology of sexuality, Harank explained, people had not been given the means to understand that sexuality was one of God's most beautiful gifts:

> Henri was part of that tragic generation which simply had no tools to work with that gift. Here was Henri in a Church which didn't honour sexuality or give him the tools to deal with the area of sexuality, and which was quite violent in a number of its teachings with regard to homosexuality. How was he going to make that a part of his writings, his life and his intimate relationships? He couldn't, and it was because of the fear.

Towards the end of his life Nouwen was put under pressure from some members of the gay community to be more open about his sexuality. But because he had suffered all his life from fear of rejection of any kind, he became troubled, not so much by being outed, but by the possibility that people would reject him and his writings if the truth about his sexuality were disclosed. This took an enormous emotional, spiritual and physical toll on his life and may have contributed to his early death. Privately he had been in touch with his publishers about writing a book on homosexuality, but had told them that he was not 'emotionally free' to do it. Harank comments:

> I think Henri wanted me to remind him gently that there was this huge gap between what he wrote and what he lived. His decision to go to L'Arche and to live in a community of broken and wounded people was a desire to close that gap. When he had his breakdown because of a broken friendship, he was forced to face the paradoxes and contradictions of his own life, especially his sexuality. But thank God for a community of people who knew the meaning of brokenness, fragmentation and woundedness in very incarnational ways because, living in a community like that, he was forced to face the contradictions and paradoxes of his own life.
>
> The dyke broke in terms of his trying to hold together pieces of his life that were being stretched. The tension became so great that something had to break. Henri suffered a total collapse of strength and energy, except for his writings. Writing was his blessing and his curse: a blessing because it was a way for him to deal creatively with the darkness of his own life and, through that gift, he was able to share that with others in some very profound ways. But for people who knew him, there was always the curse of the dissonance between his living and his words. Writing allowed him to control what he wanted to record. His true friends served (when they could) as the people who kept him humble about who he was and what he was trying to live – and helped him to realise that he had to be somewhat accountable for what he wrote.

Nouwen's journals suggest that he sometimes felt like a beggar in friendships, being all too aware of that 'same old pain that has been with me for many years and never seems to go completely away'. He expected the consideration of other people, but grew to realise that friends were not divine and could never fulfil all his longings. Yet he believed that the bond of friendship was 'stronger than sexual union can create, deeper than a shared fate can solidify, and it can be even more intimate than the bonds of marriage or community'. Blessed are those, he said, who laid down their lives for their friends.

After a lifetime of being a good shepherd, he understood that such laying down might, in special circumstances, mean dying for others. In view of his own global ministry and pastoring of others, there were many who saw his sudden death in that way. He had always wanted to die in the company of those he had loved, so, despite receiving visits and calls from many of his friends during his last days, there was a terrible irony in the precise circumstances of his death, in a coronary care unit, in the presence of a frantic medical team battling to save his life after the second heart attack in a week. Among those at his bedside during those final days was the director of Daybreak, Nathan Ball. But he was not only there in his official capacity. They had known each other for a decade and had been especially close. It was a platonic friendship which opened up so much in both of them, and was a major cause of Nouwen's breakdown. In the last decade of his life, much of his world revolved around this one person to whom he referred in his writings. Nouwen was conscious of the centrality of this friendship in that he once warned Ball that biographers would inevitably approach him after Henri's own death. Ball vowed never to speak about their relationship, and asked not be quoted in any section of this book. He would not talk about what was clearly a deeply loving friendship between two intellectuals, an extrovert and an introvert, who shared a great love of the spiritual and needed each other for different reasons.

It was Nathan Ball, along with members of Henri's family, including his father, who gathered around the bedside after Henri's death, grieving the loss of a loving brother, son and special friend. His life, which had always seemed in perpetual motion, ended abruptly, back on Dutch soil where it had begun one winter's day, 64 years before.

II
MIND

9. A Priest is Born

IT WAS A timely arrival. The birth of Henri Jozef Machiel Nouwen on 24 January 1932, in Nijkerk on the edge of the Veluwe Hills in central Holland, fell on the feast of St Francis de Sales, patron saint of writers. In past centuries the Nouwens had been blacksmiths who, as well as shoeing horses, had specialised in artistic forge-work, such as locks and ornaments. They came from the province of Limburg in the south of the Netherlands. Henri's father, Laurent Jean Marie Nouwen, who was to become an eminent professor of tax law at the University of Nijmegen, came from a family of 11. Henri's paternal grandfather had been the town clerk of Venlo, while his grandmother had brought up all the children. They were pious Catholics: one daughter became a nun, and Laurent spent a few months in a Dominican seminary testing his vocation.

Henri's mother, Maria Huberta Helena Ramselaar, was one of an artistic family of eight from Amersfoort in the middle of Holland. Her mother had been an enterprising woman who had turned her late husband's little general store into a thriving business which brought the family prosperity. They too were traditional Catholics, though not as strict as the Nouwens. Maria was a gentle, knowledgeable and devout woman with interests in languages, literature and mysticism. Her elder brother, Toon Ramselaar, became a priest in the archdiocese of Utrecht and a Vatican adviser on Jewish–Christian relations.

Henri was born nine months after Laurent and Maria married and, for an elder son who was to have his share of anguish over the years, even the delivery had its complications, his mother being in labour for three days. Such was the concern for their welfare that prayers were offered for their survival, but after such a painful birth, a strong bond was to develop between them. Henri let his mother Maria read everything he was writing, and corresponded with her regularly. The relationship with his patriarchal father was less harmonious and, although Laurent was proud of his son's ambition and desire for leadership (except when it challenged his own), Henri was never convinced of his father's unconditional love – at least, not until relatively late on in life.

Almost as soon as Henri was able to talk, his questions revolved around whether or not he was loved. Among his first words from the playpen were, 'Do you really love me?' – at other times he was restlessly trying to climb out of it and go somewhere else. Throughout his life, his problems were always with his father, never with his mother. His anxieties as to whether he was truly loved were projected on to God, and were a profound and permanent aspect of his later adult vulnerability. Light is thrown on these anxieties by the theories of John Bowlby (1907–90), a groundbreaking British psychiatrist and psychoanalyst. Bowlby believed that foundations for relationships later in life were laid in early childhood in what he called 'secure attachment' to parents, especially the mother-figure. If this attachment were secure, the child felt loved, supported and appreciated by the parents from early in its life, predisposing the child to approach relationships in the future with confidence and trust. Peter Naus, a social psychologist with whom Nouwen talked through his anxieties, commented:

> Those who believe in this theory would probably say that Henri had not been securely attached, in the sense that he always seemed to be searching for affection and was never quite sure if people appreciated him. Yet the mother–son relationship suggests a very strong attachment – so why was it broken? One possibility is that, for whatever reason, Henri almost at birth had a need for security, affection and love that exceeded by far what could normally be provided for a child. There was something early in his life, outside the control of mother or father, which somehow threatened that bond.

But there may have been another explanation. In infancy Henri was always chronically hungry and, as an adult, began to wonder if this was connected with his anxious temperament. Much later on in life his mother apologised for having brought him up in accordance with the doctrine of a German doctor who had advocated that the grasping nature of young children should be tamed by restrictions of food and physical touch.

By all accounts, Henri was an energetic child, always moving about. He was also cross-eyed and clumsy, feeling humiliated at school when he was the last choice for a sports team. At home, he was less inhibited. If his friends wanted to play Cowboys and Indians, he would agree to take the less popular role as an Indian on condition that they, in turn, would become his altar servers as he played the part of a priest saying Mass. As soon as his mother detected a priestly vocation in her lively son, she asked the carpenter of her mother's department store (where she did some part-time book-keeping) to build him a child-size altar and got her seamstress to create some small vestments. By the time he was eight, Henri had converted the attic into a children's chapel where he not only played Mass, but gave sermons to his parents and relatives and inaugurated an entire hierarchy with bishops, priests, deacons and altar servers acted out by his friends, along with his brother Paul. His grandmother bought him, not toys and sweets, but chalices and patens. In all of this, Henri had to be the leader or stand out in some way. Encouraged by his father Laurent to develop skills of independence and critical thinking, he seemed naturally to draw others to himself and found himself mixing with the real leaders of society through the friendships his parents had cultivated.

But it was by no means all a game. For him, playing the priest had a serious motivation; it was a sign of being marked out by God. At the same time, his grandmother gently introduced him to a life of prayer and encouraged him to form a personal relationship with Jesus. Likewise, the Virgin Mary also played an important role in his religious development. He loved the May and October devotions, building little shrines to her, singing hymns in her honour and praying with rosaries. His brother Paul is convinced of the authenticity of Henri's early vocation, and commends their parents for respecting it too – they never tried to push him in any other direction.

The call to priesthood seems to have been complemented by a remarkably early awareness of his own sexuality. He later said that he was just six years old when he first realised that he had a homosexual orientation. It is not without significance that his deep feeling of being set apart by God for a life of service in the Church appears to have emerged at the same time as he was discovering something about the nature of his self-identity. But it was only towards the end of his life that he accepted the extent to which spirituality and sexuality were interconnected.

Henri always remembered the beginning of the second world war, and his parents crying. He was seven when Hitler's army overran Holland. During the German occupation the Nouwens managed to shield their children from Nazi terror, but they could not prevent them from seeing their Jewish friends and neighbours being led away to the concentration camps. Henri's father carved out a secret place under a windowsill in an attic room where he remained for days reading by candlelight, never certain whose footsteps he might hear outside the door. One day in 1944, soon after the Allies landed in Europe, German soldiers forced their way into the home, attempting to take Laurent into forced labour. The family had no time to warn him – indeed, when he heard the footsteps outside the door that day, he thought it was his own father bringing him food. Finely tuned instincts, however, led him to remain silent until he was spoken to and the soldiers, after carrying out a search of the room, continued their hunt elsewhere. Maria, who spoke German fluently, was able to talk to the Nazis in their own language and, while she never collaborated in any way, she knew how to charm them and win their respect.

Determined to ensure that Henri's schooling would not be disrupted by the war, Maria Nouwen convinced the Crozier Fathers, a small group of young priests, to start a school of their own in the neighbouring village of Bussum; Henri and six other friends continued their elementary education there. Facing ultimate defeat, the German occupation forces stepped up their campaign of fear, which was then compounded by the 'hunger winter' when, cut off from electricity, fuel and food, thousands of Dutch men, women and children cycled into the countryside to find something to eat. Henri and Paul used to go on their bicycles to get potatoes and other vegetables from friends who had a farm. At home, his parents would sometimes invite friends around to read poetry or to look at each other's art work. United by a common threat, the art-loving friends came from a variety of social and religious backgrounds, teaching Henri much about respect and tolerance. He later wrote that, against the backdrop of a constant fear of death, he had learnt from his parents something about God which would be hard to appreciate for a generation without memories of bomb shelters or the destruction of large cities.

Maria Nouwen loved life and lived it for others, especially for her husband, children and grandchildren. Like Henri, she loved the beauty of flowers, trees, mountains and valleys; of French cathedrals and old village churches; of Italian cities such as Ravenna, Florence, Assisi and Rome – and of the picturesque landscapes around the family's holiday home in the mountains of Switzerland. In *In Memoriam*, his tribute to her, he writes about recognising the strength of their relationship as he watched her dying:

> The only thing that seemed important was that we were together. She was looking at me with the same eyes with which she had so often looked at me – when I went to the seminary, when I became a priest, when I left to live in the States: eyes expressing a love that could never be separated from pain. Maybe that was what had always touched me most deeply – her eyes, in which love and sadness were never completely separated. How often had I seen tears in her eyes when I left again after a day, a week or month at home! How often had I looked into that lovely face, which expressed so beautifully that love causes pain!
>
> I can still see her waving from the quay of Rotterdam Harbour as the large ship *Statendam* slowly left its berth, taking me on my first trip to the United States. I can still see her waving as I passed the 'Passengers Only' sign and walked through the airport gates. I can still see her waving from the door of the house as I was driven away in my brother's car. And the clearest memory of all because it happened hundreds of times – I see her waving from the platform as the train rolled away from the station, making her figure smaller and smaller. Always there was a smile and a tear,

joy and sadness. From the moment of my birth when her tears merged with smiles, it has always been that way.[1]

Perhaps Nouwen had an unnatural idealisation of her as the perfect mother? It was certainly the one human relationship in which he had absolute trust. Henri's younger brother Laurent, a business lawyer, recalls that, after her death, Henri spoke of the way in which she had passed on the love of God – and he prayed that together the family would be open-handed to give love and to accept the love of each other.

When Maria died of cancer in 1978, Henri felt as though he had been cut loose from his anchor. He was also deeply hurt when, having sent the text of *In Memoriam* to his father, he failed even to receive a note of gratitude. A few months later, he wrote *A Letter of Consolation* for him. The opening chapter begins somewhat ambivalently: 'Often I feel sad about the great distance between us'.[2] He goes on to reflect on his upbringing:

> Father, you are a man with a strong personality, a powerful will, and a convincing sense of self ... You have achieved what you strove for. Your successful career has rewarded your efforts richly and has strengthened you in your conviction that success in life is the result of hard work ... Experience has taught you that displaying weakness does not create respect and that it is safer to bear your burden in secret than to ask for pity. You never strove for power and influence, and even refused many positions that would have given you national recognition, but you fiercely guarded your own spiritual, mental and economic autonomy ... One of your most often repeated remarks to me and to my brothers and sisters was, 'Be sure not to become dependent on the power, influence, or money of others. Your freedom to make your own decisions is your greatest possession. Do not ever give that up.'
>
> This attitude – an attitude greatly admired by mother and all of us in the family – explains why anything that reminded you of death threatened you. You found it very hard to be ill, you were usually a bit irritated with the illnesses of others, and you had

very little sympathy for people whom you considered 'failures'. The weak did not attract you.[3]

Friends talk about Laurent Nouwen as a traditional patriarch, the stern taskmaster who, like a good Dutch father, called his eldest son to achieve more and more. Only later in life did they come to realise how much they were alike and how much they really loved each other. Henri's brother Laurent recognises that, as the eldest son, Henri was always trying to live up to what he thought were his father's expectations of him. Yet, he pointed out, there was little in his brother's writings about living up to the expectations of a demanding God. Through prayer and study Henri had learnt that this loving God loved humanity before humanity loved him – so people were already the beloved of God without having to do anything: 'Henri might have been prepared for that insight by his struggles with a demanding father, but he never perceived God that way'. Other friends, though, believe that Henri was very wounded by his father, and was always distressed by his father's attitude towards him.

Shortly before his death in 1997, at the age of 94, Henri's father Laurent spoke about his son:

> He was very generous and always bought me gifts. He was very proud of his father and he would always try to impress me by saying, 'I'm a great man, father, I have been a success'. I was very proud of his success. When he left Holland to go to the States he had nothing – no money, no relations, nothing. When he had money, he gave it away. He was a very devoted son but also very human. I miss him a lot. He was always writing and visiting. He had much of his mother in him, eager, always working.

However, from childhood, Henri always felt drawn towards another relative – his mother's brother Toon ('Uncle Anton'), who was a Roman Catholic priest. While still a boy, Henri was given a communion set by Toon Ramselaar, who was to have a deep influence on the young priest-in-the-making. Henri's boyhood fantasies of presiding at the altar remained with him vividly. Apart from a few fleeting thoughts of becoming a naval captain, mostly because of the influence of the men with their blue-and-white uniforms and golden stripes parading along the station platform of his home town, Henri always dreamed about one day being able to say Mass, as his Uncle Anton did. Toon Ramselaar's influence should not be underestimated. To the young mystic, he was the embodiment of mystery, perhaps even a Jesus-figure, whom Henri had to emulate. Toon stood for everything to which Henri aspired.

At the age of 12, Henri pleaded to go the minor seminary, but his parents felt he was too young to leave home and suggested he attend a local school near Amsterdam. His father told him that he ought to wait at least six years before making a decision about the priesthood, though Henri was ready to start training there and then. After the war, the Nouwens moved to The Hague where Henri finished his school education with the Jesuits at Aloysius College. In 1950, at the age of 18, having passed all his secondary examinations, Henri finally embarked on the road to priesthood.

10. Holy Ground

THE 18-YEAR-OLD Henri Nouwen began his training for the priesthood in 1950, a decade or so before the second Vatican council which was to bring about radical changes in the Church, not least in Holland. He initially entered the final year of the minor seminary in Appledorn where Toon (by now, Monsignor A. C. Ramselaar) was president – as well as being a pioneering figure in strengthening links between the Roman Catholic Church and Israel. After a year, Henri moved on to the major seminary at Rijsenburg near Driebergen to follow a six-year programme (two years of philosophy and four of theology). There he began to make a name for himself.

Louis ter Steeg was a few years younger but soon learned about Nouwen on the Rijsenburg grapevine:

> He belonged to a well-to-do family and most of us were from modest backgrounds. He was the nephew of the minor seminary president so had a kind of aura which was both social and charismatic. All the students liked and admired him so he was elected as senior of the community, which meant that he was a representative in front of the professors and, when the bishops came, he was the speaker. Effectively he was head boy. He was a very kind person. Even then he had a charism of being easy to approach and he talked with people freely.

Students were allowed home only once every six months, but Nouwen combated any feelings of loneliness with hard work. He read prolifically, day and night, and signed on for the Newman Club to delve into the thinking of John Henry Newman who converted from Anglicanism to Roman Catholicism. Father Frans Haarsma, professor of dogmatics, and the Club's supervisor, remembers Nouwen as hard working and hard praying, with an intellect which was not very original but very sharp: 'He was always making notes during the classes and when he handed them in they were better than what I had said in the lessons. I was absolutely persuaded that he would be a fine priest.'

Close to the seminary was a postgraduate institute for Protestants training for the ministry. In an ecumenical initiative, courageous for the day, the Catholic and Protestant students started to meet on a regular basis. Nouwen was apparently keen for this to happen – and it might have prepared the ground in which the seeds of his ecumenical vision were later sown. As a teenager, Henri had noticed how Roman clergy refused to speak to Protestant ministers if they passed them in the street – and he was later conscious of the insularity of his own upbringing. By the time he left the seminary, as he later recalled,

> I had only met – and that quite cautiously – a few Protestants, had never encountered an unbeliever, and certainly had no idea about other religions. Divorced people were unknown to me, and if there were any priests who had left the priesthood, they were kept away from me.[1]

His time as a seminarian also proved to be foundational for his travelling and his writing. Although seminarians tended not to go abroad, he succeeded in venturing to Donegal in Northern Ireland, from where he wrote his first articles for the Dutch Catholic Press. He recollects the experience in *The Genesee Diary*:

> I remember very vividly my hitchhike travels through the dark, melancholy hills of Northern Ireland. I wrote stories about the storytellers of Donegal in the Dutch newspapers and, while Kerry and Killarney left hardly any memories in my mind, Donegal I will never forget.
>
> There was something sombre but also profound and even holy about Donegal. The people were like the land. I still see vividly the simple funeral of a Donegal farmer. The priest and a few men

carried the humble coffin to the cemetery. After the coffin was put in the grave, the men filled the grave with sand and covered it again with the patches of grass which had been laid aside. Two men stamped with their boots on the sod so that it was hardly possible to know that this was a grave. Then one of the men took two pieces of wood, bound them together in the form of a cross and left silently. No words, no solemnity, no decoration. Nothing of that. But it never has been made so clear to me that someone was dead, not asleep but dead, not passed away but dead, not laid to rest but dead, plain dead. When I saw those two men stamping on the ground in which they had buried their friend, I knew that for these farmers of Donegal there were no funeral-home games to play. But their realism became a transcendent realism by the simple unadorned wooden cross saying that where death is affirmed, hope finds its roots.[2]

Back at the seminary, Nouwen continued to make connections between the world and the Spirit. Although pleased by his publications, he was convinced that his message of hope would chiefly come through his priestly identity. He was confident, intelligent and charismatic in communication. When it came to preaching, he outshone everyone with his powers of expression and theological insight. There were already suggestions that he would continue his studies after ordination and become a seminary professor. There had never been much discussion at home as to whether or not he had a vocation. His father had urged him to travel more before entering the seminary – but Henri had been, as ever, in a hurry. Moreover, he was delighted to be following in his famous uncle's footsteps at last and gaining the affirmation of students and staff. But his fellow students recognised his need for close companionship in an environment where students were encouraged to be friends with everyone, but no one in particular.

The climate of clerical formation was one of intellectual and spiritual purity, a disciplined life of supplication and sublimation, although to Nouwen at the time it was not as lugubrious or oppressive as it might seem today. Seminarians had to learn to be available for others and to be single-minded about building up the Church, the body of Christ. To serve unstintingly and lead holy lives, however, their own bodies had to be kept rigorously in check. They were to shower in light robes so they never saw each other fully naked and they had to sleep with their arms crossed at the top of their chests, above the bed-covers. The body was not to be trusted. Prone to sinful and destructive meanderings, it was the mule to be whipped on the way to the kingdom. Years later, when some friends were laughing at a 1940s manual they had found about teaching sex to children, Nouwen refused to find it funny: 'That's what it was like for us in the seminary', he protested. 'You don't understand what it was like.'

On 21 July 1957, in St Catherine's Cathedral, Utrecht, Henri Nouwen was ordained by Archbishop Bernard Alfrink, primate of the Netherlands, soon to become a cardinal and a leading progressive at the second Vatican council. The archbishop laid his hands on Henri's head, dressed him in a white chasuble and invited him to touch his golden chalice, his hands bound together with linen cloth. In *Can You Drink The Cup?*, Nouwen explains that he had always dreamed about being able to say Mass as his Uncle Anton had. When the archbishop handed him a special chalice of his own, he felt ready to start life as a priest:

> The joy of that day still lives in me as a precious memory. The chalice was the sign of that joy. Most of my classmates had chalices made for their ordination. I was an exception. My Uncle Anton, who was ordained in 1922, offered me his chalice as a sign of his gratitude that a new priest had come into our family. It was beautiful, made by a famous Dutch goldsmith and adorned with my grandmother's diamonds. The foot was decorated with a crucifix shaped as a tree of life, from which golden grapes and grape-leaves grew to cover the node and bowl. Around the rim of the foot these Latin words were engraved: '*Ego sum vites, vos palmites,*' which means, 'I am the vine, you are the branches'. It was a very precious gift and I was deeply moved to receive it.[3]

The ordination was a memorable day for the Nouwen family and his parents, in particular, were quietly proud. Henri's brother Laurent, then only 13, remembers being

> quite impressed by him in the black 'battledress' and I had the feeling that he was a very gifted and a very driven person. We

were very happy with him, but no more than we were pleased that Paul was a good lawyer or my father a professor. The ceremony was full of pomp and I can still see the great distance between the clergy on the one side and the people on the other. We felt as if we were the consumers of the Church and not participants in it.

The next morning Father Nouwen celebrated his first Mass in the sisters' chapel of the seminary:

I stood in front of the altar, with my back to the sisters who had been so kind to me during my six years of philosophical and theological studies, and slowly read all the Latin readings and prayers. During the offertory I carefully held the chalice. After the consecration I lifted it high above my head so that the sisters could see it. And during communion, after having taken and given the consecrated bread, I drank from it as the only one allowed to do so at that time. It was an intimate and mystical experience. The presence of Jesus was more real for me than the presence of any friend could possibly be. Afterwards I knelt for a long time and was overwhelmed by the grace of my priesthood.[4]

Later he said another Mass in the parish church of Our Lady of Lourdes in Scheveningen near The Hague where the family was living. A social party and dinner followed. In subsequent years, as soon as there was any possibility of expressing something spiritually at home, Henri took over from his father and did the praying at the table. He didn't have to play at being priest any more.

Nouwen remained a priest of the archdiocese of Utrecht throughout his life, but had an ambiguous relationship with the Church there. In the 1960s he was seen as a progressive and socially orientated priest while many of his colleagues were conservative. In the 1970s and 1980s, as he discovered the value of spirituality in America, those same fellow priests became more political about the way the Church was being run and, as Nouwen saw it, relegated the spiritual or ignored it altogether. To them, Nouwen became a pious conservative, frightened of making a stand on social issues because he wanted to be friends with the right, the left and the middle.

The second Vatican council, which Nouwen attended between 1962 and 1965, inaugurated a period of renewal in catechetics, ecumenism and pastoral methodology. The Dutch National Pastoral Council even proposed that priests be allowed to marry, a proposal rejected by Rome. Indeed, for several years during and immediately after the second Vatican council, the Dutch Catholic Church was the advance guard of the future of Catholicism, an image which faded with the onset of internal dissension and polarisation, and the growth of pastoral demoralisation and frustration. The appointment of conservative bishops, aimed at healing the cracks, only seemed to make matters worse. Polarisation within the Church in Holland seemed on a greater scale than anywhere else in the European/North American Catholic Church – but it was only a stage in a process of change. The decisive issue was the speed with which the Dutch Church grasped what Vatican II was all about. In articles Nouwen referred to 'the tragedy' of Dutch Catholicism, and confessed to feeling like a stranger among his own people. He found churches locked, people uninterested in prayer or the Eucharist and an increasing number of families torn apart by divorce. Nouwen believed that the Dutch Church was failing to address the spirituality of the people with whom it had lost touch. The boundaries were being pushed back too far. But he cautioned against viewing Holland as more liberal than other countries, pointing to the fact that issues were simply more openly discussed there.

But just as his uncle had been an exception in his time, applauded for his work in Jewish–Christian relations, so too did Nouwen have exceptional status conferred upon him by people increasingly impressed with his success in the secular world and with his ability to make connections. And just as some Dutch priests had had mixed feelings towards the prominence of Father Toon Ramselaar in his day, so too did they towards his nephew. Both men were from the higher echelons of society, and had managed to make their own distinctive marks in Church and society – whereas other priests from more modest backgrounds had equal talents, and maybe even better scholarship, but had not gained such popular acclaim and public appeal. Nouwen, who had modelled himself on his uncle and was always connected with him in the minds of other priests, later became angry that he was not respected by his Dutch colleagues. Many Dutch priests, however, resented the fact that Henri had been allowed to roam the world while they had had to stay behind and live within the Dutch context, with all its problems.

His bishop, Cardinal Adrianus Simonis, noted Nouwen's unhappiness about the liberal direction of the Church in Holland and about the lack of welcome from his fellow priests there. For many of them, his spirituality was too soft and sentimental, lacking hard political clout. Cardinal Simonis understood Nouwen's lack of popularity in the Netherlands:

> Here, we have been through a big crisis, with priests becoming anti-hierarchic, anti-celibate and anti- the moral doctrine of the Church. Harrie (as he was known here) didn't fight against Rome and the views of the pope. The modern priests and people in the Church here wanted him to take up positions in discussions, and he wouldn't do that. That is one of the reasons why he was less accepted here. In his writings he was not an academic theologian but a Christian speaking out of his experiences of the Gospel. That's why he isn't mentioned much in seminaries.
>
> Yet although he rarely referred to the pope or the institutional Church, in his way of writing Nouwen was a Roman Catholic. You could taste that, and in *Can You Drink The Cup?*, I find the soul of Henri Nouwen. I always considered him a secular priest with the whole world as his diocese; and I realised that he would never be at home with the spirituality and secular culture of Holland.

Holland was not a place to fan the flames of Nouwen's own enthusiasm for spiritual living and, not surprisingly, his books ended up being published across the border in Belgium, where he had a keener following. However, in the last years of his life, Dutch Catholics mellowed towards his writings, while the Protestants relished his emphasis on the Bible. Ruud Bunnik, an old seminary friend, thinks that Nouwen's books are unlikely to make any significant breakthrough on his native soil: 'Here, the problems of secularisation are experienced on a deeper and more far-reaching level than in, for example, North America'. Bunnik believes that Nouwen was too restless and insufficiently systematic to take part in the more technical debate about the renewal of Church and theology:

Henri did not deny that ecclesiastical structures could hedge in and enfeeble the Gospel message, but he did not see it as his vocation to take an active role in trying to change them. He was a man of personal spirituality which starts from the individual person and returns to it. A question which I cannot really answer, but which has to be asked, is whether the deepening of personal insights carries with it the risk of isolating people from their ecclesiastical and social contexts. It may lead to the fragmentation of the self and such an emphasis may jump on the dubious band-wagon of present-day individualism.

Whatever his sadness over the demise of spirituality in the country of his birth, Nouwen looked back to his ordination as one of the most important days of his life. Yet almost from the very first weeks, his ministry was to move in its own unique direction. Few Dutch priests of the time had as much freedom as he did. It was customary for the newly ordained to be sent off to parishes, but the archbishop asked Nouwen if he would pursue further studies in theology at the Gregorian University in Rome with a view to becoming a professor back in the seminary. But the courteous and independently minded Father Henri had other ideas: he asked and received permission to read psychology at the Dutch Catholic University of Nijmegen, and soon found himself on the threshold of a whole new world.

11. A Meeting of Minds

IN SEPTEMBER 1957, Henri Nouwen enrolled at Nijmegen for what would amount to seven years' doctoral research in clinical psychology. Psychotherapy was already replacing spiritual and moral guidance as the primary method for relieving mental and emotional disorders, while psychologists and psychiatrists were increasingly viewed as 'the new priesthood'. To keep up with the times, clergy had started having psychological training, but there were concerns that their counsel would become more psychological and less spiritual. It was rare, but by no means unknown, for Roman Catholic priests to enter the field; Nouwen was among a number of priest-students eager to connect ministry and theology with a variety of new disciplines.

With his father a professor of tax law at the same university and his uncle a renowned priest, Nouwen was something of a marked man. For a time, he got involved in his uncle's project of improving relations between Roman Catholics and Jews, organising all kinds of meetings, some with VIPs, to bring the different groups together and forge a better understanding of the state of Israel. But he was just as interested in the powerless people as in the powerful.

Peter Naus, a student of social psychology, got to know Nouwen as a result of his engagement to Anke who, unlike Peter, was not a Roman Catholic. Before the marriage it was recommended that she become a Catholic too, and Henri was asked to give the instruction:

Our conversations were at least as important to me as they were

to Anke because Henri opened up totally new perspectives for me
on church teaching and the Bible. It was a much more open
approach than I had been used to, and I found it very refreshing.
I came from a very traditional background and, although I was
used to asking important intellectual questions in other spheres
of my life, I was still afraid to do that with my own religion – but
Henri made it a lot easier in those pre-Vatican II days.

Throughout his time at Nijmegen Nouwen stood out for his enthusiasm
and intensity. With his theological education and the blessing of the
Church, he seems to have been active in all kinds of meetings for
students who were amazed by his proclivity to talk. Although it was a
Catholic university, many students tended to be anti-clerical and
Nouwen clearly had a rough ride at times, though he won many friends
and admirers too. He helped in an institution for difficult young people,
joined a work placement programme in the mines of South Limburg
(no doubt remembering van Gogh's work as an evangelist among
miners) and gained experience at Unilever in Rotterdam. He also
became a part-time chaplain in the army, and in one of his books,
Nouwen described the wide leather belts, girded around his waist and
across his chest and shoulders, which had 'given me prestige and power'
and encouraged him 'to judge people and put them in their place'.[1]

Ever keen to travel, Nouwen also arranged for an unpaid position
with the Catholic Emigration Service as a merchant naval chaplain on
the Holland–America line. His job was to serve as a pastor, chiefly to
people emigrating from the Netherlands to North America. He often
talked about being on board ship and passing the Statue of Liberty and
the imposing Manhattan skyline. He did some parish work on the
stopovers and managed, through correspondence with a Boston
cardinal, to meet the famous psychologist Gordon Allport with whose
work at Harvard he had become familiar. Like Nouwen, Allport had
an interest in religion and pastoral psychology which countered the
academic trends of the time. During their meeting Allport advised
Nouwen to finish his psychology studies in Nijmegen and enrol in the
programme of studies in religion and psychiatry at the Menninger
Foundation for Psychiatric Education and Research in Topeka, Kansas.

But there was still much work to pursue in Holland. Nouwen became particularly influenced by the psychologist of religion, Professor Han Fortmann, himself a priest of the archdiocese, and undertook research on Anton Boisen, the father of the clinical pastoral education movement (whom he was later to meet). But in order to be awarded a full doctorate, he was told that he would have to include more statistical evidence and scientific evaluation. Nouwen was apparently furious and refused to co-operate, feeling he was being 'forced into a straitjacket'. Like most Dutch students, his research work entitled him to the degree of Doctorandus, meaning 'someone who still has to become a doctor'. It is not equivalent to a British or American doctorate. Further action was needed.

Dr Seward Hiltner, who was undertaking pioneering work in pastoral theology at Princeton Theological Seminary and who taught at Menninger four days a month, once recalled that, early in 1964, he received a long and meticulously handwritten letter from an unknown Catholic priest at Nijmegen, explaining that if he remained there and finished his doctorate in psychology, the faculty would give him the freedom to relate it to theology, but he felt inadequate to fulfil such an integrative task. He could only justify dropping out at that crucial stage if he could get direct help in integrating psychology with theology and pastoral care. Was there anything in the USA, he continued, that could help him at this critical juncture? Hiltner had never had such a self-authenticating letter. Like Allport, he recommended that Nouwen spend a year at the Menninger in a 'golden age of religion and psychiatry' where he would have the chance to meet some of the leading figures in the field. So Nouwen applied, and was accepted.

Peter Naus vividly remembers Nouwen's last day at Nijmegen:

> There was a party after graduation, and it was one of the few times I saw Henri unequivocally happy. Usually, even if he was having a good time, there was an undertone of seriousness, nervousness or tension. But on this occasion he seemed to have no restrictions or ties. He was just having good fun and I remember him dancing La Bamba. He was elated – and that image has stuck with me.

Nouwen was excited to be heading for the United States. The Menninger Foundation had been founded by Karl Menninger and his brother, William, who had pioneered certain methods of psychiatric treatment in the USA. Their work attempted to merge the psycho-analytic understanding of behaviour in the treatment of hospital patients with the use of the hospital's social environment so that all members of the clinic's staff – nurses, therapists, orderlies and even housekeepers – had a role to play in helping the mentally ill to recover.

What pleased Nouwen was that the Foundation practised clinical pastoral education, a programme of professional training through the long-term supervision of ministers and theological students working alongside men and women suffering mental illness in hospitals, prisons and social agencies. There he would be able to combine psychology and theology in a more practical way than he could in Holland, and he knew that the practitioners of the respective disciplines did not regard each other suspiciously as they tended to elsewhere.

Nouwen could not have been there at a more exciting time as he launched himself into new learning patterns, expanding his knowledge of clinical work and developing crucial skills. He also had to improve his English and this helped him communicate at a deeper level with the patients with whom he loved to work – and they soon found they could trust him. In combining his theological interests with his new-founded clinical knowledge, Nouwen enhanced his reputation. Unlike several of the Catholic priests, ministers and rabbis there, Nouwen had no problem in bridging the gap between ministry and psychology. His counselling and therapy skills were deeply ingrained, as was his faith and spirituality: in him, the two were seamlessly integrated.

When Nouwen's former supervisor, Professor William Berger, who taught the psychology of culture and religion at Nijmegen, visited Nouwen in America in 1965, he encountered two divergent evaluations of him:

> Seward Hiltner was very full of praise of him – this had something to do with the fact that he was giving lectures, addressing the spiritual life and fascinating students at a time when young people were rebelling against institutionalised religion. He was one of the people who could overcome that resistance. His business was spirituality and he usually wore his collar in those days. Hiltner was much more fond of him than the famous Dutch psychologist

Dr Paul Pruyser, who assured me that he did not expect much scientific work from Henri Nouwen. Pruyser said that Nouwen was too full of himself – and I don't believe he ever changed his mind.

Highly precise and scientific psychology was far from Henri Nouwen. His enormous spiritual hunger was so overwhelming that he had no patience with wasting his time and energy doing scientific work. He was on the frontier between the educational and psychological sciences, more a preacher than a researcher.

One of his most enterprising studies followed a visit he made to Hiltner's teacher, Anton Boisen. Nouwen had huge admiration for Boisen, the founder of the clinical pastoral education movement, who had served as a Presbyterian minister in rural parishes before becoming chaplain at Worcester State Hospital, Massachusetts, and Elgin State Hospital, Illinois. In his clinical work, Boisen had tried to lead students towards deeper theological insight by teaching them, in hospital settings, to view psychiatric patients as 'living human documents' whose pain and healing could cast light on the nature of religious experience. Nouwen had studied Boisen's work at Nijmegen – now he wanted to meet him in person.

He discovered him in a small room behind the dining room, sitting in a wheelchair. Nouwen found his language slow and difficult to understand, but recorded a vivid account of their meeting, a year before Boisen died:

> Most remarkable were Boisen's direct and open questions to me: What do you think about the messianic claim of Jesus? Who is God? What influence do you think that nuclear power has on the idea of God? Will this world survive? By these many intrusive questions he kept me close to him and didn't allow me to leave . . . Who is God? What is your answer? Boisen challenged me to a straight and open answer. When I asked him the same question he replied: 'God is the internalisation of the highest values of our social relationship, and Jesus Christ is the man in whom the apostles found these highest values represented'. He showed an obvious preoccupation with the end of the world and his own

personal death . . . The fact that I was a priest intrigued him,
especially in relation to celibacy.[2]

Nouwen was grateful to have met this man whose suffering had become
a source of creativity: 'Seeing a man so closely and being able to
experience how a deep wound can become a source of beauty in which
even the weaknesses seem to give light is a reason for thankfulness'.[3]

Nouwen's vigorous approach to research took his mind away from
the sense of loneliness he felt in a new culture, and a certain confusion
over where his life was leading. At Menninger he became more acutely
aware of his homosexuality which he saw as a disability, and it started
to disturb him greatly. He knew that the sharing of it would not elicit
much sympathy in church circles, and an understanding response from
fellow priests could not be guaranteed. The uncertainty of whether he
was loved by his father was one thing; the conviction of his sexual
orientation was another.

This uncomfortable realisation in his early thirties coincided with a
political awakening, as Nouwen aligned himself with the struggle of
Martin Luther King Jr and the protests of the black Civil Rights movement into which he channelled some of his energies. He also became
more at ease with the spiritual climate of America so, all in all, the
1960s became a time of new awareness, both without and within. He
later stated that he became 'spiritually adult' during his time in Kansas,
where academic rivalry was turned into collegial co-operation. Emotionally, though, he remained adolescent because so much of his own
personal struggle was repressed and he had no means of dealing with
it effectively in the Church – and his spiritual identity was always
uppermost in his mind.

Nouwen's reputation as clinical psychologist and dynamic speaker
was raising his profile in parts of America, thus boosting his self-
esteem. Here was a gifted priest from a famous Dutch family on the
threshold of an exciting academic career in the combined world of
psychology and spirituality. He stood out from other students and, just
as people had started talking about him back in Holland, so too was
his name being whispered within certain circles of influence in the
United States. Alert psychologists at the University of Notre Dame in

South Bend, northern Indiana, got wind of his reputation and Nouwen was invited to join their new psychology department.

Nouwen accepted, but he knew he had to sort out his own psychological confusions which were clouding his sense of vocation. While on a long trip from Miami to Topeka, he decided to stop off at the Cistercian monastery of Our Lady of Gethsemani, Kentucky (Thomas Merton's home for 27 years), in the hope of finding someone to whom he could talk. When the guest-master learned that Henri Nouwen had studied psychology and was at the point of joining the faculty at Notre Dame, he introduced him to John Eudes Bamberger, a monk and a psychiatrist. Father Bamberger – who later became abbot at Genesee – recalled (without breaking any confidences) that Nouwen was going through a difficult time in his life, experiencing deep (and, for him, unparalleled) anguish over his vocation: 'He came with considerable stress and crisis and I think he left in peace'.

Nouwen later referred to his meeting with Bamberger in a published journal, but did not specify what had been on his mind:

> John Eudes listened to me with care and interest, but also with a deep conviction and a clear vision; he gave me much time and attention but did not allow me to waste a minute; he left me fully free to express my feelings and thoughts but did not hesitate to present his own; he offered me space to deliberate about choices and to make decisions but did not withhold his opinion that some choices and decisions were better than others; he let me find my own way but did not hide the map that showed the right direction. John Eudes emerged not only as a listener but also as a guide, not only as a counselor but also as a director. It did not take me long to realize that this was the man I had needed so badly.[4]

Nouwen returned to Kansas in a more relaxed frame of mind, reassured about his vocation and now keen to live it out in another world. As he prepared to move to the University of Notre Dame, he looked back on his years at the Menninger Foundation as a time of growth. When, many years later, the journal *Pastoral Psychology* named Nouwen Pastoral Theologian of the Year, Seward Hiltner, himself an American Presbyterian minister, revealed the depth of Nouwen's commitment at Topeka:

I still have nearly 200 pages of a not quite completed, thoroughly realistic, but extraordinary imaginative account of Henri Nouwen's ministry to one particular person during the Menninger period. This was an offender before the law, young, with many of the usual handicaps of family and social background. Nouwen neither attempted nor made any heroic interventions. But he stuck with his young patient to understand everything he possibly could. The unpublished 'case history' is a model not only of careful reporting but also of professional-level concern. The Menninger Foundation mix of theory and practice was apparently just what Henri Nouwen wanted and needed at the time.[5]

12. Connections

THE UNIVERSITY of Notre Dame, near South Bend, Indiana, was founded in 1842 by the Congregation of the Holy Cross, a French religious community led by Father Edward Sorin who sought to establish a great Catholic university in America. Originally it comprised a men's college, an elementary school, a college-preparatory school, a vocational ('manual labour') school and a novitiate. A sister school for women, St Mary's Academy, was opened in 1843. In its early days, the college offered a standard programme of humanities, rhetoric and philosophy, to which modern languages, music and art were added and, later, science, law and engineering, along with an academic press and a library. In the 1920s the university was reorganised into colleges of arts and letters, science, engineering, law and business administration.

Under the presidency of Father Theodore M. Hesburgh CSC from 1952, the university's undergraduate and graduate programmes were strengthened. With the development of the largest Catholic university press in the world, Notre Dame became a place where the Catholic Church could do its thinking, especially on education, culture and parish life. The aerodynamics of glider flight and the transmission of wireless messages were also pioneered there, but it perhaps became best known for its football team, its newly expanded 80,000-capacity stadium and its marching band, the Band of the Fighting Irish.

When Henri Nouwen arrived as visiting professor in pastoral psychology in 1966, it was still a men's university. (It was not to become a co-educational undergraduate university for another six years.) Father Hesburgh was looking for ways of revitalising the curriculum, one of which was a new department of psychology. While the second Vatican council was still in session, Father Hesburgh was already seeking ways of integrating its theology into the spiritual and intellectual lives of students and staff. After the close of the council in 1965, its full implications were causing upheaval among Catholic congregations of North America, who were beginning to open their windows to the unpredictable winds of ecclesiastical change. There was both ex-citement and revolt: the Mass was changing from Latin to English, priests were starting to face the people, parishes were becoming less cloistered and more socially engaged, and there was an atmosphere of ecumenism among denominations and other faith traditions. Nouwen had attended sessions of the council in Rome and was invigorated by the air of renewal which subsequently swept through Catholic Christendom.

Much of Nouwen's own theology was clearly shaped by Vatican II. The Church was to be seen as a mystery or sacrament, and not primarily as an institution, which was completely in line with his deeper intuitions. The Church was the whole people of God, not just the hierarchy, clergy and religious; its mission included action on behalf of justice and peace and should involve the laity in their own apostolate. The word 'Church' embraced all Christians. God used other Christian Churches and non-Christian religions in offering salvation to all, so the Catholic Church was not the only means to salvation. Not all official teachings of the Church were equally binding or essential to the integ-rity of the Catholic faith, while the dignity of the human person and the freedom of the act of faith formed the foundation of religious liberty for everyone, over against the view that 'error has no rights'.

Eager to help people connect their lives with the new insights of Vatican II, Nouwen was something of a fresh breeze at Notre Dame as he encouraged searching clergy and congregations to imbibe the spirit of the council which many had regarded as the most significant religious event since the Reformation. Father Don McNeill, who founded and directs the university's Center for Social Concerns, recalled the August day in 1966 when, as a newly ordained priest, he had his first encounter with Father Nouwen during a concelebration of the Eucharist:

His hair was all over the place and he was running around making sure the cruets for the wine and the bread were taken care of before the Mass began. I didn't know who he was. I even wondered if he was someone who was able to celebrate the Eucharist. But when he began to preach there was an immediate magnetism – all of us were awestruck by his passion and insights. As he continued the Mass, his reverence and emanation of light released us from our stereotypical expectations of priesthood.

I also participated in a course he was teaching on pastoral care and counselling. It was magnificent. The courses I studied in Rome were in Latin, but Henri's dynamism was so captivating that I had to rethink my approach to theology and what I was going to be doing as a priest. Henri used experiential learning and helped us develop journals and case studies, based on our ministries. Students and others in need became sources for our theological reflection. It was a whole new way of doing theology.

Some Protestant seminaries used clinical pastoral education. In the Roman Church our use of psychology was often pragmatic and compartmentalised. It was a time of confusion for us. Henri integrated the best wisdom of forward-looking European theologians with clinical–psychological insights from Holland and the Menninger Foundation. He had a way of integrating psychology and theology, and bringing it to life in exciting terms linked with our contemporary experience of the 1960s and beyond.

As always, Nouwen cared about his students and their personal lives. He was the first to recognise their goodness and gifts and, with the same attention, was willing to help them through any crisis. He was very curious and deeply interested in all that went on in people. He was sensitive to people's sufferings and wanted to do something about them. Because of his own woundedness, the concept of the wounded healer came naturally to him – but not in the sense of 'I've had my problems so I can now understand yours'. It was at a much more fundamental level.

The sporting spirit of Notre Dame raised some questions. Nouwen was attracted by the opportunities and vision the university offered, but had a more ambivalent attitude towards its overtly competitive ethos. Nouwen went along to some of the Notre Dame football games with Don McNeill, himself a former athlete (they were still exchanging their opinions on the idea of competitiveness six weeks before Henri died). Nouwen didn't understand everything that was going on in the matches, but he was amazed by the size of the players and the roughness of the sport, wondering how it all connected with the Christian message. He objected to people's self-esteem being based on competition that showed they were better than someone else. He cringed when students said that they were only happy if Notre Dame was the number one team in the country. Yet he also loved watching the game.

When Nouwen and McNeill – along with Douglas Morrison – were writing the book *Compassion*, they decided to include competition among the themes. But the issue was sometimes difficult, even among the authors themselves. Nouwen disagreed with aspects of McNeill's approach, and won the day on what eventually appeared in print:

> This all-pervasive competition, which reaches into the smallest corners of our relationships, prevents us from entering into full solidarity with each other, and stands in the way of our being compassionate. We prefer to keep compassion on the periphery of our competitive lives. Being compassionate would require giving up dividing lines and relinquishing differences and distinctions. And that would mean losing our identities! This makes it clear why the call to be compassionate is so frightening and evokes such deep resistance.
>
> This fear, which is very real and influences much of our behaviour, betrays our deepest illusions: that we can forge our own identities; that we are the collective impressions of our surroundings; that we are the trophies and distinctions we have won. This, indeed, is our greatest illusion. It makes us into competitive people who compulsively cling to our differences and defend them at all cost, even to the point of violence.[1]

Nouwen's one-year visiting professorship was extended to two years, during the course of which he engaged with, connected and reconnected people in ways few others could. He was an enthusiastic teacher and by all accounts highly respected by the students. He made a point

of establishing himself on campus and he quickly got to know the
people in power too.

Father Hesburgh, the president of Notre Dame, had approved of
Nouwen's appointment and felt he had much to contribute to psychology at a time when those trained in classical behaviourism tended
to be distrustful of what went on inside people. They understood
psychology as a science, whereas Nouwen put a lot of emphasis on
people's experience, not their behaviour. It was the inner life that
mattered. Peter Naus, a Dutch friend who spent a year teaching with
Nouwen at Notre Dame, believes that his spirituality came out of the
psychology he had been exposed to, rather than the other way round:

> Henri's books almost all start with human experience to which he
> gives a spiritual meaning. His core concept, the wounded healer,
> is a very profound spiritual concept – but it's also a very profound
> psychological concept within a phenomenological, not a behav-
> iourist, tradition. The power of Henri's writings was that people
> recognised their own experiences in them. He would say that if
> people cannot connect their own experience to what you are
> talking about, you might as well forget it.
>
> Henri found a way of connecting the psychological with the
> transcendental approach, so he would say to pastoral people, 'Do
> not stay at the psychological level, you have to bring something
> else, you have to clarify the transcendental dimension. As a pas-
> toral counsellor you have to show how human experience can be
> elucidated by reference to the Gospel.' On the other hand, he was
> always very clear that you couldn't talk about a spirituality which
> was disembodied, as it were, of human experiences – so he found
> his own unique solution for bringing the two levels together.

But Nouwen could not hide his own dissatisfaction about being solely
a psychologist. The longer he stayed in the profession, the more he
realised that he would have to go on asking psychological questions
which would only elicit more psychological answers. He wanted to
'make available the light of the Spirit', and free himself from a life
to which he was beginning to feel enslaved. At the same time, he had
seen the development of the charismatic movement in the Catholic
Church and been attracted by its focus on personal renewal and

community. He believed that, by concentrating on inner conversion and the eradication of evil from the human heart, by stressing personal love and the creation of small communities of prayer, many deeply committed Pentecostals were basically saying that the only way to change this destructive world was to start with a change in one's own heart – a position with which he fully agreed.

Notre Dame was the only Catholic university in the United States at which Nouwen taught full-time. He felt at home with its ethos, but knew he needed a wider ecumenical perspective. While the authorities were indebted to him for his service, they insisted that if he were to teach there permanently as a professor, he would need a doctoral degree.

In 1968 Nouwen returned to Holland where he worked at the Pastoral Institute in Amsterdam and the Catholic Theological Institute in Utrecht, teaching seminarians. For a while he lived in a community of professors who recognised the signs of loneliness in him – that he expected more from others than they were able to give him. This need for friendship and community produced a restlessness in him – he was looking for so many people and so many places, driven by his need of real affection, a factor of unrest in his life.

During this time Nouwen got stuck into his further studies at the University of Nijmegen. He realised that, as a priest and pastoral counsellor, it was important for him to deepen his theological insights and he hoped that his work in psychology in the United States could be reworked into a doctoral thesis in theology. But, as with his psychological research several years before, there were hurdles. He presented a text in the spirit of Hiltner, a case study which he had been working on in America. It was a good piece of work but, according to his supervisor Professor Frans Haarsma, the theological side was not sufficient for a doctoral thesis. His interest was not strictly scientific, but more practical – and he wasn't prepared to start again on a wholly new thesis. But, passing exams in pastoral theology, psychology, sociology and catechetics, he was awarded another Doctorandus qualification. (All would not be lost, however, as American institutions later showered him with honorary degrees including doctorates.)

Nouwen did not settle back in Holland. His name was now becoming known in the United States where his articles had started to appear in

newspapers, his lectures on pastoral psychology had been published
in book form and he was gaining a reputation as a teacher and speaker.
He regretted the way in which the Dutch Church was drifting away
from what he considered to be its spiritual values and sacramental life,
and he knew that Holland, in the aftermath of Vatican II, would not
be the soil in which his new-found insights would germinate. There
was a lukewarm response to his publications and he was not offered
any professorship at Nijmegen which he might have expected. All in
all, Europe did not look like the continent for him.

At one point, Nouwen resigned from his teaching job and lived for
a year as a student in a rented room – but found he was soon forgotten:

> People I had hoped would come and visit me didn't come; friends
> I expected to invite me remained silent; fellow priests whom I
> thought would ask me to assist them in their Sunday liturgy didn't
> need me; and my surroundings had pretty well responded as if I
> were no longer around. The irony was that I always wanted to be
> alone to work but when I was finally left alone, I couldn't work
> and started to become morose, angry, sour, hateful, bitter, and
> complaining. During that year I realized more than ever my vulner-
> ability.[2]

Encouraged by the transatlantic reaction to his first publication, he
submitted a text based on his theological thesis which would became
the book *Creative Ministry*. He also managed to get published in Dutch
a study of Merton, which was later translated in English. Like an actor
who had tasted Broadway and relished it, Nouwen kept up his
American connections while he was back in The Netherlands. From an
address in Utrecht in March 1970, he sat down in front of his typewriter
with yet another proposal – this time for a manuscript which would
eventually become his most famous book, *The Wounded Healer*. The
letter, addressed to Betty Bartelme, religious editor at Doubleday,
explained that it would be a pastoral book consisting of three substantial articles around the question of 'How do we face the world of
tomorrow?' He ended by pointing out:

> I have been reading the prison letters of George Jackson and I
> have this strange feeling that this book has really changed me

very much. If I will write more things in the future it certainly will be different. I think I am getting less sweet if you know what I mean. I very much would appreciate a quick note from you. Time is becoming very precious to me and I can hardly keep up with my own change of feelings.

There were indeed many changes afoot. The offers were not only coming by way of publishers – he was being headhunted by academics too. The prestigious Yale Divinity School, a leading American Protestant seminary, invited him to apply for a post as a pastoral theologian. Initially, he had turned down the offer and affirmed his commitment to the Church in Holland. But he began to realise that the Dutch were not as interested in him as the Americans, and that he was more likely to have greater influence across the ocean. Six months later he was approached by Yale for a second time, interviewed and appointed to the staff. But the conditions were laid down not by the interviewing panel or by the appointments board – but by the candidate himself. He would be pleased to join the faculty, but only on his own terms and in his own time.

op, left] Henri's father, the late Professor Laurent Jean Marie Nouwen, at his home Geysteren, outhern Holland. (Photo: Ron van den Bosch 1993)

bove, left] Henri with former Yale students Yushi Nomura (centre) and Bobby Massie at the twenty-fth anniversary of his ordination in 1982. Yushi became a teacher in his native Japan and Bobby n Episcopal priest in Boston, USA. (Photo: Mary P. Carney)

bove, right] Henri with Abbot John Eudes Bamberger at the Abbey of the Genesee during the :lebrations to mark the twenty-fifth anniversary of his ordination to the priesthood in 1982. 'hoto: Mary P. Carney)

[top, left] After-dinner reflections: Henri with Jean Vanier at Trosly in 1983.

[top, right] Henri with his father at Connecticut Hospice, USA, in 1982. After the death of his wife, Mr Nouwen asked to visit the hospice, where one of Henri's friends, Mary P. Carney, is a nurse. (Photo: Mary P. Carney)

[above, left] The real road to Daybreak, 1986: Henri looks on as friends at Harvard load the removal van. (Photo: Mary P. Carney)

[above, right] For Father Henri, the eucharistic life was about letting go of resentments and choosing to be grateful.

[left] Henri with Adam Arnett, the 'silent, peaceful presence' at the centre of his life at Daybreak. (Photo: Dutch TV/Jan van den Bosch)

[top, right] A man for others: Henri with young friends at Daybreak. (Photo: Peter Doll)

[above, right] Preaching, for Henri Nouwen, was not about converting, but about developing a spiritual way of life.

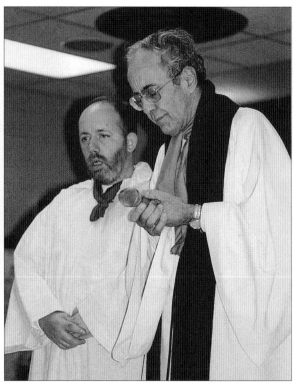

[top, left] 'I'm coming here to do battle', said Henri when he arrived at the South Park Community Trust in Surrey, England, with an icon of St George and the Dragon. During a time of deep inner struggle, the image was a symbolic reminder of the demons he was confronting.

[top, right] Preaching in pairs. Bill van Buren, a core member at Daybreak, reflects on life at L'Arche with Father Henri. 'He was our best pastor, but also my best friend.' (Photo: Peter Doll)

[above] True friends: Henri in his room at the Dayspring with his secretary, Connie Ellis. (Photo: Jutta M. Ayer)

[top] Part of Henri's extensive library at the Dayspring. A print of a detail from Rembrandt's *The Return of the Prodigal Son* hangs on the left.

[above, left] Wearing a favourite Latin American stole, Father Henri points out the features of a Guatemalan cross to his godson, Gabriel Gavigan, in Surrey in 1992. (Photo: Bart Gavigan)

[above, right] Henri being 'born again' as a clown on his sixtieth birthday in 1992. 'He who is called to be a minister is called to be a clown.' (Photo: Peter Doll)

[top, left] The Flying Rodleighs in mid-air: for Henri, not just an exciting showpiece, but a whole picture of life. (Photo: Ron van den Bosch)

[top, right] Trying it for himself: Henri preparing for a flight on the flying trapeze. (Photo: Ron van den Bosch)

[above, left] Reliving his experience with the trapeze artistes at the home of the McNeill family in Illinois, 1995. 'Just stretch out your arms and hands and trust, trust, trust.' (Photo: Thomas B. McNeill)

[above, right] The Lighter Side: Sister Sue Mosteller and Father Henri Nouwen entertain 'on horse-back' in a play at the Winter Garden Theatre in Toronto. The performance – part of the twenty-fifth anniversary celebrations of L'Arche, Daybreak – was staged in January 1995. (Photo: Doug Wiebe)

[top, left] Body language: Henri Nouwen explaining a point of theology with his entire being. He was speaking to a friend after morning Mass at Peapack, New Jersey, in April 1996. (Photo: © Neal McDonough)

[top, right] Henri Nouwen with the Archbishop of Chicago, Cardinal Joseph Bernardin, at a Catholic conference on disability in the spring of 1996, just a few months before their deaths. (Photo: Pathways Awareness Foundation)

[above, left] A Croatian edition of *Letters to Marc about Jesus*, found next to a church in Bosnia which had been destroyed by the Mudjaheddin. (Photo: Diana L. Chambers)

[above, right] Henri's nephew, Marc van Campen, subject of *Letters to Marc about Jesus*. Marc is now an attorney at law and tax adviser in Amsterdam.

[above, left] For Henri J. M. Nouwen, putting ideas down on paper could lead to 'inner places hardly knew were there'. Here he is writing his spiritual journal during a retreat at Guernevi California, in 1996. (Photo: Kevin F. Dwyer)

[top, right] Sunflowers adorning the grave of Henri Nouwen in King City, Ontario. (Photo: Mar Carney)

[above, right] Photo: Kevin F. Dwyer.

13. The Art of the Teacher

SITUATED IN New Haven, Connecticut, Yale is the third oldest university in the United States. The founding fathers of 1701 were committed to 'the grand errand' of disseminating 'the blessed reformed Protestant religion in this wilderness'.[1] The establishment was originally chartered by the state and called the Collegiate School, but a Puritan leader, Cotton Mather, concerned about the growing tolerance of religious dissent at Harvard, encouraged a wealthy British trader, Elihu Yale, to contribute to the new institution. He made a series of donations to the school – and it was renamed in his honour. The initial curriculum focused on classical studies and an unyielding obedience to orthodox Puritanism. In 1882, four years after the separation of Church and state, the Divinity School was founded. It was the new era of professional schools, not only in theology, but also in subjects such as medicine and law – and was necessary because parish ministers were too busy to train apprentice clergymen. That a Roman Catholic priest would one day become one of its most popular professors would have been unthinkable.

An opportunity for Henri Nouwen to join the staff arose in the late 1960s when a vacancy occurred for a professor of pastoral theology. Nouwen was no stranger to Yale: he had visited the university some years before and had spent time with James E. Dittes, professor of pastoral theology and psychology. It was Dittes who chaired the search committee which eventually interviewed a number of candidates for the prestigious post. Two were recommended, one of whom was

Nouwen. He went through the appointments process and was offered the job of associate professor. But he was very reluctant to make such a commitment, and agreed to go to Yale only if he were given two years to make the transition.

But by the time he arrived, Nouwen seemed to have changed. He had been appointed largely as a discerning clinical psychologist who could help seminarians become more aware of their psychological realities and the needs of parishioners. He and Dittes were meant to be close colleagues: Nouwen was to lean more towards the psychology side, while Dittes was to concentrate on the theology side. But two years later, when he came to take up his appointment, he had abandoned his reliance on psychology and was into spirituality and theological issues. These were what he wanted to teach – leaving Dittes responsible for the psychological side: 'He'd gone through a very understandable evolution', said Dittes, 'and probably a desirable and attractive one'.

Nouwen also insisted right from the beginning that he would not be forced into contributing the kind of academic articles usually expected of the Yale elite. He would be writing books and papers from his own unique perspective. The dean of Yale Divinity School was Colin Williams who showed particular affection for Nouwen, providing a welcoming atmosphere where he could follow his own heart in what he taught and wrote about. Nouwen climbed the ladder without a formal doctorate, eventually becoming a tenured professor of pastoral theology.

Nouwen's initial appointment in 1971 also broke new ground in that he and Sister Margaret Farley (now professor of ethics) were the first two full-time Roman Catholic appointments to the Protestant faculty. They were also to become the two most popular members of staff. Margaret Farley recalls:

Henri was not exactly what Yale Divinity School had expected. This was a time when spirituality was still suspect among Protestants but now, across the United States and the world, it has become a primary concern of all religious denominations – and Henri was a major figure in all of that. His presence here, from the moment he began, was so charismatic that he immediately awakened students in a way that was phenomenal. That sometimes made it difficult for him to relate to his faculty colleagues, and not all of them appreciated him.

With his early books gaining a reputation across America and beyond, and selling well, publishers were eager to have his latest scripts. Many of his lectures were turned into paperbacks, including *With Open Hands*, *Ageing*, *Out of Solitude*, *Reaching Out* and *The Way of the Heart* – works which were considered by other pastoral theologians to be extremely signficant in their field. But as his popularity and fame grew, the faculty at Yale found him something of an embarrassment. Each year faculty members were expected to present a list of their publications and, where possible, indicate how their work was being received in their field – but it was always Nouwen who outshone his colleagues, not only by writing a book a year, but also by being foot-noted in so many pastoral theology texts. Some people were concerned that he had an undue influence on students because many were coming to the Divinity School especially because of him.

Nouwen offered a vision of ministry grounded in contemplative life and flowing out of it. Although he began teaching the psychology of religion and pastoral psychology, he gradually developed courses such as 'Ministry and Spirituality', 'The History of Christian Spirituality' and 'Prayer and the Spiritual Life'. He was a highly organised teacher and his notes were concise and immaculately handwritten. He was also aware that physical space had a significant influence on the quality of personal encounters, so he always sought out the most inviting classrooms for his students. To teach was to 'create a space in which obedience to the truth is practised'.[2]

Beyond the physical space, there was also a prayerful dimension to his classes, which always began with biblical readings, silence and intercessions. Not only did this cultivate an interior quietude, but it was also a conscious acknowledgement of the gospel text, 'When two or three meet in my name, I shall be there with them' (Matt. 18:20). This discipline created a space in which attention was directed to Christ, in whose name the students were to minister.

Nouwen aimed at giving them a space in which to be themselves. John Mogabgab, his teaching assistant at Yale (now editor of the spiritual journal *Weavings*), recalls that Nouwen sought to make visible the often unnoticed points of contact between typical human experiences and the deeper reality of God's spirit at work in the world:

> Just as the early Christian writers could appeal to a common fund of philosophical categories, methods of thought and cultural ideals to introduce the educated person of their day to the truths of Christianity, so Henri was able to use such daily experiences as loneliness, anger, joy, friendship and business to instruct his students in the ways of the Spirit, and to persuade them of the essential relation between spirituality and ministry. Henri himself most often described this effort as an attempt to see the connections between their own life stories and the one great story of God's redemption of the world in and through Jesus Christ. The many pastoral examples, personal anecdotes, psychological observations and theological analyses that went into building the floor, walls and ceiling of Henri's lectures were aimed at helping students gain a new vision of their vocation as Christians.[3]

For Nouwen, the classroom, the prayer and the lecture were all placed in the service of obedience to the truth. In a spiritual sense, this meant hearing how much God loves humanity and responding to that love in the freedom which it creates. Obedience involves a movement to God in response to a divine, loving initiative towards humankind which fully expresses and embodies God's own being. Nouwen did not believe that intellectual formation could be separated from spiritual formation. No methods, skills, techniques, films or field trips could replace the influence of the teacher because the essence of all religious teaching was witness, proclaiming 'something which has existed from the beginning, which we have heard, which we have seen with our own eyes, which we have watched and touched with our own hands, the Word of life – this is our theme' (1 John 1:1–2). It was hardly a philosophy to endear him to traditional academic approaches in theology, but Nouwen did not waver in his conviction:

> We are not asked to teach a discipline like mathematics, physics, history or languages, but we are called to make our own faith available to others as the source of learning. To be a teacher means indeed to lay down your life for your friends, to become a 'martyr'

in the original sense of witness. To be a teacher means to offer your own faith experience, your loneliness and intimacy, your doubts and hopes, your failures and successes to your students as a context in which they can struggle with their own quest for meaning. To be a teacher means to have the same boldness as Paul, who said to the Corinthians: 'Take me as a model as I take Christ' (1 Corinthians 11:1). To be a teacher means to say to those who want to learn what Jesus said to his disciples: 'Come and see' (John 1:39).[4]

Strongly influenced by Orthodox writers, Nouwen believed that prayer, community and ministry are integral parts of true theological under-standing – in other words, that the study of theology itself needs to have a prayerful quality about it. He used the story of the annunciation to illustrate what he meant. Mary's first response to the angel's greet-ing – 'Rejoice, you who enjoy God's favour! The Lord is with you' (Luke 1:28) – was fear. Mary was 'deeply disturbed by these words and asked herself what this greeting could mean.' (Luke 1:29). For Nouwen, this is where all theology starts. God broke into history and Mary, after hearing the word, did not run away but started to ask what the painful interruption might mean, and discovered it to be a moment of revelation. According to Nouwen, the theologian responding in faith to the situation of the moment discovers God's active presence in the midst of pain and, trusting in that presence, dares to raise a question such as Mary's – 'But how can this come about?' (Luke 1:34). A theo-logical question is not an attempt to disqualify what is present but a prayerful request to be more deeply led into the truth.

Nouwen argued that the final words of Mary at the annunciation – 'You see before you the Lord's servant; let it happen to me as you have said' – show clearly the aim of all theology. They create the inner space in which God's word can happen to us: 'The purpose of theological understanding is not to grasp, control or even use God's word, but to become increasingly willing to let the word of God speak to us, guide us, move us, and lead us to places far beyond our own comprehension.'[5]

Nouwen did not deny the importance of critical analysis in reading historical texts, but he felt it could only bear fruit in the context of obedience – that is, attentive listening – to the truth. However, if biblical criticism is no longer practised as part of 'true obedience', theology quickly loses its doxological character – praising God in the present moment – and degenerates into a 'value-free' science subjected to fruitless disputes and arguments. Nouwen reminded his students that the first usage of the word *theologia* within the Christian tradition had referred to the highest level of prayer. The Desert Fathers had spoken about three stages of prayer: the *praktike* (the discipline of bringing the whole person with all thoughts, feelings and passions into the presence of God); the *theoria physike* (the contemplation of God's creation and providential plan as it becomes visible in nature and history); and the *theologia* (a direct intimate communion with God). Only since the Enlightenment had 'theology' developed into one academic discipline among others, increasingly involving analysis and synthesis, and less and less related to the experience of union with God. But the original connection between *theologia* and prayer must never be lost – nor could theology be 'done' outside a community of faith.

Nouwen's vocation was to affirm students in their own sacred journeys and then, in common vulnerability, enter with them into the search, allow their questions to resound in the depths of his soul, listen to them without fear and discover the connections with his own life. No fresh insights, though, would ever develop unless they came from a source which transcended both pupil and teacher.

Nouwen's own wisdom reached out to young people in compassionate and life-changing ways. Students who went to discuss their difficulties with him felt the full focus of his energy on them – he offered his total attention. Similarly in class, he treated their comments or struggles with the course as symptoms of the pain in their lives. He wanted to help them get to that pain and allow God's Spirit to touch it and heal it. As a trained psychologist, he was not at a loss for creative strategies in dealing with distraught people.

Yet, reflecting on his teaching career at a later date, Nouwen believed that he had failed many times to live up to his convictions. Sometimes he felt that he had given sermons instead of good theological education; that he had given in to contemporary controversies to 'stimulate the curious mind rather than stir the listening heart'. On other occasions he sensed that he had been so eager to be relevant that he had not paid enough attention to difficult fundamental issues, and he confessed that there were times when he wanted to prove himself to students and colleagues instead of helping them to discover God's ways in their lives. There were moments when he had been far too personal, and others when he had been too distant.

The verdict of the students, though, was positive. His course on Vincent van Gogh, while raising the eyebrows of more traditional theologians, drew in vast numbers of people from the New Haven area who came to regard the lessons not so much as lectures but as opportunities to gain insight into their own experiences. Students felt that Nouwen, with his Dutch accent and his own yearning for deeper purpose and closeness to God, somehow began to take on the character of van Gogh. Henri's own struggles, and his openness to the struggles of others, led him to understand van Gogh and to reveal van Gogh's compassionate being to his students. Van Gogh also became a guide and a teacher to Nouwen, whose future classes on compassion were fuelled by his intimate knowledge of the artist's life. There were many of Nouwen's students whose lives were changed through his teaching. It wasn't just what he said but how he said it. His lecturing style was warm and disarming, rather than cool and inhibiting.

His affection and respect for his students extended well beyond the classroom. Every week he had an open house for students between 8 and 10 p.m. The first hour he would serve wine, juice, cheese and crackers, then at 9 p.m. they all gathered in the living room and shared what was on their minds, perhaps something they had not understood in his classes. At 9.45 the chatter stopped as Henri got out his Liturgy of the Hours prayer book and they all said Night Prayer together.

When Yushi Nomura, from Tokyo, visited the campus for the first time, he had already heard that Henri Nouwen, the famous writer, taught there. Yushi turned up at the Divinity School during the Christmas vacation – the only person around was the caretaker, who seemed nice but a little odd:

> I was impressed that they employed people like that. I was a stranger there, but this man came up to me, saying 'Hi, I'm Henri. What's your name?' – so I said, 'Hi, I'm Yushi, nice meeting you'. I didn't know how long to keep the conversation going for, then

he just said 'Nice meeting you, Yushi', shook my hand and walked away.

When term started, I was persuaded by one of my friends, who had loved Nouwen's books, to see if I could enrol on one of his courses – and I thought at least I should see what type of person the famous professor was. I looked into one of the crowded classrooms, full of students trying to grab seats, so I stood at the back until I could catch sight of the man. Then I saw the janitor walk in – it was that guy called Henri who had spoken to me that day by the noticeboard. I thought he must be coming in to clean the blackboard and prepare the room. And then he started to teach . . .

When Holly Whitcomb was a first-year student, she had a similar encounter at a start-of-year square dance:

I danced with this man who I thought was a homeless person. I thought how fine it was that they invited these people off the streets of New Haven to come into the assembly hall and dance. He had strange hair and a wild look in his eyes. After dancing with him, I asked another student who the man was. She said, 'Oh, that's Henri Nouwen. You'll have him for spirituality.' I was totally shocked that this man wasn't homeless at all! I think Henri would have appreciated being mistaken in that way because he wanted to be identified with the disenfranchised.

Holly, who later became a minister in the United Church of Christ, and a retreat leader, sometimes felt overwhelmed by the academic content of the courses – was this really the best way to prepare for parish ministry? Henri taught her spiritual survival skills for the heart – tools which allowed her to survive the business of being a pastor and to feel that she could be attentive to the inner resources that would do her good and enable her to reach out more effectively.

Despite his shambolic appearance, Nouwen was a highly organised and efficient lecturer. Marjorie Thompson (now director of the Pathways Center for Christian Spirituality in Nashville, Tennessee) joined his courses at Yale after hearing him give a retreat: 'When he led a quiet day he always seemed very centred, and when he taught a course he was very clear about what he wanted to convey. In the midst of all the words and gestures there was a tremendous focus on what he was communicating.'

Not all of his students went on to become ministers; some became teachers. Yushi Nomura, who now teaches in Tokyo, paid tribute to Nouwen for his inspiration. Nouwen enabled him to penetrate the spiritual meaning of the Christian Scriptures and then make connections with the eastern spiritual tradition of Zen Buddhism. Nouwen often used Zen stories in his teaching and, during discussions on the Desert Fathers, Nomura's mind always went back to the Zen monks he had seen in the Orient. Instead of taking notes, Nomura quickly sketched images in the margin. When he handed in his essay, he submitted his revised pencil drawings as well:

> Henri was more impressed by my drawings than by my essay and, without my permission, he took them to his editor in New York. He then told me what he had done and asked if I was interested in doing them all again for a book. The publishers obviously couldn't sell a book about the Desert Fathers painted by an unknown Japanese student – so their condition was that Henri would write the introduction, which he did.

Desert Wisdom was published as stories translated, handwritten and decorated by Yushi Nomura. After Nouwen's decision to approach the publisher without even consulting the artist, there was a certain irony in his words on the opening pages: 'I am grateful for the opportunity to introduce this splendid book because from the moment the plans for this project were first expressed, I have felt very closely connected with their realization.'6

If Nouwen was exceptional in the kind of courses he chose to teach, he also stood out for the open way in which he celebrated the Eucharist every evening in a small octagonal basement chapel. Everyone was welcome to receive the sacrament – and almost everyone did. If he was absent, it was an Anglican, rather than a Roman Catholic, priest who stood in for him. When Nouwen had Catholic friends staying with him, he invited them along to the Mass, and they often expressed surprise at the number of people going up to the altar: 'Are they all Roman Catholics?' some asked. 'No, but we do things differently here',

Nouwen answered. During the giving and receiving of peace, he encouraged people not just to shake hands with their friends but go over to strangers – his whole idea of Eucharist was about bringing people together. His understanding of the Eucharist was that it was a gift to humanity, and not to be used as a weapon in denominational debates.

Nouwen also found God through music, and could play the piano magnificently, often immersing himself in his favourite classical pieces during impromptu recitals in the common room. These renditions also helped him to relax, a discipline which did not come naturally.

His generosity was often in evidence. He once met a woman in New Haven whose spirits needed lifting, so he decided to send a bouquet for her birthday – not only on the one occasion but every year. He was a master of the small gestures which affirmed the dignity and value of people. On another occasion he agreed to go the bedside of a sick woman who had read all his books and been transformed by his words, but had never met him. She knew nothing of the visit until one day, shortly before her death, she looked up from her pillow to be introduced to Father Henri Nouwen standing beside her. She was so amazed to see him that she began to wonder if her medication was causing hallucinations.

On the highways around New Haven, though, his reputation was less revered. Driving with Henri was an act of faith, not only because he put his foot down, but also because he could become so absorbed in conversation that he would take his mind off the road and his hands off the wheel. And his depth perception was such that he would hit the brakes as soon as he saw a car coming out of a side turning 100 yards away. As John Mogabgab put it:

> If you weren't speeding with Henri, you were jerking to a stop and starting up again. I once made the mistake of asking him what time we would reach our destination; he looked at his watch . . . which unfortunately wasn't on his wrist at the time. We were driving at about 50 mph along a country highway when he literally turned halfway round and began rummaging behind the front seat on the floor of the car, looking for his watch. At that point I volunteered to look for it!

It was not only Nouwen's distractions which could make him a socially unpredictable figure in the university world. He was not necessarily aware of the tactful way of doing things and, while never a man of ruthless cunning, he laid himself open to accusations of being a social manipulator. Jim Dittes recalls a farewell dinner party for an associate chaplain at Yale Church of Christ; the hostess had arranged that everyone should present their own gifts quietly during the informal, pre-dinner part of the evening:

> I noticed that Henri did not appear to have a gift with him. Then, during the formal part of the evening, when everyone was sitting around the supper table, Henri stood up and began making his speech and presenting his gift then. That seemed to be vintage Henri Nouwen. He would find his way of doing things in a promi- nent, public and manipulative way, rather than going along with what the hostess had requested. Henri was probably wholly unaware that he was doing things inappropriately, and he would have been terribly chagrined if anyone had pointed it out. There was a dimension of insensitivity to the world here and now which might have been the cost of being terribly sensitive to the more transcendent dimensions of things.

Whatever the motivation, Nouwen always did things his own way, but, whatever his shortcomings, he left his mark on his students – if not on Yale itself. There continues to be great interest in spirituality at Yale, and clearly Nouwen was there at a time of increasing openness in the churches when budding pastors were eager to receive his message. But he never totally fitted in, and rarely contributed much to general policy-making or faculty decisions. After he left Yale in 1981, the Divinity School did not try to replace him. The job description changed, and there were calls for the new lecturer to be more theologi- cally systematic. Despite Nouwen's international reputation and his impact on many lives, his portrait is not hanging in the hall of fame, nor are his books prominent on reading lists. There is no sense that 'Nouwen was here'.

According to Jim Dittes, Nouwen was a rarity:

> He was a pastoral theologian, somebody who made theology exis- tential enough to become a living theology. He thought intuitively,

and that sort of person doesn't come to the seminary very often. He was an important figure to many people and I would rate his contribution highly – but I don't think he was original. He was a skilful artist. He was an intriguing mixture of somebody absolutely self-confident and somebody troubled. He had a huge ego and would place himself at the centre of things, combining that with a kind of wistfulness or sense of self-confusion. He was searching for something. I don't know what it was and I suspect he never found it.

Jim Dittes was among a number of colleagues who supported Nouwen when his mother died in October 1978, at the peak of his Yale career. She was taken ill while visiting Henri in the USA, and was flown back to Holland where surgery revealed widespread cancer. Henri flew back to be with her. Despite the physical distance between them, they had always been extremely close. His mother had followed every decision he had made, discussed every trip he had undertaken and read every article and book he had written.

Nouwen later said that it had been for his own good that she had died. While her death was an agonising wrench, it was also 'God's way of converting me, of letting his Spirit set me free'.[7] He believed that the person who had taught him so much by her life would teach him even more by her death.

14. Silent Cloisters

DURING HIS decade at Yale, Nouwen took full advantage of sabbaticals, which included his becoming a fellow at the Ecumenical Institute in Collegeville, Minnesota, and scholar-in-residence at the North American College in Rome. It was appropriate for him to read, write, talk and lecture in two contrasting academic settings – and to slow down as well. It was perhaps more surprising that he also decided to spend two six-month periods at an isolated Trappist monastery in upstate New York, close to Lake Ontario. In 1974, and again in 1979, the frenetic man of words entered a place of silence and took part in the Cistercian cycle of observances, from vigils to Night Prayer, which meant getting up just after 2 a.m. and going to bed before 7 p.m.

Ross, one of the 'family brothers' associated with the community, looked back on the early days in the monastic life of Nouwen the novice: 'My memory is of someone doing 100 mph in a 30 mph limit – he was really struggling, and he really yearned for God, while perhaps not always realising how close God was, because he was always ahead of himself.'

Nouwen, who was 42 at the time, described the experience as being like a stranger in paradise, but his desire to live as a monk, rather than as a guest, was not an overnight dream but the result of many years of restless searching. While teaching, lecturing and writing about the importance of solitude, inner freedom and peace of mind, he kept stumbling over his own compulsions and illusions, only to discover that his vocation to be a witness to God's love was just becoming another exhausting job. What was it that was driving him from one book to another, one place to another, one project to another? Perhaps he was speaking more about God than being with God? His writing about prayer might even have been keeping him from a prayerful life. In his concern for praise from other people, was he slowly becoming a prisoner of expectations instead of a priest liberated by divine promises?

As he looked closer at his life, he realised he was caught in a web of paradox:

> While complaining about too many demands, I felt uneasy when none were made. While speaking about the burden of letter writing, an empty mailbox made me sad. While fretting about tiring lecture tours, I felt disappointed when there were no invitations. While speaking nostalgically about an empty desk, I feared the day on which that would come true. In short: while desiring to be alone, I was frightened of being left alone.[1]

Although the monks did not usually admit temporary members, they were prepared to make an exception for Nouwen after their abbot, John Eudes Bamberger, put forward a proposal and asked them to vote on it. Having first given spiritual direction to Nouwen eight years before, Bamberger knew him to be searching for his identity in God; a seven-month stay, from Pentecost until Christmas, would certainly be beneficial.

Nouwen continued to receive spiritual direction from John Eudes who listened to his specific concerns over feelings of anger, many of which seemed to relate to his experiences of rejection: a visitor had not asked him how he was getting on, students whom he had helped had not written to thank him, a few monks had seemed unfriendly . . . John Eudes pointed out Nouwen's difficulties with what he termed 'nuanced responses': he might have good reasons for feeling rejected; but his responses were not in proportion to the nature of the events. The people whom he felt had rejected him did not mean that much to him in any case – but their distance opened up huge chasms into which he plunged. Nouwen wrote in his journal:

We tried to explore the reason for this. Somewhere there must be this need for a total affection, an unconditional love, an ultimate satisfaction. I keep hoping for a moment of full acceptance, a hope that I attach to very little events. Even something rather insignificant becomes an occasion for this full and total event, and a small rejection then easily leads to a devastating despair and a feeling of total failure. John Eudes made it very clear how vulnerable I am with such a need because practically nobody can offer me what I am looking for. Even if someone did offer me this unconditional, total, all-embracing love, I would not be able to accept it since it would force me into an infantile dependency which I, as an adult, cannot tolerate.[2]

Nouwen soon became aware that, in a world of monastic obedience, he was not able to stand out in the ways he had elsewhere. His teaching, preaching and writing styles were all very different from those of other priests of his era, and they helped to put him centre-stage. His long introspections at the Genesee were to put him in touch with some home truths:

I have always had a strange desire to be different than other people. I probably do not differ in this desire from other people. Thinking about this desire and how it has functioned in my life, I am more and more aware of the way my life-style became part of our contemporary desire for 'stardom'. I wanted to say, write or do something 'different' or 'special' that would be noticed and talked about. For a person with a rich fantasy life, this is not too difficult and easily leads to the desired 'success'. You can teach in such a way that it differs enough from the traditional way to be noticed; you write sentences, pages, and even books that are considered original and new; you can even preach the Gospel in such a way that people are made to believe that nobody had thought of that before. In all these situations you end up with applause because you did something sensational, because you were 'different'.

In recent years I have become increasingly aware of the dangerous possibility of making the Word of God sensational. Just as people can watch spellbound a circus artist tumbling through the air in a phosphorized costume, so they can listen to a preacher who uses the Word of God to draw attention to himself.[3]

After several weeks of repeated spiritual and physical exercises, Nouwen conceded that the less he was noticed, the less special attention he required; and the less he was different, the more he could live the monastic life. The mystery of God's love was that in sameness lay the discovery of uniqueness, which has nothing to do with specialities but everything to do with an intimate relationship on a divine scale. *The Genesee Diary* was a turning-point for Nouwen in that, for the first time, he opened up parts of his soul to his readers and revealed his petty-mindedness as well as his deeper struggles. There was something real about his writing, yet these self-disclosures came only after spells of concentrated prayer and labour. As well as keeping the Liturgy of the Hours, he was expected to work on the hot bread line, wash boxes of raisins, peel potatoes, press sheets, paint and collect granite rocks for the new church. In the daily round of monastic chores, Nouwen's flair for the unpractical became manifest.

Brother Christian, who worked alongside Nouwen in the bakery, described the problems he had with mechanical, routine tasks of any kind – not to mention equipment: 'I had to tell him everything, even how to use a can opener. I could see he wasn't cut out for our life – the confinement, solitude, was too much for his personality.'

Nouwen might not have realised the extent to which he would have to engage physically with all the building work that needed to be done in the construction of the new church. He worked with six-inch to ten-inch heavy steel nails, hammering them into solid oak beams one after another. He did his share of rolling boulders too – it was a tough physical challenge.

One night Nouwen had a dream about Thomas Merton which seemed significant. Nouwen and a group of sisters, in civilian dress, were waiting for Merton to give a lecture, then suddenly he had appeared, 'bald-headed and dressed in an all-white habit'. He left to get his notes, and all the sisters vanished, returning in immaculate white robes to listen to the master. In the dream, Nouwen left the room to look for Merton whom he found in brown trousers and a yellow T-shirt. He was busy fixing something. Asking questions about nails and screws, Nouwen tried to help – but Merton didn't answer. Then he started to clean an old yellow bench with sandpaper and repaint it. Nouwen asked where he got the sandpaper and paint but, again, he did not reply, except to invite assistance with a silent gesture. The sisters were waiting back in the room for his talk, but it didn't make sense to tell him so. Just as Nouwen started to paint, he woke up. His interpretation of the dream was that the spiritual life consisted not of any special thoughts, ideas or feelings but was contained in the most simple experiences of everyday living.[4]

Nouwen had written one of his first books on Merton. The two had met on 7 May 1967 while Nouwen was visiting Gethsemani. (There is a reference to the meeting in volume 6 of Merton's journals, *Learning to Love*, although Merton didn't cotton on to his name, alluding to him as 'Father Nau'.)[5]

Many people have tended to cast Nouwen in the same mould as Merton, seeing him as Merton's successor, but John Eudes Bamberger, who lived in the same community as Merton for 18 years, has a different view:

> I think there would have been a fruitful exchange between them but there weren't many who were really soul-mates with Merton. Anybody who thinks Nouwen was the Merton of his generation either didn't know Henri or didn't know Merton. They were very different types of people and they wrote to a different audience from different levels of experience. Henri was basically a teacher and a communicator on the popular level, whereas Merton wrote for a more specialised group in terms of his personal experience. Merton was basically a poet, a literary figure. The opinions people had of his writings didn't influence Merton very much, unless they were artists.
>
> Merton was my spiritual director and my teacher, and I worked with him for ten years, so I knew his style very well. Henri's style was very different from Merton's. I think Merton was an unusual type of person; I don't think Henri was. He was not gifted in at all the same way Merton was. Merton had a terrific amount of energy and also an unusual kind of intelligence. Henri was very

devoted and reasonably intelligent, but he wasn't extraordinarily intelligent like Merton.

Nouwen was such a sympathetic person that he could identify with his audience far more deeply than Merton could. Merton identified with his audience at a certain level and then, if they didn't get it, that was their problem. Unlike Nouwen, that wouldn't have worried him too much. On a personal level, however, Merton was inclined to go as far as he could to agree with people, which was why (according to Bamberger) many were misled by him because, in reality, he might not really agree with them at all. Bamberger continued:

> Henri was identifying deeply with his own spiritual values and finding his way into prayer. He was bringing together his emotional life and his life of prayer, then relating them to daily experience which is the monastic approach. Prayer for a monk is a way of life. It's not just one activity among many, or even the most important activity. It is something which permeates the whole of one's existence, and I think Henri was trying to approach that. In seven months nobody achieves that, and he was smart enough to know it. I think, during one phase, he thought that he might do better to think of becoming a monk – but that was just a normal, understandable attraction. I don't think it was ever a serious issue for him. Whereas Merton was a very deeply committed monk and, although other people tried to get him to leave the monastery, he himself said that he never really took that seriously, except for five minutes once. With Henri it was quite the opposite, and for very good reasons. He felt that his time here worked, that it helped him very much to point out the ways he could approach his spiritual life while still remaining active.

The first that Bamberger knew of Nouwen's detailed record of his sabbatical was when he received in the post the manuscript of *The Genesee Diary* and was asked for his opinion:

> I thought this journal would be helpful – in a way that Merton's work wasn't – because Henri's difficulties were the kind the average person has when they come here. His time here was one of struggle. He had peace up to a point but, as the diary shows,

he had all kinds of emotional struggles which almost everybody has. Merton had them too, but he didn't write about them. He wrote about his experience from the point of view of someone who had assimilated and reinterpreted it, then expressed it in a highly literary way, but he did it with such naturalness that an unsophisticated reader would be led to think that that was the way it worked, but it didn't.

It's like reading the prophet Isaiah, who was a great poet and a deeply religious, contemplative person. There aren't many people who are capable of that kind of experience – but many people can learn a lot from it. You can take what you're up to, but you won't function the way he did. That's the difference between the two people. What Henri experienced was a kind of large version of what the average intelligent, devoted and serious person will soon run into.

The months at Genesee helped Nouwen to grow in confidence, not least when visitors turned up at the abbey wanting to discuss spirituality. Bamberger suggested that Nouwen went and talked to them, but at first he found it an unnerving experience: 'Don't I need to prepare?' he asked. 'If you need to prepare after more than 20 years as a priest', Bamberger replied, 'what are we talking about here?' Nouwen had to learn to draw on his own inner resources in a naturally spontaneous way. The personal approach began to emerge in his books, and *The Genesee Diary* sold well because it was such an honest account of his monastic interlude. He had discovered how poor, weak and incapable he was. Readers might have expected a blissful account of his spiritual journey, but ended up being told about his anger and resentment – not all of it superficial:

> Today: the feast of Christ the King. No easy feast day for me since I have always associated this feast with a certain triumphalism in the Church and with a militant spirituality, both of which were so much part of my pre-Vatican II Jesuit formation. It also is the day in which I am always confronted with the problem of authority in the Church because it makes me realize how many people in the Church like to play king in Jesus' name. Finally, it is the day in which I have to deal with my own unresolved struggle with

obedience and submission, a struggle of which I have again become very conscious in a monastery such as this where the abbot is such a clear-cut authority figure.[6]

After a further five years at Yale, Nouwen returned to the abbey in 1979 for another six months. He seemed a little more at ease with the routine, but on that occasion he lived away from the community. The abbot didn't notice any remarkable change and thought that Nouwen still hadn't found the place he was looking for. Like Merton he seemed to feel that, unless he was writing things, he wasn't fully experiencing them. There was a gravitation in both men towards writing too much. On Nouwen's second sabbatical, he compiled *A Cry for Mercy*, prayers from the Genesee. He returned a third time as a family brother before going to Latin America. In July 1982, shortly after returning from Peru, he celebrated the twenty-fifth anniversary of his ordination, inviting friends from different periods of his life to share it with him at the abbey. Despite the simplicity of the setting, it proved to be an expensive and elaborate affair, with representatives from different religious traditions and backgrounds, a good many of them with impressive contacts. The Quaker writer Parker Palmer, who was master of ceremonies for part of the time, felt Nouwen's energies had turned the quiet abbey into a three-ring circus – almost literally:

> He actually hired a circus tent to put up in the grounds, and there were film crews and famous people from round about. Henri paid for us to be there for two and a half days and there were probably 150 people. But one face in the crowd kept haunting me. Finally I went over to him and discovered that he had been on the front covers of magazines the world over: he was the secret service agent who had pushed Ronald Reagan into the automobile as he was being fired at in the assassination attempt. I asked if he had been a friend of Henri's for a long time and he said, 'No, I just met Henri two weeks ago in Washington and he gave me a plane ticket to come to the celebrations'. Henri was a kind of equal opportunity friend. Whether you were great or small, he would reach out to you in many ways. He wasn't just climbing the social ladder – but he liked the company of challenging and interesting people who had had unusual experiences.

But there was an undercurrent to the event which is said to have infuriated Nouwen. The abbey had a policy, in accordance with diocesan guidelines, that only Roman Catholics should receive Holy Communion. A notice outside the chapel doors was a clear reminder. But Nouwen had invited many non-Catholics to the Mass and expected them to be able to take the sacrament as they always did from him. The abbot insisted that there should be no exceptions on that occasion, and Nouwen made it clear to his friends that he was far from happy. In the years that followed it became a talking point and might have accounted for a certain cooling-off on Nouwen's part in his relationship with the abbey. 'If he was hurt, that was his problem', says John Eudes Bamberger. 'As a Roman Catholic I believe in the discipline of the Church and he knew that. I never had any indication of his feelings at the anniversary.'

As Nouwen continued his priesthood, the spiritual dimension of the psychological life became more urgent for him. His monastic interludes brought him to more of an integrated understanding of the two worlds. He was highly sensitive to the different psychological layers which constituted the realm of personal relationships and was finely in tune with the dynamics and values of the spirit but, to survive as a priest–psychologist, he had to bring them together, a quest pursued not only at the Genesee, but throughout his adult life. While the world of the cloister answered some of his deeper questions, it did not quench his restlessness or end his search for community. From the monastic acres, he turned to the mission fields.

15. The Mission

FROM THE moment he left Europe for Yale, Henri Nouwen's mind was turning towards the potential connections which could be made between North and South America. He made a number of short visits to Mexico, Chile and Paraguay, coming to realise that ministerial training in the United States must include the millions of Spanish and Portuguese speakers whose destiny was bound up with that of their English-speaking brothers and sisters. His excursions led only to limited involvement but they served to deepen his conviction about the spiritual unity of the Americas. In 1981, he left Yale and moved back in with the Trappists at the Abbey of the Genesee to prepare himself for a more systematic discernment of a possible vocation in Latin America. The question, 'Does God call me to Latin America?', had been niggling for many years: now the time had come to confront it. But, as so often with matters of vocation, there were to be surprises.

During the retreat he felt at times 'too tired, too preoccupied with personal struggles, too restless, too busy, too unprepared'[1] to make the transition but, as the end of his stay grew closer, he responded to a growing sense of call. After leaving the abbey, he returned for a week to Yale where the eucharistic celebrations, expressions of friendship and many conversations stirred within him a profound sense of mission: he felt he was being sent out with the affection, support and prayers of those who loved him most. Nouwen thought he might well be going for the rest of his life – a decision which bewildered some of his friends in academia, but impressed others. He knew he was losing a certain prestige by giving up his job at Yale, but he was equally aware that he was testing a call to work in a countercultural world. As always, it was a sense of vocation which motivated him above all else.

Peru was his central base. After flying to Lima, he was introduced to his new community of Maryknoll Fathers and Brothers. When they heard he was coming, the community members had joked about the need to be careful what they said over lunch or it might end up in a book. On his first day, he went straight into town for the procession of the Lord of the Miracles, the second largest religious devotion in Latin America. On returning for lunch, he remarked that he had already seen so much, he could write a book about it. A few grins went round the room.

Indeed, that very spectacle was to open the pages of his journal *¡Gracias!*:

> Peru: from the moment I entered it, I felt a deep love for this country. I do not know why. I did not feel this when I went to Chile or Bolivia in the past. But looking at the busy streets of Lima, the dark open faces and the lively gestures, I felt embraced by a loving people in a way I had not known before. Walking through the busy streets, looking at the men, women, and children in their penitential dress – purple habits with white cords – and sensing the gentle spirit of forgiveness, I had the strange emotion of homecoming. 'This is where I belong. This is where I must be. This is where I will be for a very long time. This is home.'[2]

After several days, Nouwen flew to Bolivia and its 'garden city' of Cochabamba, situated some 2600 m (8500 feet) up in the Andes, where he was to spend the next few months, chiefly at the Institute for Spanish Studies which was run by the Maryknolls. The normal basic course was six months but, as Nouwen could already speak several languages, the tutors felt a shorter period would be sufficient for him. None the less, it was an intensive experience in the high altitude – four hours of individual classes daily, with a different team of four teachers every fortnight, lots of private study and weekly lectures on the cultural reality of Latin America. Every day, the professor-turned-pupil attended two individual classes with language drills, one conversation lesson and a grammar class in a small group. Altogether he had 14 different teachers. The language school's director, Father Gerry McCrane, was aware of some of the other tensions and conflicts in Nouwen's life:

> He was trying to disengage from an intense and demanding life to focus on Spanish, Latin America and his possible presence here. But he still received many calls and invitations from around the world. All of us realised, without having to state it explicitly, that indeed here was someone who had left all things to follow Jesus – and all things meant not only his family and friends, but also such prized achievements as tenure at the prestigious Yale university. He was restless with it all too, wondering just what this might mean for him and where he might serve the kingdom of God, given his unique background and experience.

Nouwen also heard more first-hand accounts of the political situation and the courage of some church leaders in a climate of fear and chaos. Ronald Reagan was shaping his policy towards Central America, convinced it was a hotbed of communism posing a huge threat to the borders of the USA. Rutilio Grande, a Jesuit priest from El Salvador, had been martyred in 1977, and in 1980 the Archbishop of San Salvador, Oscar Romero, had been gunned down in a hospital chapel while celebrating Mass, because of his vigorous defence of the poor and powerless against the military and the wealthy classes. Bolivia was going through its own internal turbulence. Between 1978 and 1984 there were 15 different governments. At times there was strong repression by the military, great inflation, financial instability and a scarcity of basic products. Trade unions had been suppressed. The Catholic Church protested vehemently and had, in Monsignor Jorge Manrique, a fearless leader backed by the Episcopal Conference, but the bishops and their clergy were faced with frequent attempts to intimidate and silence them. Many priests were arrested and jailed. Some were held incognito for days, and several were killed indiscriminately. It was a time of despair.

Nouwen learned quickly about the interplay of power and the drug wars as well as the poverty, desperation and bravery of the Bolivian people, all of which would no doubt have added to his burden of adjustment: 'Coming here must have been especially difficult for Henri', said Father McCrane. 'To leave centre-stage and to plunge into being a student in the middle of the Andes is a major personal adjustment and challenge, physically, psychologically, spiritually – in every way.'

For many students, this sudden and dramatic displacement resulted in the surfacing of the old, unresolved conflicts and troubling childhood experiences which arise when traditional defence systems are down. Nouwen saw this new awareness of vulnerability and dependency as an opportunity for mental and spiritual growth:

> One of the most rewarding aspects of living in a strange land is the experience of being loved not for what we can do, but for who we are. When we become aware that our stuttering, failing, vulnerable selves are loved even when we hardly progress, we can let go of our compulsion to prove ourselves and be free to live with others in the fellowship of the weak. This is true healing. The psychological perspective on culture shock can open up for us a new understanding of God's grace and our vocation to live graceful lives.[3]

By this time he was seriously thinking about joining Maryknoll as an associate priest for, perhaps, five years – but he was advised to move slowly and to view Latin America as part of a longer discernment process. Returning to the Maryknoll base in Peru at the beginning of 1982, Nouwen went to live in a *barrio* (slum) in the northern part of Lima. He stayed with a family at Pamplona Alta – their small house consisted of four brick walls painted pink, and a covering made of sheets of metal. His room looked out over a sandy desert of neighbouring homes for the poor. Rather than having lots of time to be helpful, as he had expected, Nouwen found that, as for everyone else there, physical survival was a daily challenge. At first he thought it appropriate to share some of his privileged background with those who were poor – but he quickly realised that he was going to receive far more than he could give:

> It is a simple, but happy family; but not without the fears and anxieties of most poor people. I do not think they are eager churchgoers, but the walls show many pictures of Jesus, Joseph,

and Mary. I am glad to live with these people. They teach me about life in ways no books can.[4]

In the 100,000-strong parish, 70 per cent of the inhabitants were younger than 20. The children came alive for him. As he walked down the road, they showed their affection towards him by clutching his fingers – one finger per child. The children's acceptance, and the spontaneity of their parents, helped Nouwen through the depressions of his first weeks and, as he was to explain later, literally hugged him into life, teaching him that life was now, to be shared and to be thankful for. The poorest of the poor knew a certain joy even in the midst of suffering: no regime or economic injustice was going to deprive them of their deep awareness of the giftedness of existence in the mystery of God. Nouwen learned from them all the great virtues like gratitude, joy, playfulness: 'The kids were wonderful', he said. 'I'm not romanticising. They were also suffering a lot, they missed a lot, they were quite often in great pain because of a lack of clean water. I am amazed how God loves the poor.'

In a section of the house next door lived three Maryknoll missionaries. They were aware of Nouwen's struggles, his culture shock, his vulnerability – these were the common reactions of newcomers to Lima. They also noted his instinctive grasp of one of the key aspects of liberation theology – a connection to the grass roots and to people in the neighbourhood: 'Henri certainly got into that', said missionary Larry Rich. 'He embraced the people there when he gave homilies at Mass on Sunday mornings. His enthusiasm was very clear – he loved the people.'

Both the cultural reality of the poor and the humanity of their struggle for survival placed Nouwen in a situation of powerlessness from which he entered into a new dimension of trust. During those years 'mission' was attempting to move away from the image of dominance and arrogance which had previously characterised the presence of the Church. Now, missionaries were themselves called to conversion. Henri was quickly aware of this challenge and the struggle it presented for his own heart. His vulnerability and trust of God's presence in these unknown realities created for him an incarnation of this mission shift. As Maryknoll priest Pete Byrne commented:

From his writings one would have thought he was a secure man, with great personal certainty. He was in fact struggling to know and understand both himself and the God he sought to proclaim, so he came to the mission searching. He was on a journey of discovery. He shared both his doubts and his wonder, non-judgemental and yet challenging. He arrived as mission itself was attempting to come to a rebirth. He came as one searching for the face of God already present among a people, and was willing to be a sharer in that discovery.

Nouwen's experience in Latin America created a social dimension in his own spiritual journey. He became aware that the pilgrimage with God in the world is a pilgrimage with God's people in their struggle for liberation from all the social, political and economic forces which deny their dignity, create their hunger and allow their oppression. By living with the poor, he knew at first hand the meaning of poverty, where there is no food, no water and no shelter; he experienced insecurity in being unsafe in the streets because of military control and political domination. He came to realise that religious expression is more about a group of people searching for God's love in the ordinary events of life and death in their neighbourhoods, rather than in the rituals of institutions or churches. In turn, Nouwen gave the missionaries the insight that 'mission' was not defined by where they were but by what they shared and attempted to proclaim wherever they were, and he is remembered as a member of the community who had the blessing and privilege to encounter God in the 'Blessed of the kingdom living in Peru'.

While he was in South America, Nouwen attended a series of lectures in which Father Gustavo Gutiérrez first presented his main themes of a spirituality of liberation, and which were to form his book, *We Drink From Our Own Wells*. It was an unusual learning event because 2000 pastoral workers and students turned up, not only from Peru, but also from Chile, Brazil, Colombia, Paraguay, Uruguay, Argentina, Panama and Nicaragua. The words from the lips of the founding father of liberation theology were not perceived as an imported way of thinking but as an expression of what they had come to know in their own daily experiences of living the Gospel. Most of the students had grown up in poor *barrios* and were already actively involved in the process of liberation. Although Nouwen had been a little uneasy at first about the political overtones of liberation theology, he came to accept that it could not be reduced solely to a political movement. The struggle to which the God of the Bible called people was much larger than the struggle for political or economic rights. It was a struggle against all the forces of death wherever they became manifest – a struggle for life in the fullest sense.

Nouwen underwent almost a conversion in Peru as he began to realise how individualistic and elitist his own spirituality had been, and to discover the ways in which his thinking had been dominated by influences within his own North American tradition, with its particular emphasis on the interior life. Only when he took fully on board what Gutiérrez had called the 'irruption of the poor into history' did it register just how 'spiritualised' his own spirituality had become:

> It had been, in fact, a spirituality for introspective persons who have the luxury of the time and space needed to develop inner harmony and quietude. I had even read the Gospels in a rather romantic way. I had come to pray the Magnificat as a sweet song of Mary. I had come to look at the children of the New Testament as innocent, harmless beings, and I had come to think of humility, faithfulness, obedience, and purity primarily as forms of personal piety.[5]

Father Gutiérrez, who had read Nouwen's books, got to know the writer while he was in Lima. As the continent slowly moved towards democratisation, they shared many conversations in both Spanish and English about the poverty, oppression and terrorism which continued to overshadow the halting process of change. 'Liberation theology was something new for him', said Gutiérrez:

> From his experience here, and later in Nicaragua, where he had to be well protected by the police, he did very beautiful work in the field of reverse mission in the States. He was very influential in the States and, in my view, his presence there was more important for us. He did it so well in speeches and through his book *¡Gracias!*

He told me once that, before coming to Latin America, he had not been conscious of the link between political and social commitment, and a spirituality – how people could be open to social and political issues for very spiritual reasons. But he went on to become very good in demonstrating to the First World this connection between the two. Coming from another background, he astutely perceived the meaning of this political commitment, the question that we as priests here ask: how do we engage with the poor if we are not against other people, against oppressive structures which marginalise the poor? From my experience, for many people in the States and in Europe it is difficult to understand these things – if you are against poverty, you are seen as a politician, not a spiritual person. With Archbishop Oscar Romero the case was very clear: he was very spiritual but he was against poverty, against injustice, against the causes of poverty. Henri was so open to learn, and at one point he was very radical in his expressions. He told me that, from then on, his spirituality would have to be different. I think he was exaggerating because I had read his books before his visit and they were very beautiful books, even for very socially committed persons.

Father Gutiérrez rates Henri Nouwen as one of the best spiritual leaders of the twentieth century, not only for his work in bridging the worlds of social justice and spirituality, but also for stressing the importance of a contemplative dimension in the spiritual life, which should always be part of any active commitment to social change:

Spirituality is the essential question of Christian life because following Jesus Christ is at the core of what it is all about, and Nouwen was right there. But he also helped us, as he helped others, to understand the meaning of a spirituality in our own concrete situations. And he was such a fine person when it came to understanding suffering. He said that sometimes you had to be close to someone only because that person was suffering. He was exceptional in many ways but especially in helping Christians to be Christians.

Gutiérrez invited Nouwen to write the introduction to the English

translation of *We Drink From Our Own Wells*. In it Nouwen crystallised
what reverse mission meant for him:

> Although I had gone there hoping to be able to give, I found myself
> first of all the receiver. The poor with whom I lived revealed to
> me the treasures of a Christian spirituality that had been hidden
> from me in my own affluent world. While having little or nothing
> they taught me gratitude. While struggling with unemployment,
> malnutrition, and many diseases, they taught me joy. While
> oppressed and exploited, they taught me community.[6]

It was his conviction that the spiritual destiny of the people of North
America was intimately connected with the spiritual destiny of the
people of South America. What was happening in the Christian communities of Latin America was part of God's way of 'calling us in the
North to conversion'.[7]

Accepting that he was not being called to live as a missionary priest
in South America, Nouwen returned to the United States to strengthen
those connections. Whatever else he did with this experience, he
opened up a lot of people to understanding the Church in South
America and the reality of liberation theology. He had access to people
who might not otherwise have heard about such issues. Gustavo Gutiérrez helped him to understand more clearly what was going on – and
his South American companions noticed that he seemed more at peace
as a result.

16. Brainstorms

INSPIRED BY Gustavo Gutiérrez, Henri Nouwen returned to the United States in March 1982 to think through the implications of his experiences. He went back to the Abbey of the Genesee and continued to live privately, away from the community, as he sought to work out what 'reverse mission' (being a missionary from the developing countries to the developed world) might entail in practice, and how it might fit in with his priesthood. Nouwen was still without a job but, learning that he had decided not to become a missionary priest, influential figures at Harvard started writing to him to see if he would consider taking a position there.

Founded in 1636, Harvard (in Cambridge, Massachusetts) is the oldest university in the United States. It was named after an English Puritan minister, John Harvard, who left the original college his books and half his estate. At its inception, Harvard was under church sponsorship, but during its first two centuries, it gradually became liberated from both clerical and political control. Nouwen knew that its strict religious ethos had long evaporated and it had become the citadel of American intellectual life.

Making it clear that he no longer wished to teach full-time, Nouwen eventually reached another compromise: he was appointed as a divinity professor to teach for six months of every year, giving him freedom to pursue his other interests, which included spending time at a theological centre in Peru. In the late autumn he moved to Massachusetts to prepare for his first teaching semester at Harvard the following

January. When that ended, he went off to Latin America again, travelling first to Mexico where he became a student at the Center for Economic and Social Studies in Mexico City, and then moving to Nicaragua where the Sandinistas were fighting the American-backed Contras. He visited some Maryknoll friends, celebrated Eucharist in villages and met many peasants, listening to their stories and praying with them. He also met some of the Sandinista leaders including Tomas Borge, drawing attention to the apparent contradictions of their declaration to create a more compassionate country. Nouwen returned to the USA for a six-week tour, telling North Americans what he had seen and heard. The intensity of the programme exhausted him, but he completed it. While many in Latin America saw his efforts as laudable initiatives to act as a witness of oppression, some in the States started to question his motives. Just as Merton had been challenged over his right as a cloistered monk to talk about the social ills of the modern world, so, it was suggested, Nouwen really didn't have the experience or the expertise to be speaking so passionately about the Third World. Perhaps the underlying concern was that Nouwen, man for all parties, was identifying himself too strongly with the left – but there were also cynical suggestions that this might just be a means for Nouwen to write another book or become an instant expert on Latin American affairs.

'It was spiritual work – not political', Nouwen insisted:

> Though my message had political implications, I was basically calling Christians to consciousness about what was happening there. When I finally finished the tour, I was absolutely exhausted. Not just tired. My soul was somewhat broken. It was as if someone was saying to me, 'Are you trying to save the world? Where is your heart in all this? Who holds you safe?' I felt I was losing my soul and that God was not supporting me.[1]

In addition to his teaching at Harvard, he was working on his Latin American journal *¡Gracias!* He asked Peggy Ellsberg, a doctoral student, to be his personal editor on the journal, which needed a great deal of rewriting before publication. She recalls:

> He was a one-man cottage industry while he was at Cambridge

and had a lot of people doing lots of different jobs. On his kitchen table he had about ten pounds of sugar, lots of coffee and a couple of boxes of chocolates. He had an apartment to begin with, and he had a little altar there where he would say Mass every day. Then he moved to one of the university's staff properties, the Carriage House, where he got more support.

He was very gifted with friendship which is why it was so easy for him to attract people like me who would come in with a very small job in mind, and the next thing we knew we would be spending portions of every day with him – and having a wonderful time. His greatest line to me was, 'Don't concern yourself with anything but the Lord. Ask yourself what has this to do with the Lord and, if the answer is nothing, then just drop it.'

When Nouwen moved into the Carriage House – a university home a world away, in distance and decor, from the Peruvian slum where he had lived – he hired a cook so he could entertain a range of guests, from Russian Orthodox priests and Jewish rabbis to right-wing evangelical Protestants and Marxist-Leninist writers – all of whom had little in common except that Nouwen's books had spoken to them in some way. Only Henri Nouwen could have got them all together in one room.

There was a pluralistic dimension to the critically intellectual atmosphere of the Divinity School. Some students were following a master of divinity ministerial degree programme before being ordained in Protestant denominations; a number were preparing for professional lay ministry in the Roman Catholic Church; others were exploring their spiritual lives in a non-confessional context. With his international reputation before him, Nouwen taught at Harvard with a Pauline determination to 'know nothing except Christ crucified', and he elicited strong responses of both support and objection. His assistants met in the Carriage House before any course began, to discuss its structure, then talk about spiritual matters and pray. Nouwen's courses made their way into the record books of Harvard Divinity School in terms of student attendance. The room in which he taught was usually overflowing with 300 students – not so much there for another lecture, more for a spiritual experience. Although there was a great crowd whenever he spoke, the small group of 'aides' around him did not go unnoticed, and light-hearted comparisons to Jesus and his disciples were made. From the outside, it looked as if Nouwen had swiftly settled back into academia, but the critically intellectual atmosphere of Harvard was not for him. His teaching assistant, Michael O'Laughlin, was aware that Nouwen felt far from home at Harvard:

> He was trying things. He had tried being a monk, tried being a missionary priest, now he was back talking about reverse mission, trying to influence American society and even public policy concerning Latin America. Harvard had a policy of tolerance which was in fact, as I experienced it, a policy of intolerance whereby everything is tolerated and the worst of all possible sins is to suggest that you have something to tell someone about the spiritual life. Henri was doing this right and left. In his second year, Henri made an even stronger point of flying in the face of this and being more Christian than he had been in the first year, which just increased the tension around him. There were students who were vocally non-Christian – it was very disturbing for them that he became so explicitly Christian in his teaching.

Nouwen gained support from a number of friends including former Yale student Peter Weiskel, whom Nouwen invited to join him for a fortnight's trip to Guatemala to visit a friend, Father John Vesey. Vesey had asked Nouwen to visit him in Guatemala and pray with him and the Indian people. It was an extremely violent time and the state department had issued a warning to travellers – but none of this mattered to Nouwen who could only focus on the need to support his friend.

They toured around Guatemala for ten days, meeting Father Vesey and the local bishop, and absorbing the atmosphere of the countryside and its villages. Nouwen kept a diary and asked Weiskel to take pictures. Although there was no mention of a book then, the words and the photographs eventually formed *Love in a Fearful Land*. Because of the increasing threats to Vesey's life, Nouwen wanted to make the priest's work central to the story so that he might have an easier time there:

Every time John spoke to his people during the time Peter and I stayed with him, I was struck by his lack of fear. He used plain words that needed no interpretation. They were the words of the teachers and prophets of Israel, the apostles and evangelists, and of Jesus himself. They were words I had heard often before in Holland, France and the United States. But in Guatemala they were like the double-edged sword coming from the mouth of the Son of Man (see Revelation 1:16; 2:12). Words about justice and peace, forgiveness and reconciliation, conversion and new ways of living together that had never shocked me before, now struck me as extremely dangerous. Stan [Vesey's predecessor] used them and he was killed; John is using them and he risks his life. They are not used to irritate or provoke, but to proclaim the truth of God's kingdom.[2]

Peter Weiskel is convinced that Nouwen wrote the book in order to keep John Vesey alive: 'People always came first. It was a constant refrain at Harvard that everybody wanted to talk about issues – but for Henri it wasn't the issues which mattered. Even in the Latin American experience, it was the people.'

The demand on Nouwen to lecture and preach never abated. With his books continuing to pour off the presses, he found himself in ever-increasing circles of people who wanted to get to know him. One such seeker, who later became a friend, was psychotherapist Robert A. Jonas, who first heard Nouwen speak in 1983, when he was completing a doctorate in psychology and education at Harvard:

Henri's presence in the lectures was extraordinary. He would exhort his listeners to live Christ's reality right now! He would declare ultimate truths and announce the Good News without a trace of self-doubt. He used Scripture in a way that I had never heard, suffused throughout with the keen insight of a post-Freudian psychologist. I felt at the time that Henri was a mixture of evangelical preacher, Harvard intellectual and Catholic saint. His passion overflowed – quite outside the bounds of ordinary human experience. In his public presentations I, and so many others, were simply awestruck. Before I met Henri I had begun to learn Buddhist meditation – this Eastern spiritual path seemed more

profound than the Christianity that I had grown up with. As a
Harvard graduate student I would have been embarrassed to admit
it – but Henri's presence brought Jesus alive in a way that went
straight to my soul.

Chanting Taizé songs and proclaiming the Gospel on his tiptoes was
not exactly the accustomed style for a professor at Harvard. Within
the confines of the academic structure, Nouwen felt frustrated, lonely
and unappreciated – a tension which had also emerged at Yale in his
final years there. Harvard was another engagement with the intellectual
life, but he knew he loved the spiritual life more. Nouwen wanted to
be in a faculty where more members prayed, but he didn't see much
praying going on, so he felt marginalised.

Nouwen also discovered at Harvard that when he tried to talk about
Latin America, everyone really wanted him to talk about prayer and
contemplation, asking him about the inner life, the spiritual life
and ministry:

> Even though I was integrating a lot of the Latin American dimen-
> sions, I was focusing on the life of the spirit. I loved it. But at the
> same time, I had the feeling that Harvard was not where God
> wanted me to be. It's too much podium, too much publicity, too
> public. Too many people came to listen. Plus Harvard is intensely
> competitive. It's not an intimate place. It's a place of intellectual
> battle. On the one hand, I loved being there – I made some
> beautiful friends. But at the same time, I didn't feel it was a safe
> place where I could deepen my spiritual life. I had to pray more.
> I had to be quiet. I had to be in community.[3]

One occasional visitor to Harvard was Jan Risse who had founded the
L'Arche community in Mobile, Alabama, and was one of the movement's co-ordinators in North America. She was asked by Jean Vanier,
one of the founders of L'Arche, to make contact with Nouwen after he
had mentioned the community in his book, *Clowning in Rome*. The
two met and Nouwen was invited to attend a L'Arche covenant retreat
near South Bend, Indiana, where he had a number of long talks with
Vanier whom he invited to Harvard. During his subsequent visit to the
Divinity School, Vanier guessed that Nouwen was going through a

period of fragility and vulnerability, but at the same time became aware of just how popular Nouwen was with students:

> He was an incredible teacher. I sensed just how much the students loved him, but there was something going on which meant he knew he couldn't stay. It might have been a growing loneliness. Or it might have been the discrepancy between who he was and what he was living in an interior and personal sense, and the acclaim he was receiving from the students. My feeling was that somewhere there was a discrepancy between those two elements which became almost unbearable for him.

17. Icons

THROUGHOUT HIS teaching and writing career, Henri Nouwen reached deep within himself to discover his true identity in God. Whatever he learned, he passed on through his lectures and books. During the 1970s and early 1980s his output burgeoned as he became one of the most influential stars in the constellation of spiritual guides. Certainly much of what he continued to write proved not only helpful to people but transformative too: thousands the world over had their shaken spiritual lives restored by his words. But readers could not have realised the extent to which Nouwen was struggling with severe depressions, exhaustion and intense feelings of loneliness. He sought some help from psychologists and psychiatrists, but never stayed with them for any length of time. He also mentioned to friends that his prayer life wasn't touching some things he needed to explore. Was the eagerness to minister and the constant round of globetrotting lecture tours a means of diverting himself from his own inner truth?

There was a constant tension at the heart of Nouwen's personality between being a priest – and a famous one at that – and living with the painful knowledge of his sexuality, which he described as a handicap, another cross to bear. He had lived with the conflict for a great many years and, in personal terms, it was to remain largely a secret which dared not speak its name. However, he had first tackled homosexuality from a pastoral standpoint in the late 1960s, in an article for the *National Catholic Reporter*, advocating a relaxed and unfearful Christian approach. While at Yale in the 1970s, he had distributed to students an article called 'The Self-Availability of the Homosexual' which he had written for a book entitled *Is Gay Good?* It was an essay about the need for gay and lesbian people to be themselves in all circumstances, for both their spiritual and emotional health. 'This was in 1973 so it was incredibly enlightened for that period and it certainly made me feel I could gain support from him', said Chris Glaser, the first and only openly gay person at Yale Divinity School during those years. 'Henri was the most supportive of all the professors. His availability for me was part of a broader context of his support for a lot of folk. In addition he had a particular concern for people who were marginalised, and so I fell into that category.'

Glaser, who was reading for a master of divinity degree but was prevented by his Church from becoming a Presbyterian minister because he was gay, learned from Nouwen that celibacy was a gift:

> He did have a strong sense of his vocation as a celibate priest, and he would sometimes talk with me about that when I had a bad relationship. He would say that maybe I should consider celibacy as a vocation. He didn't expect gay people to be celibate but he did expect them to be in a relationship, and to be in a covenant relationship, as he would expect heterosexuals to be in a covenant relationship. And that was against his Church's teaching.
>
> I was a Protestant – and he dealt with me on that basis; he didn't expect me to adhere to Roman Catholic thought and teachings as he would had I been a Roman Catholic. A Catholic priest friend of mine, who was gay, was more directly challenged by Henri. Part of it was the expected celibacy of priesthood.

During his years at Harvard in the early 1980s, Nouwen seemed to take a particularly hardline approach with students towards homosexuality. Some claim he was ruthlessly unsympathetic to a number of gay men at that time because of his allegiance to Church teaching, telling them that the only way they could be acceptable to God was strictly to obey the Church's law on celibacy because homosexuality was an evil state of being. One person claimed that Nouwen had begun taking Catholic doctrine 'in a very Northern European way, interpreting it literally and basically crucifying people on it'.

Such a position seems surprising in view of his compassionate nature. Perhaps, as a loyal servant of the Church and a world-renowned priest, he felt obliged to uphold traditional teaching – but more probably he was becoming more acutely aware of his own struggles in this area and his warnings to students might have been reminders to himself. Whatever the reason, it suggests that his own state of mind cannot have been peaceful. Michael O'Laughlin, Nouwen's teaching assistant, confirms the depth and intensity of his depression and his needs at that time. In some desperation, it seems, Nouwen sought advice from a Franciscan-run centre in New Orleans which ministered to homo-sexual men and women. There, in a state of perplexity over ecclesiastical law and his own calling, he happened to meet an icono-grapher from New Mexico called Robert Lentz, from whom he had ordered an icon of St Francis the previous year. Lentz recalls their meeting:

> I only spent a short afternoon with him but he struck me as being incredibly tense and nervous and under a great deal of stress. He seemed to be an incredibly shy person, a very private person, and to allow very few people into his life. He was looking for spiritual guidance, and his tenseness around these sexual issues made me feel very uncomfortable indeed.

Nouwen then told Lentz – himself gay and a former monk – that he wanted to commission a second icon from him, one that would help him to consecrate his homosexual emotions and feelings to Christ. Lentz had recently seen in a collection of old icons an image of Christ with St John the Evangelist, not in the characteristic pose of the Last Supper where John reclines on Christ's chest, but depicting Christ sitting on a throne while John approaches him virtually bowing, a formal yet affectionate image:

> I suggested that a variation of that image might be what he was looking for, somebody coming to Christ and offering their feelings, their emotions and their sexuality to him. He liked the idea very much and it led to the image which I painted called *Christ the Bridegroom*. The old image had come from Crete and I had not seen it anywhere else. I made my own interpretation of that

ancient icon, and sent it to him. He liked it very much and wrote
to me saying it was exactly what he had been looking for.

For Nouwen, art was always an important means of coming to grips
with the struggles of his heart, and for that reason alone he valued it
intensely. But it must have taken enormous courage for him to order
a personal icon because of the need to explain precisely what he needed
it to do for him. *Christ the Bridegroom* became a metaphor for his
own struggle and liberation. He placed it opposite his bed so it was
the first thing he saw in the morning and the last thing he saw at
night. Sometimes he moved it to other places – for example, he used
to lay it on the floor of a chapel, slightly raised, surrounded by freshly
cut flowers and sumptuous cloths, so it drew people in with a remarkable intimacy. During his times of greatest mental anguish and distress,
it was perhaps a physical reminder of what he most wanted; for
someone who talked so passionately about the Word made flesh, the
icon became a means of grounding his own struggle in the incarnation.

Lentz sympathised with Nouwen's fears because he himself had just
been expelled from a monastery for being gay, even though he wasn't
a practising homosexual. He also had privileged access to Nouwen who
had to open up deeply so that the iconographer could create the right
image for him:

> No one could understand some of Henri's problems at Harvard,
> or why he ordered that icon from me, without recognising that
> he was a homosexual human being who was basically being grilled
> over the fire of church law and his own conscience, as formed by
> another era of spirituality. That explained why he looked so tor-
> tured. I think Henri never had any doubt in his mind that he was
> a celibate man – and that was always my intention in my own
> monastic life as well. Henri was an incredibly emotional man, and
> it may have been difficult for him to be celibate with strong
> feelings for people. But part of his reason for wanting the icon
> was to have a visual aid enabling him constantly to say, 'This is
> what I offer to you, Lord. I offer you all of these feelings, all of
> this confusion, and I want to remain celibate'.
>
> I went through the same phase in my own life as a Catholic
> and a homosexual and, while I say all this with some vigour, I say

it also with compassion, because I can understand how a person reacts against gay people in the way Henri did at Harvard, simply because of the nature of the Roman Church and its inquisitorial qualities – especially if you buy into the power structure, which every male religious and every priest does. You have some investment in that power and in some ways you are then bound by that power much more than others in the pew.

Nouwen's reputation as a popular exponent of the Christian faith was also making increasing demands on him as his books continued to dominate the religious market. He had to maintain a Catholic stance in his own mind if he were to continue to be influential as a Catholic preacher. He knew too that he was a man of connections who had access to (and perhaps some influence in) the halls of power – he had even preached to the US Congress during one of their prayer breakfasts. Henri Nouwen was a name on everybody's lips, one of the golden boys whom everybody looked up to and admired. He had become an icon in his own right. To reveal his clay feet would be a betrayal of those who respected him. In any event, part of him needed the adulation. But being on a pedestal had a price, when reactionary lay people in the Catholic world seemed to be lying in wait for the scent of scandal so they could be the first to tip off the authorities.

It was difficult for Nouwen to know whom to trust. He certainly guessed that there were a great many other priests in turmoil for the same reasons, and that some of them were leaving the Church, a move he deplored. Abandoning the priesthood was out of the question for him, so he had to find ways of coping with his struggle. The constant frenetic activity, which was burning him out, was probably the classic means of escape.

He had important relationships with colleagues and students, but he found personal friendships hard to sustain. Seminary prohibitions about getting too close must have haunted every encounter and may have explained his tendency to strike up conversations of deep intimacy with strangers instead. His driving force was to know the full mystery of God in everyone he met and, on a practical level, this left a lot of people thinking they were in his intimate circle when in fact they were not. While he searched for God in every human being he met, and often made people think they were entering into trusting new bonds of friendship with him, in reality he tended to keep everyone at arm's length and there were things that even his most intimate friends did not know about him. None of it was deliberate – he could never be accused of hypocrisy, because the one person who could not see what was happening was Nouwen himself. He was not trading on other people's intimacy but was a professional intimate who had simply never learned another way of dealing with people; it only exacerbated the dilemma over the extent to which he should share the secret of his sexuality.

Jean Vanier felt convinced that Nouwen would benefit from being in a place where there would be permanent relationships. At the professional level, the constant flow of students at Harvard was unsettling, as were the tensions which existed between him and some other members of staff. At the deeper level, there appeared to be a need for a personal relationship as well as a community relationship, 'so I invited him to spend a year at Trosly and he seemed very touched'.

But Nouwen was not one for making rash decisions and needed to pray through his options carefully. To leave Harvard for L'Arche in Trosly, France, would be the most radical step yet, and he sought the advice of a great many friends and spiritual advisers. Before finally deciding to leave Harvard, Nouwen also undertook his second 30-day silent retreat following the spiritual exercises of St Ignatius Loyola (the previous one had been some years before, when he was deciding whether to leave Yale). The exercises constitute hard, specific guided meditations towards a radical conversion to serve Christ and his mission, to bring the kingdom into the world. Nouwen kept private handwritten journals during those retreats, and might not have left either institution had it not been for the power of their experience in helping him to make what in both cases turned out to be life-changing decisions.

Nouwen had first visited the L'Arche community at Trosly in 1983. Jean Vanier's assistant, Barbara Swanekamp, had put Rublev's icon, *The Holy Trinity*, on the table where he was staying and, after gazing at it for many weeks, he felt a deep urge to write down what he had gradually learned to see. When he visited the following year, Barbara had replaced that icon with *The Virgin of Vladimir*. During that third visit in 1985, his own spiritual life had become so connected with the beauty of icons that he felt compelled to write about two more icons – Rublev's *The Saviour of Zvenigorod* and *The Descent of the Holy Spirit*.

It was also through Nouwen's contemplation of icons that he was slowly able to move from an inner world of fear to an inner world of love, along the lines of one of his previous books – but it was a long process of conversion. Just as *Christ the Bridegroom* had become a powerful form of meditation for him, so looking at the four icons became a consolation in times of spiritual dryness, fatigue and depression. It safeguarded an inner space during periods of distraction. By talking about the icons, reading about them but mostly by gazing at them, just like the Byzantine Fathers, he gradually came to know them by heart, as he had learned the Our Father and the Hail Mary half a century before. It took Nouwen a long time to *see* the icons, but they became for him windows looking out upon eternity:

> Icons are not easy to 'see'. They do not immediately speak to our senses. They do not excite, fascinate, stir our emotions, or stimu-late our imagination. At first, they even seem somewhat rigid, lifeless, schematic and dull. They do not reveal themselves to us at first sight. It is only gradually, after a patient, prayerful presence that they start speaking to us. And as they speak, they speak more to our inner than to our outer senses. They speak to the heart that searches for God.[1]

Icons offered him a glimpse of heaven. Just as Western spirituality, through St Benedict, had emphasised listening, so Eastern spirituality, through the Byzantine Fathers, had focused on gazing: looking with complete attention at these sacred images of an eternal mystery. For Henri Nouwen they gradually stilled the anxieties of his mind, leading him to the inner room of prayer and drawing him ever closer to the God of love.

III
BODY

18. Slowly Through the Forest

HENRI NOUWEN'S decision to go to L'Arche was a turning-point in his life and a major change of direction, but it was based more on what he hoped to receive than on what he had to give: he was looking for somewhere to belong. When Jean Vanier had said, 'Maybe we can offer you a home here', he knew that was what Nouwen's heart desired and he was certain it would also lead to a more radical living-out of Christian discipleship. Founded in 1964, L'Arche is an international organisation of women and men with intellectual and physical disabilities, who create a home together with assistants from many different backgrounds and faith traditions. Assistants, as well as core members, often come to L'Arche wounded by circumstances, accidents, structures, rejection, abuse – and for a range of other reasons.

The community at Trosly-Breuil near the forests of Compiègne, an hour from Paris, was not unknown to Nouwen because he had made previous visits there, the last occasion as part of a 30-day Ignatian retreat. As he walked the streets of the French village that August afternoon in 1985 without seeing a person or a car, the noisy, crowded and competitive environment of Cambridge, Massachusetts, seemed worlds away. There was tranquillity in the woods to think and pray, a stillness in the air broken only by joyful birdsong and an occasional barking of Alsatians. Nouwen would not be actively involved in the community and would have the freedom to travel wherever and when-ever he wanted; nevertheless Jean Vanier offered him a year's accommodation in a section of his mother's house. Pauline Vanier and Henri became close friends.

In Nouwen's heart was a need for a permanent intimacy, which was answered to some extent by a spiritual friendship which he developed with the Dominican priest, the late Thomas Philippe, who had co-founded L'Arche with Jean Vanier. On his first visit to Trosly, Nouwen had concelebrated Mass with Père Thomas:

> As I stood beside him behind the large rock that was the altar of the Trosly-Breuil chapel, I sensed that I was in the presence of a man in whom immense suffering and immense joy had become one. I knew that people from all over France, very simple and very sophisticated people, very poor and very wealthy people, young and old people, came to visit and listen to him. From early in the morning to late at night, there were people sitting in the small waiting-room in front of his hermitage-like living space. I knew that this old priest, in his eighties, hard of hearing, slow in walking, unable to celebrate without a tall chair to support him, and fragile in health, was an immense source of faith, hope, and love for countless men and women who experienced deep inner darkness.[1]

Nouwen was drawn to the man's luminous presence and felt understood by him in depth. He would later say that, at a time of great anguish, Père Thomas became for him the most tangible manifestation of God's compassion he had ever experienced: 'It seemed like the depth of my inner pain had called forth from him the depth of God's compassion'.[2] Jean Vanier thought the relationship partly explained the change in Nouwen during his year at Trosly and gave him renewed hope that, mysteriously, his own aching loneliness could become an instrument of God for the healing of others:

> Somewhere at the heart of Henri was that cry for a permanent intimacy. He found that with Père Thomas, and I think he really sensed that Père Thomas had understood him in depth. It changed him – it was quite amazing, but with that great cry for intimacy and friendship, the question was: where could he live his ministry

as a priest of Jesus? He loved Jesus and wanted to reveal the name
of Jesus.

Despite the sense of security he experienced at Trosly, Nouwen knew
that he would not be able to stay in that particular community. In
October 1985, he spent a week at the L'Arche Daybreak community
near Toronto, where he had the first glimpses of where his new
vocation might lie. Two days after his arrival at Daybreak, one of the
core members, Raymond, was seriously injured in a car accident and
Nouwen moved naturally into the role of pastor. On his own initiative
he went to the hospital, visited the community's ten homes, talked
to assistants about Raymond's condition and urged them to place a
photograph of Raymond on their dining-room tables so they would
remember to pray for him. He told Raymond's father to bless his son
in case he died. The fearful and grief-stricken father said he did not
know how to do that. 'I will show you', replied Nouwen. 'Bless your
son and say good things to him. Tell him that you love him and speak
to him about God.' Raymond eventually recovered.

Nouwen came to feel intimately part of the intense joys and sorrows
of the community and, after he had returned to France, the leaders
realised what a gift he had been. They wrote asking him to come to
Daybreak to live as their pastor, initially for three years. They urged
him to discern the call with his spiritual director and talk it over with
his bishop, although they also pointed out that they had no salary to
offer him. Deeply moved by the letter, Nouwen had never felt called
in such a direct way. He had many spiritual directors and did not know
which one to turn to; and, while he was not sure his bishop knew
where he was, he would go and seek his permission to go to Daybreak.

Back in France Nouwen continued to struggle with his old cravings
for affirmation. When Robert Jonas, one of his American friends, failed
to visit Trosly as planned, he felt sad, hurt and rejected, especially as
he had made all kinds of arrangements to welcome him. Jonas apologised for having unintentionally hurt his friend and tried to explain
the competing commitments that had prevented him from visiting
Nouwen until later in the year. He thought the matter was finished,
but was surprised to receive what felt like a public reprimand in
Nouwen's subsequent book, *The Road to Daybreak*. In later discussions

with other friends of Nouwen, Jonas realised that, in this instance, Henri had given him a role in an inner drama which had been going on throughout his life. There always seemed to be people who were abandoning Nouwen, failing to make him the centre of attention, often unwittingly causing him deep pain.

Jean Vanier felt that Nouwen never really knew the origins of his loneliness but viewed it as an unanswered craving which came out in phenomenal anguish, a pattern of behaviour not unknown by artists:

> Aristotle said that if you are not loved, you seek admiration, and you saw with Henri that double movement: the sense of not being loved and the feeling of loneliness – and a terrific need for admiration. And through all of that, the power of God was working, and that's where I see the mystery.
>
> It's said of Aristotle that he loved all that was human, and it was also true of Henri – his whole contact with the circus people, music, painting; he was incredibly gifted, incredibly cultured. So in him there were these different elements: loneliness, culture and a deep sense of psychology – and he brought all that to revealing Jesus.

Vanier recollected the talks Nouwen gave entitled 'What is the glory of God?'. They revealed deep insights from his everyday existence and contact with people. Many people talk about the gospels but don't relate them to experience. Nouwen shed light on reality through the gospels and shed light on the gospels through experience. That was part of his incredible genius. Although he could seem little and needy, crying out for the love of human beings, he was also yearning for an experience of God, and that was another part of his mystery.

Many talk affectionately about him in the various homes around the picturesque French village. Etienne Bourdaire, a young man unable to speak, makes circles in front of his eyes to indicate that he is talking about his bespectacled friend Henri. He then puts his hand on his heart and lifts it upwards to explain that Henri is now in heaven. It was Etienne who, through his sign language, reminded the community that 21 September 1997 was the first anniversary of Henri's death. Most assistants had forgotten, but Etienne had remembered.

Simone Landrien also became a close friend of Henri's. On the side of her staircase, she sticks pictures of community members, living and dead. The display is divided between earth and heaven. When Henri died, she moved his picture from one side of the display to the other, where he can now be seen in the community of saints: 'I moved Henri up to heaven', she smiled. 'I feel his presence more now than when he was alive, now that he is in the bosom of the Father of the prodigal son.' Simone, who is among the many devoted helpers at L'Arche, keeps a small archive of Henri's writings in a nearby office where she has a range of books, documents and tapes, including a copy of a letter Nouwen sent to friends back in Boston while he was at Trosly, in which he wrote:

> Being at L'Arche in France is a real gift. 'I feel very much supported by the community, and am having ample time to write. Once, a few years ago, my spiritual director asked me: 'What do you really want?' Without hesitation I answered: 'Time to pray and write'. He said: 'Well, maybe your desire shows you your vocation'. I never thought that I would ever find the place to live that vocation, but now I am closer to it than ever. Prayer is still hard. It feels as if the busy years in Cambridge are still crowding my heart and mind. I still feel driven to do too much. But at least I am in the right place to learn to pray again.

Nouwen particularly liked to spend time in the oratory where the Blessed Sacrament is exposed from morning until night. A long-time lay assistant, Mirella Di Sabato, once walked into the small room and noticed 'this huge long body on the floor, a full-length prostration'. It was Henri praying – he remained in that position for a long time, and Mirella had an overwhelming sense that he was in the presence of God and God was with him.

The longer he stayed at Trosly, the more unified and more centred he became. Nouwen willingly gave homilies in French, and beforehand might go for a walk through the forest to practise his pronunciations with a friend: he had to get the words right. The congregation recognised in him a gift of speech – Mirella noted that 'each individual heart present was touched in a different way, transformed and deepened'. Such was the nature of his prophetic presence that, through Nouwen, many people found themselves experiencing the divine.

The Road to Daybreak detailed Nouwen's many conversations, thoughts on God, age-old struggles and dilemmas, journeys around Europe and trips back to North America. It named all the people who were important to him during this period, friends about whom he comments without inhibition. However, one 'deep and nurturing friendship'[3] which began at Trosly was to trigger a profound emotional response in Nouwen, and was to affect him at his deepest and most painful level of need for the rest of his life. Nathan Ball was then a Canadian assistant in his early thirties in whom Nouwen recognised a deep compassion, someone who 'is becoming a friend, a new companion in life, a new presence that will last wherever I will go'.[4] Nathan came from a Baptist family in Calgary; he had been received into the Catholic Church and, soon afterwards, he went to Trosly to live and work with the handicapped. His own brother, who had been disabled, had died a few years before. In his published journal, Nouwen openly shared his feelings for Nathan:

> Over the past few months we have gradually come to know each other. I was not aware of how significant our relationship had become for me until he left for a month to visit his family and friends in Canada. I missed his presence greatly and looked forward to his return.
>
> Two days ago he came back and tonight we went out for supper together. I felt a need to let him know how much I had missed him. I told him that his absence had made me aware of a real affection for him that had grown in me since we had come to know each other. He responded with a strong affirmation of our friendship from his side. As we talked more about past experiences and future plans, it became clear that God had brought us close for a reason. Nathan hopes to begin theological studies in Toronto in September and plans to live at Daybreak during that time. I am filled with gratitude and joy that God is not only calling me to a new country and a new community, but also offering me a new friendship to make it easier to follow that call.[5]

The journal charted Henri's preparation for another venture into the countercultural – and it also focused on Nathan as an intelligent and sensitive person in whose company Henri felt protected and secure:

I will never think about this year without a deep gratitude for my friendship with Nathan and our long hours of sharing our joys and pains. Often it seems to me that the main reason for my being in Trosly was to be given this friendship as the safe context for a new vocation. Whatever happens at Daybreak, I am not going to be alone in my struggle, and Nathan will be there with me to keep me faithful to my promises.[6]

Many people admired his decision, at the age 54, to abandon the prestige of an upwardly mobile life for an unglamorous future of downward mobility, but some of his friends seriously questioned whether Nouwen was doing the right thing. These reservations are summed up by Donald Reeves, rector of St James', Piccadilly, in London, who met Nouwen for the first time a few months before he joined Daybreak:

He told me that he was going to live in a community where people didn't know how famous he was, among those who couldn't read his books. I found that absolutely admirable in one way, but I wondered how natural it was for him to do that and whether he was making an enormous statement about something. The way he talked about it struck me as being rather like a pose or a statement; it didn't seem to come from the heart. I felt that if he really meant this, he wouldn't actually have told anybody. He would have just done it.

Jean Vanier admits that joining the Daybreak community was not a natural step for Nouwen because he didn't know what he was going into and what it would be all about. Nouwen had taken risks before, when he had left Holland for the United States and when he had moved from North America to South America – but, in many ways, the decision to go to Daybreak was the most daring. Anxious for a home, he was uncertain about how he would fit in and frightened by the demands the community might put on him – in the past he had always managed to hold a free rein within institutional life. As the time approached, he looked forward to a new place of belonging but looked back on the liberties he might lose. His sense of vocation held him safe – but why was one of America's most distinguished and independently minded professors, who had made his name in his country's centres of academic excellence, being drawn to a small, unknown community, where people with disabilities live together, sharing life in community? Many people pondered the reasons and so did he:

> I was living in accordance with God's love for me as a university professor, but at one point it felt that there was a conflict between my career and my vocation, that my career no longer allowed me to continue my vocation. Then suddenly I was at a loss. Finally I discovered L'Arche and L'Arche discovered me. I was invited to do something I wasn't prepared for. I didn't know anything about mentally handicapped people. I'd never studied them. I'm totally impractical in the first place, but God called me there, and in this case God's will was not totally in line with my specific talents.[7]

Perhaps it was the wounded part of him which wanted to forge a bond with other wounded people? Or perhaps it had more to do with the prophetic dimension of this famous priest who was responding to the needs of a hidden community, searching for a new vision and identity? It could have been both.

19. Rite of Passage

THE CONVOY of vans wound around the shores of Lake Ontario and headed north towards Richmond Hill, an hour's drive from Toronto. On the way the entourage had stopped off at the Abbey of the Genesee. Now it was heading full speed for Daybreak. Among those waiting to greet the new assistant was Sister Sue Mosteller CSJ, who had worked there since 1972:

> I can remember him coming in the driveway with all his friends from Harvard. Most people come with a backpack, but he came with his vans and all his furniture – we didn't know where we would put it. That was the beginning of many surprises as Henri made the shift. It took him a while to get out of the classroom and just become Henri – friend, brother and pastor. He loved an audience and he loved to teach. He wanted to teach us, to have classes here, and we kept saying, 'Get to know us first. Don't be the teacher first; be the pastor first and then we'll see.' And although he didn't like that much at the time, he grew to love being pastor.

Nouwen later spoke of his deep inner sense of not being simply called to do a certain job, but to live some particular kind of life. Notre Dame, Yale and Harvard had all been professional choices. The call to L'Arche had emerged from his own need for a community and for a home he had never found in the United States:

The community called me and said maybe we can offer a home for you. That's not what the universities ever said to me: they said maybe you can do a job for us. The community said that if Daybreak really felt like home for me, then maybe I could make it my home as a priest and therefore become the pastor. I could only be a good pastor if this was a good home for me.

Nouwen was yearning to integrate the mind and the heart, but it was here also that he was to learn much about the body. The sun was rising on a whole new landscape for him. It wasn't simply a movement towards countercultural thinking, but a commitment to the life of the Beatitudes: 'blessed are the poor'. He joined L'Arche in the first instance as an assistant, working and living alongside the core ('handicapped') community members. He was involved in some pastoral duties – but his work as an assistant enabled him to learn about the community's ethos. Members of the Daybreak community recognised the prophetic nature of his choice: 'For him to make the journey of his heart and come to live among us in L'Arche was very prophetic. Our society goes against such choices. People strive to get into universities, to make a name for themselves, to have status and success. He had that, but he chose another way.'

Living in a L'Arche community is difficult for many of the new assistants, but for Henri, who had lived alone for much of his life, it presented particular challenges. Being on time for supper, for example, was not a natural discipline, and at first he found ordinary conversation with those who were slow to articulate a difficult new experience. He used to invite visitors every day so he could engage in less mundane matters – almost every night there would be three extra guests at the dinner table, even though he hadn't thought to tell the cook before-hand. There were evenings when community members simply wanted to be together without Henri rushing over and introducing his friends – so there were rough patches in the early days, both for New House, where he lived, and for Henri himself. The nature of his personality inclined towards wide spaces and lots of activity, so the community had to keep reining him in and rechannelling his energies. 'In the end we just had to give up and accept that he was unique', said Sue Mosteller. 'The wonderful thing is that he learned to talk about community in a very brilliant way but he didn't live it very well. He could never get a hold on it.'

There were other practical adjustments to face as well. In his first week, Henri emerged from his room with a pile of dirty shirts and underwear: 'Who do I give my laundry to?' he enquired, only to be given an impromptu lesson in washing-machine technology. But it was never one he fully grasped and, when his clothes started to shrink, change colour and rip apart in awkward places, someone else took the job on. He hardly knew how to make a cup of coffee, and had never seen anyone fry steak. Washing-up with Henri was also novel, not just because of his clumsiness, but also because he could become completely distracted by a conversation. Once when it was his turn to put the dishes away, he started an absorbing discussion with friends he'd invited for a meal. After a quarter of an hour, the washer began to wonder why they had used so many utensils in preparing dinner. He then discovered that, instead of putting them in the cupboard, Henri had, like a man under hypnosis, simply been walking over to the washing-up bowl and putting the clean dishes back in the water again.

It was therefore with some trepidation that the community assigned him to Adam Arnett, a 25-year-old man who could not speak or move without assistance, and who suffered from frequent seizures. Adam was among five core members who lived in New House, one of the eight houses which made up the Daybreak community. Henri's job, like that of the other four assistants in New House, was to live with the handicapped and carry out a range of duties, most of them alien to him. He was responsible for taking care of Adam and doing his morning routine, which meant waking him at 7 a.m., taking off his pyjamas, dressing him in a bathrobe, walking him to the bathroom, shaving his beard, giving him a bath, making his breakfast, sitting close beside him as he ate, supporting his glass as he drank, brushing his teeth, putting on his coat, gloves and cap, getting him into his wheelchair and pushing him over a road full of potholes for his day programme, which lasted until 4 p.m.

Nouwen acknowledged that he was terrified when first asked to look after Adam. He was awkward, but open to learning. He asked many questions time and again and called for help until he felt safe and able to do the job well. Through the discipline he came to learn the sacredness of touch and felt honoured that the weakest and most disabled man in the entire community had been entrusted to him, the least capable of the carers. His whole life had been shaped by words, ideas and books, but his priorities were starting to change. He realised that Adam was offering him his body in total vulnerability – and being near to Adam's body brought him closer still to Adam. It was an encounter which inevitably was to find its way into print:

> I must confess that there were moments when I was impatient and preoccupied by what I was going to do when I had finished Adam's 'routine'. Then, without being conscious of his person, I started to rush him. Consciously, but mostly unconsciously, I hurriedly pushed his arms through his sleeves or his legs through his trousers. I wanted to be sure I was finished by 9 a.m. so I could go to my other work. Right here I learned that Adam could communicate! He let me know that I wasn't being really present to him and was more concerned about my schedule than his. A few times when I was so pushy he responded by having a *grand mal* seizure, and I realised that it was his way of saying, 'Slow down, Henri! Slow down.' Well, it certainly slowed me down! A seizure so completely exhausted him that I had to stop everything I was doing and let him rest. Sometimes if it was a bad one, I brought him back to his bed and covered him with many blankets to keep him from shivering violently. Adam was communicating with me, and he was consistent in reminding me that he wanted and needed me to be with him unhurriedly and gently. He was clearly asking me to follow his rhythm and adapt my ways to his needs. I found myself beginning to understand a new language, Adam's language.[1]

The bond between them deepened as Henri started talking to Adam, even confiding his secrets to him, telling him about his moods and frustrations, his easy and difficult relationships, and about his prayer life. Adam became for him like a confessor, silently listening with his whole being, offering his hesitant friend a safe place. When Henri was working elsewhere or becoming anxious over something or someone, he thought of Adam as the silent, peaceful presence at the centre of his life, someone who seemed to 'call me back to stillness at the eye of the cyclone'.[2] He saw the tables turning as Adam became his teacher, taking him by the hand, walking with him through the wilderness of his life. He discovered in Adam a person who enabled him to become not only rooted in Daybreak but in his own inner self. The things he most desired in life – love, friendship, community and a deep sense of belonging – were there in the beauty of someone who uttered not a word:

> His heart, so transparent, reflected for me not only his person but also the heart of the universe and, indeed, the heart of God. After my many years of studying, reflecting, and teaching theology, Adam came into my life, and by his life and his heart he announced to me and summarised all I had ever learned.[3]

Although he was to receive immense support from the whole community in that first year, his truest teacher and healer was Adam, even though Nouwen might not have realised it until long after. Nouwen saw Daybreak as the place of Adam's public ministry. He believed that Adam, like Jesus, had been sent into the world to fulfil a unique mission not in action but in passion. His was a life of suffering, of daily epileptic seizures, of total dependence on other people's actions and decisions. He could do a few things for himself, such as jumping on the bed, pushing a vacuum cleaner down the stairs or lifting his spoon or cup, but he could never determine where to go, with whom to be or what to do. He lived every moment waiting for others to act on his behalf, but all the action around him did not diminish his passion which, to Nouwen, became a profound prophetic witness, challenging people to believe that compassion and not competition was the way to fulfil a human vocation.

At Daybreak Nouwen felt loved, appreciated and cared for, and he never questioned the move he had made. Surrounded by so many different handicaps, he discovered more and more of his own, and found his defences weakening. In a caring environment, without pressure to prove himself or a lecture circuit to rush out on, he was confronted with his own reality as never before: a very insecure, needy, and fragile person who came to see Adam as the strong one: 'The fact that my handicaps were less visible than those of Adam and his housemates didn't make them less real.'[4]

Nouwen's prophetic ministry at Daybreak started immediately, as he reached out to other people both in the community and in the surrounding area where he often preached. People were instantly struck by the power of his message and his compassion for them as individuals. He had the skills and experience to tune in sensitively to what they shared with him.

Although L'Arche did have a spirituality of its own, there was not a great deal of spiritual leadership or theological expertise at Daybreak. There was much to think through because people came from various religious traditions – and there were a number of highly motivated assistants from different backgrounds for whom being at L'Arche was a way of living the spiritual life. The staff knew that spirituality was an issue which had to be addressed, but it was not high on the agenda. As their priest and pastor, Nouwen called them to lead a spiritual life, and to worship together more regularly. He brought to them a sacramental presence. When he first came to Daybreak, the community's spirituality was at the margins; but by the time of his death, it was in the centre. The changes, though, did not happen overnight and the development of an ecumenical spirituality was a difficult process, as Sue Mosteller recalls:

> He started with his desire to celebrate the Eucharist every day and he ran right into the wall because, being an ecumenical community, people didn't want the Roman Catholic Eucharist to be the main act of worship every day. He had to adapt, and we looked at other kinds of liturgy; this grew into a very beautiful rhythm of worship for which Henri was responsible. He began to pastor by listening and then, through his homilies, talking with us as a community and individually.

At first, he struggled to find the right words – the academic tone was hard to lose. There were also times when he used language which was childish and inappropriate, so he had to find his own way and learn how to communicate. Then he realised that people with disabilities heard his words not so much with their minds as with their hearts. It was not necessary to talk in a new way but with a simplified message.

As he settled in at Daybreak, Henri explored a whole new adventure in grace among people who were broken in their bodies but had a lot of wholeness to give in their hearts. Previously he had been used to people being quiet and paying attention to him; as the primary celebrant at the Eucharist, he wasn't used to a group of people who made all kinds of godly sounds that weren't part of his vocabulary. He had to discern what these new voices of God meant in his life. He was at first distracted and annoyed by the lack of silence in the eucharistic celebration, but he was open enough to learn gradually that this brought a new dimension to Eucharist: the broken ones of God, who could not give a verbal homily, brought a new understanding and love to the Eucharist, the broken body of Christ. The community ended up being the primary celebrants of the Eucharist, and he was able in his best moments to receive that grace and gift from the community.

Nouwen continued to feel uncomfortable among people who did not share his own verbal dexterity and background, finding it a trial to sustain a presence with them. Added to this were his problems in finding a balance between being rooted in the day-to-day demands of the community and all the demands of wanting to write and responding to invitations. Before he employed his own secretaries, Daybreak appointed a group to help him work out a sensible means of planning. Nouwen never wanted to turn anyone down, but was constantly complaining of having too much to do and feeling tired. His fame brought some problems for the community too, according to Joe Egan, who was director of Daybreak when Nouwen arrived:

> A lot of visitors came to see Henri and not Daybreak. So there were sometimes tensions around the number of people at liturgies who wanted to meet Henri rather than the core members. He was a difficult fellow to hang on to. Henri had an incredible sensitivity to people when he met them on a one-to-one basis and people quickly started to meet with him but he also had three left hands and three right hands. He couldn't make any sandwiches but he was willing to try new things. There was a whole passage from academic life to community life. For a number of years he talked about semesters but we had to tell him that our concept of time didn't include semesters. Like all the assistants he learned by

watching other people on the spot but he picked it up quickly. With Adam he was very comfortable and he did it very faithfully.

During that first year at Daybreak, Nouwen was invited to give a Lent talk at St Paul's Church, Harvard Square, Massachusetts, on the theme of peace and non-violence. The church was packed with intellectuals from Harvard, Yale, Boston University and Massachusetts Institute of Technology. It was the first time Nouwen had been back in Cambridge since joining L'Arche, and he decided to take John, one of the core members, with him. The pair were a powerful presence in the church and Nouwen began to speak about what he had learned from Adam. But the reactions from some people in the pews were hostile, as Elizabeth Buckley, now a hermit at Daybreak, observed:

> People walked out asking how this great intellect, this former professor, could say he's learning from a man who can't even speak or walk. He got some hard letters from people and later said, 'I think if some of them had had stones they would have thrown them at me'.

Many continued to criticise him for moving to L'Arche, one woman even writing to ask, 'Why are you living with those retarded people? They don't even understand you. People away from there need you much more.' Nouwen began to discover during that first year that, far from being something to be ashamed of or embarrassed by, woundedness could be a gift. To be wounded was to be blessed. It was not a theology with which everyone would agree, but for Nouwen, the community of L'Arche was confronting him increasingly with his own wounds. And the sight scared him. In his words, it was as though the planks which had covered his emotional abyss had been taken away and he was staring into a canyon of wild animals waiting to devour him. On the surface, he had seemed to be settling into his new community, but at a deeper level he was facing an inner crisis which seemed to be mauling his very soul. What many of his new colleagues did not realise was that, away from his responsibilities at Daybreak, he had been returning to friends in England to be guided through his darkest night.

20. Inner Darkness

IN THE CHAPEL of an ecumenical community in rural Surrey hangs an icon of St George slaying the dragon. Not that the South Park Community Trust near Chobham is in any sense nationalistic: this was a symbolic gift from one of their much-loved guests. During his first year at Daybreak, in particular, Henri Nouwen visited the community on a number of occasions, and Patricia Beall Gavigan recalled the time when he strolled into the chapel one day and propped up the icon on a shelf, saying, 'I have brought this because I am coming here to do battle'. She believes he had an informed perspective on his deep inner struggle: 'He was determined and serious. He knew what he was about and why he was about it. He was going to see it through and so he had brought with him a visual image of what he was doing in his spiritual life, which was confronting his demons.'

Patricia, a writer and educator, is married to Bart Gavigan, a film-maker – they are co-founders of the South Park Community Trust. Both are experienced in the field of pastoral counselling, and they were among a number of people who offered guidance to Henri during his bleakest period. The three of them had met in the USA and quickly become close friends. Henri, who became godfather to their young son, Gabriel, would sometimes come to Surrey to write in the solitude of a small cottage in the community's grounds. He also liked visiting England to meet his British publishers and to rest.

Bart and Patricia Gavigan discerned that the essence of his struggle was his humanity rather than his sexuality. To some extent, Henri had found a home in all the places where he had been admired, but this had been built on his own success – his abilities, talents, gifts and scholarship. L'Arche was his first real home, where he had begun to deal with his own being in a realistic and incarnational way, rather than in an intellectual and theorised sense. Daybreak was a safe place where he was free to break down and face his own brokenness in all its complexity. People with developmental disabilities surrounded him every day and proved to be a constant revelation to him: they could not deny the reality of who they were, and Henri realised that he could no longer repress the wounded child in him. He started to face his own vulnerability as never before, but found that, in the context of L'Arche, this was actually life-giving and not life-threatening. The close relationship which had developed with Nathan Ball, in particular, was the trigger for many things he had never known, named, accepted or admitted. There were huge parts of his personality that he had never allowed himself to look at or consider, because being successful had been such a driving force in him. He had become a fine priest, a good scholar, a talented linguist, a brilliant teacher and a popular writer – but all of that had been only one highly developed side of his personality.

There were other areas which the Gavigans discovered were under-developed: his ability to be faithful in friendships, to trust love, to believe his value regardless of his gifts and to have significant relation-ships which were not based on what he could do or what he could produce – in other words, to be a person. Henri had, for so much of his life, lived through his gifts and, because he had a calling, his gifts facilitated his calling and his calling facilitated his gifts. Slowly and painfully Henri came to see a much wider panorama of awareness, possibility and being – one that he had always been denied or had denied himself.

The Gavigans tried to meet Nouwen on a range of spiritual, psycho-logical and personal levels which affirmed both his being and the faithfulness of God. They used many different therapeutic methods, but the essence of the counselling was to provide him with an utterly safe, comprehensive relationship which allowed him to *be*. They encouraged him 'to get into his body and into his prayer', but advised him not to drift off into meditations, so the prayer took the form of going for walks, striding around the garden, swimming or hitting a punch-bag. He had to channel the energy into his body but not lose touch with life – even washing-up was part of the 'therapy', for reasons Bart explained:

> There was a deliberate aim to keep him in life, because there was a great danger that he would go deeply into this darkness, this hole in the ground. In terms of regression here was a wounded little child, not a six-year-old, but a two-year-old or an 18-month-old, who needed to be held in a safe way with great purity. One had to keep separating out what was an agony at the sexual level and what was actually an agony at a much deeper level.

There were times when Henri doubted that he would ever emerge from the darkness. Bart reassured him, seeing in him a deep faithfulness to the normal disciplines of life, a refusal to let the extraordinary crush the ordinary, an openness to grace. His wound was large and deep, but he was responsive and had a strong desire to be healed:

> Henri was courageous and I admired him – but it was very, very dark indeed. He couldn't work out the despair in his life. This was not just a dark night of the soul, it was a dark night of everything, of the spirit, at the point of faith, at the point of his own being, desires, longings and sexuality. It was a dark night at the point of his own calling, work and writing. But he did not lose his faith.

Such inner knowledge was a terrifying discovery for Nouwen. It was as if everything he had lived by and held dear was being sieved inside him. He wanted to find God in the pain but he had no idea where God actually was in it. God appeared to be absent, but the dark void was pierced by some light through his faithfulness to the Word in terms of the liturgy and the office, his fidelity to the Eucharist and his loyalty to his pen. Here was a man who could hardly drag himself out of the door, only just manage to get out of bed, but who could still find the energy to write. Exhaustion, nausea, lassitude and despair hovered over every blank page, but he knew that writing was a grace in the darkness, a form of salvation.

Returning to Canada, Henri did his best to get on with life but he was still in a maelstrom and his feelings for Nathan bordered on the obsessive. Bart Gavigan came over to talk with some members of the community about the depression and was impressed by the integrity and openness on all sides, as well as Henri's desire, in the midst of it all, to want to live what he wrote about.

But in the weeks that followed Henri began to feel homeless, devoid of faith and abandoned. He could no longer sleep, cried uncontrollably for hours, was unaffected by consoling words of friends, was uninterested in other people's problems, had no appetite for food and lost all his appreciation of music, art and nature.

All this had been sparked by what he called 'the sudden interruption' of the friendship with Nathan Ball in whose company he had felt most secure. As he admitted in *The Inner Voice of Love*:

> Going to L'Arche and living with very vulnerable people, I had gradually let go of my inner guards and opened my heart more fully to others. Among my many friends, one had been able to touch me in a way I had never been touched before. Our friendship encouraged me to allow myself to be loved and cared for with greater trust and confidence. It was a totally new experience for me, and it brought me immense joy and peace. It seemed as if a door of my interior life had been opened, a door that had remained locked during my youth and most of my adult life.
>
> But this deeply satisfying friendship became the road to my anguish, because soon I discovered that the enormous space that had been opened for me could not be filled by the one who had opened it. I became possessive, needy, and dependent, and when the friendship finally had to be interrupted, I fell apart. I felt abandoned, rejected, and betrayed. Indeed, the extremes touched each other.[1]

Intellectually Nouwen knew that no human friendship could fulfil the deepest longings of his heart and that only God could give him what he most desired – but even that intuition did little to assuage the despair. Nathan retreated from the friendship because Henri's needs for attention and affection overwhelmed him. There was undoubtedly a love between them, but at different levels of intimacy. Nathan had received much from Henri but could not satisfy Henri's demands. Henri wrote explicitly about his dependency in the epilogue to *The Road to Daybreak*:

> As I approached the new life in community, I came to think about my friendship with Nathan as the safe place in the midst of all the transitions and changes. I said to myself, 'Well, whatever happens, at least I have a friend to rely on, to go to for support, to be consoled by in hard moments.' Somehow I made Nathan the centre of my emotional stability and related to the life in community as something I would be able to cope with. In this way my dependence on Nathan prevented me from making the community the true centre of my life. Unconsciously, I said to myself, 'I already have a home. I do not really need another one.' As I entered community life more deeply, however, I became gradually aware that the call to follow Jesus unreservedly required me to look for God's guidance more in the common life with handicapped people than in a unique and nurturing friendship. This discovery created such an excruciating inner pain that it brought me to the edge of despair.[2]

Nathan pulled back and, in the ensuing crisis, both men suffered greatly, according to friends who explain that Nathan chose not to deal with the pain at that point but immersed himself in his part-time work at Daybreak and his theological studies in Toronto. It was a different matter for Henri who had to deal with the situation there and then, because he would otherwise have been unable to function. He was in crisis, and he knew that he couldn't stay at Daybreak because his anguish was too great. To deal with his breakdown he needed not only psychotherapy, but also emotional and spiritual support. He eventually found this in a community in Winnipeg, which looked after him for the next six months and helped him to grow through his pain. He lived in a house with four or five others who joined in community events, but Henri preferred to keep to himself. He did exercises on his own, had the Blessed Sacrament in his room and prayed every day which, in the first few months, took the form of lying on the floor in an anguished litany of tears. Two 'guides' – a man and a woman – visited him every day. One form of therapy involved being held physically, as a friend recounts:

It responded to a craving within him to be held physically in a non-sexual way. The sessions took place fully-clothed on a bed for comfort's sake, but in the context of an office. There, in the arms of this male therapist, in a primal state, he could be held very tightly and weep, scream, writhe and be caressed, all the things a parent does when holding an infant or small child. He was held unconditionally with an enormous amount of nurture and tenderness, which was for him very healing.

The therapy was a clinical version of what friends had been offering him for many years, but it was not the only remedy. Nouwen also learnt how to be held in other senses – emotionally, spiritually and psychologically – but the darkness was often so deep that he had no vision of ever surviving it. He could only live by the faith of others who would tell him gently that the veil would lift. But, just as van Gogh painted masterpieces during his most melancholic phases, so Nouwen, in his months of desolation, found words flowing expressively through his pen. The 'secret' journal, which was eventually published as *The Inner Voice of Love*, disclosed how everything had come crashing down – his self-esteem, his energy to live and work, his sense of being loved, his hope for healing and his trust in God: 'I had come face to face with my own nothingness. It was as if all that had given my life meaning was pulled away and I could see nothing in front of me but a bottomless abyss'.[3] Just when people around him were assuring him of their love, care, affirmation and admiration, he had experienced himself as a useless, unloved and despicable person who had seen the endless depths of his human misery and felt that there was nothing worth living for.

Writing became a therapy, too, and almost every day, after meeting with his guides, he wrote a 'spiritual imperative', a command to himself which had emerged from the session. These were directed at his own heart where old places of pain and fearful experiences from his early years were being opened up. Despite his periods of total confusion, the notes he kept show a man of incredible faith, perspicacity, wisdom and spirituality. Throughout his exile he never became suicidal and the insights slowly drew him to an inner freedom:

Not being welcome is your greatest fear. It connects with your birth fear, your fear of not being welcome in this life, and your death fear, your fear of not being welcome in the life after this. It is the deepest fear that it would have been better if you had not lived. Here you are facing the core of the spiritual battle. Are you going to give in to the forces of darkness that say you are not welcome in this life, or can you trust the voice of the One who came not to condemn you but to set you free from fear?[4]

During his months in Winnipeg, he was visited by a number of friends including Jean Vanier, who recognised that the way in which Nouwen went through that immense suffering and came out more peaceful showed a lot about who he was. There was a greatness in his spirituality.

Other visitors included Father Don McNeill from the University of Notre Dame who believed Henri would make it: 'There was always a glint of hope in his eyes. It seemed as if he was being held and loved by God at a level which I felt was mystery.' Even when Nouwen was crying or needing to be held, his inner core trusted that God would bring him through.

In the final journal entry, Henri Nouwen told himself that he was faced with a choice. He could choose to remember his time at Winnipeg as a failed attempt to be reborn completely, or he could choose to regard it as a precious time when God had begun new things in him that would have to be brought to fruition. His future seems to have depended on how he would remember his past. He still faced a spiritual battle, and would have to ensure that his emotions did not distract him. But it was not all about words. Winnipeg had also given him the space to reflect on a painting which encapsulated the meaning of his whole life . . .

21. The Father

DURING HIS breakdown the only books which Henri Nouwen managed to read were about another Dutchman, Rembrandt van Rijn. During those bleak months he derived great consolation from studying the tormented life of the Dutch painter whose own agonising inner journey had ultimately enabled him to paint *The Return of the Prodigal Son*:

> For hours I looked at the splendid drawings and paintings he created in the midst of all his setbacks, disillusionment and grief, and I came to understand how from his brush there emerged the figure of a nearly blind old man holding his son in a gesture of all-forgiving compassion. One must have died many deaths and cried many tears to have painted a portrait of God in such humility.[1]

Just as Nouwen felt an affinity with the struggles and paintings of Vincent van Gogh, so too did he sense a connection with Rembrandt, whose psychologically penetrating work was the bitter fruit of success, loneliness, rejection and an endless stream of personal turmoil. Rembrandt's masterpiece had first captured Nouwen's attention in 1983, after an exhausting lecture tour when he was physically and mentally fatigued, alone and afraid. In the midst of his turmoil he noticed a poster on the door of an office at L'Arche in France, showing part of Rembrandt's famous painting. The embrace between father and son signified everything he wanted, both at that moment and in the years ahead. It was an image of homecoming. Just before joining Daybreak Nouwen went to the Hermitage in St Petersburg and spent hours in front of the painting, studying its every detail and relating it to his own life and longings. One of his first jobs in the new community was to hang a poster of it on the wall of his work space. Every time he looked at the depicted embrace between father and son he saw something new. For years he had instructed students on the different aspects of the spiritual life, trying to help them see the importance of living it. But had he himself really ever dared to step into the centre, kneel down and let himself be held by a forgiving God?

These thoughts recurred to him at Winnipeg as he read the parable in the Bible and studied the painting. But out of that very experience emerged insights, both about him and about the painting, which were eventually to culminate in one of his finest books. It was as though these spiritual riches could only be discovered in a state of emotional poverty. He found within the painting an enormous power, and looked at it 'from the perspective of a human being who lives a lot of pain and a lot of joy, and has a lot of yearnings, and wants to be able to get in touch with that'. The painting put him in touch with his deepest self. It became a summary of his life, but also a call for him to become something new.

Originally he identified himself with the younger son in the picture. His university teaching and involvement in South and Central American affairs had left him feeling lost. He had wandered far and wide and become part of many movements, but wanted to return home and be welcomed by his Father. Then it was pointed out to him that he might be more like the elder son. He had been the eldest child in his family, had always wanted to be a priest and never changed his mind. He had been born, baptised, confirmed and ordained into the same Church and had always been obedient to his parents, teachers, bishops and God. He had never run off or wasted his time and money on sensual pursuits – but at the same time he could recognise his own jealousy, anger, sullenness and subtle self-righteousness.

It was Sister Sue Mosteller who told him, 'Whether you are the younger son or the elder son, you have to realise that you are called to become the father'. Now was the time for him to claim his true vocation: to be a father who could welcome his children home without asking them any questions and without wanting anything from them in return. If he looked at the father in the painting, she told him, he would know who he was called to be. Daybreak needed him, not just as a good friend or as a kind brother, but as a father who could claim for himself the authority of true compassion.

So, back at Daybreak, Nouwen began to claim that spiritual fatherhood and to write the initial chapters of *The Return of the Prodigal Son*, a meditation on the themes of homecoming, affirmation and reconciliation for readers who had known loneliness, dejection, jealousy and anger. The book, dedicated to his own father for his ninetieth birthday, described the demands of 'becoming the father' in a community of mentally disabled people and their assistants, and of the 'hard and seemingly impossible task of letting go of the child in me'.[2] It also led to some revealing conclusions about his relationship with his own father:

> Recently, on looking into a mirror, I was struck by how much I look like my dad. Looking at my own features, I suddenly saw the man whom I had seen when I was 27 years old: the man I had admired as well as criticized, loved as well as feared. Much of my energy had been invested in finding my own self in the face of this person, and many of my questions about who I was and who I was to become had been shaped by being the son of this man. As I suddenly saw this man appearing in the mirror, I was overcome with the awareness that all the differences I had been aware of during my lifetime seemed so small compared with the similarities. As with a shock, I realized that I was indeed heir, successor, the one who is admired, feared, praised, and misunderstood by others, as my dad was by me.[3]

Nouwen's difficulties with his own father had prevented him from making the Father in the painting the centre of his attention: it was much easier for him to feel a bond with the two sons. But Rembrandt's portrayal made him understand that he no longer needed to use his sonship to keep his distance: he could not remain a child forever, or keep pointing to his father as an excuse for his life. Grief, forgiveness and generosity were the three ways to compassionate fatherhood. He knew he had to claim it for himself by allowing the rebellious younger

son and the resentful elder son within himself to receive the unconditional, forgiving love that the Father offered him. There he would
discover the truth of homecoming.

Just as Nouwen was grateful to Daybreak, so too was the community
grateful to him. As the second largest L'Arche community in the world,
it had experienced some difficulties in communication and Nouwen
played an influential part in overcoming them, his skills as an arbiter
coming into play. As part of the healing process he helped people
speak the truth to each other and to look more deeply into their hearts
when difficulties arose. He was a priest and a friend who was not only
trying to transform himself but the community as well. Supported by
a small group of people, he started to pick up the pieces, helping
Daybreak celebrate Advent and then writing a book for Lent. He
claimed his spiritual fatherhood and nourished the community by word
and sacrament. He was Daybreak's first full-time priest and brought a
whole new vision for L'Arche in North America. That he did not have
everything worked out did not matter. There was always an openness
to continue to go forward, as well as the recognition and acceptance
that some elements of his life were still a struggle. It was important
for him to try to heal the relationship with Nathan. Both men were
scared, but eventually there was a reconciliation and a new understanding of their friendship.

Although Nouwen returned to Winnipeg for check-ups from time to
time, he had started to feel stronger. He moved into his own room at
Daybreak's Dayspring retreat centre, which had been completed in his
absence, so his day-to-day contact with people with disabilities was
one-step removed from that of other assistants who lived in the homes.
For the first time since he joined Daybreak, he was paid a salary – the
previous year there had only been enough in the funds for his board
and lodging. He also had his own resources from his royalties which
paid for his travel expenses and his international telephone calls. He
lived modestly, though, and ran a small car. He was still accepting a
tremendous loss of privacy living in the Dayspring centre which, while
a house of retreat and prayer, could be like Grand Central Station. He
made himself available to a vast number of people, and was generous
with his time and energies – though his capacity for self-care remained

very limited. He travelled more than the Daybreak community would have liked, but they respected his vocation as a writer and a speaker.

When he began once again to accept invitations to speak all over the world, but mainly in North America, he took other members of the community with him. One of his travelling companions was Bill van Buren, who was 16 when he first came to L'Arche. Henri and Bill established themselves as a duo on the circuit – Bill did the jokes:

> As soon as Henri got up, I would take the microphone from him and talk about life at L'Arche. Then I used to say things like, 'How do you get holy water?' And Henri would ask me how you got holy water. Then I would say, 'Boil the hell out of it!'
>
> He was a good man to work with and always thanked me for the way I was with the people. He was so kind to me on trips. His greatest gift was being in community. He always brought us gifts. He used to go up to the church and I helped him with Mass. He gave me the cup and the plate for the hosts and I helped him with that. I used to pray for him every night before supper and especially when he was away, or in hospital. I started to cry when I heard he had died. He was our best pastor but also my best friend. When I die I want to be next to him. I feel he is in my heart. I know that.

Nouwen strongly believed in preaching the Gospel in pairs; after all, Jesus had sent his apostles out in twos. The audience might forget what he had said in a few days, but they would always remember the person who had come with him and that they had witnessed together. It was all about community and relationship, a prophetic means of taking the good news of L'Arche to a wider world. It was a way of allowing the unique and open gifts of core members to encounter the more defended, able-bodied members in the church or hall. They could have an experience of the Spirit through the core member who might have little to say verbally but whose presence was powerful.

By 1989, Nouwen was back on his feet, but unfortunately not for long. Early one dark winter's morning, while weaving his way through traffic across a busy icy highway near the community, he was struck by the wing-mirror of a passing truck and thrown to the ground. He had been on his way to another community house to help Hsi-Fu, who

is blind and dumb, get ready for school at 7 a.m. He had been warned
by a friend not to go because the conditions were treacherous, but he
had ignored her pleas. The driver who hit him found him crying in
pain at the side of the road. Unable to get through to the ambulance
service, the driver took him to York Central Hospital where five broken
ribs were discovered. Further tests later in the day revealed a ruptured
spleen. He had been taken in at 10.30 a.m., and by 6.30 p.m. he was
dying. The internal bleeding persisted, and Nouwen faced life-or-death
surgery, having been warned that he might not survive. He told Sue
Mosteller, who was at his bedside, that he was not afraid to die, but
was ready to go to God: 'I have had a wonderful life and I want you
to tell people how grateful I am that people have been so good to me'.
He asked her, in the event of his death, to pass on his forgiveness to
all who had hurt him, and in turn to beg forgiveness from those he
had wronged. Sue recollects his state of mind:

> He was just peaceful. His face was clear and radiant. He was not
> anguished at all. He said he was ready to go, and was surprised
> he was so peaceful about it. On a previous occasion when we had
> talked about death, he had said he was frightened of it. This was
> so different.

But he pulled through. And the following week, Nouwen's father and
sister, Laurine, flew from Holland and stayed four days. A lot of his
own inner anguish from the past was connected not only to Nathan,
but also to the relationships with his own family, in particular with his
father. One friend described the significance of that visit:

> Something very big happened when his father went to visit him
> in the hospital. It was to do with forgiveness. That's when he
> understood something in the prodigal son parable about becoming
> the father – the day he let his own father go free. He did it with
> a lot of consciousness and a lot of pain. I don't think his father
> had ever really understood his son very well, or been sensitive to
> him, even in childhood. The war was going on, his father was in
> the most important years of his career, and the Dutch culture of
> that period meant that he didn't show much affection. Henri's

heart was so sensitive that he just couldn't abide it and suffered so much.

Nouwen's experiences on the threshold of eternity inevitably provided him with inspiration for another book, *Beyond the Mirror*: 'My encounter with death told me something new about the meaning of my physical death and the lifelong dying to self that must precede it. My being sent back into life and its many struggles means, I believe, that I am asked to proclaim the love of God in a new way.'⁴ This was, perhaps, another case of reverse mission: having touched 'the other side', he could be a witness to the world of ambiguities from the place of unconditional love.

None the less when he took Carolyn and Geoff Whitney-Brown out to lunch the summer after his accident, his struggle to take up his life and work again was evident:

> He told us that what people didn't understand was that after making his peace with death and with everyone he knew, it was really hard to want to be back in all the complexity of his life. He sat in the restaurant with his arms wrapped around his head and neck, and he took off his glasses and mashed his face into different shapes, confiding earnestly, 'I get more handicapped all the time'. Then he wanted more coke and he couldn't remember that he had to invite the waitress over. He picked up his empty glass and followed her around; she knew him and kept saying, 'Sit down Henri, I'll bring it'.
>
> Then there was a moment when it all changed. He put on his glasses and leaned forward. His eyes were totally focused and alive. His whole body was at peace and attentive: 'Now tell me how you are', he said. We had corresponded but had never met, and he remembered every detail of our letters. We talked about our lives and he listened with absolute attention and deep insight. I still remember everything he said to us, and I remember, too, the respect and reverence he had for us and our life-choices. Then when we had finished, he took off his glasses, started squishing up his face again, rumpled his hair and wound his body all up in knots and we drove back to Daybreak. But this first meeting stayed in my mind as a paradigm of everything I would grow to

know and love about Henri. He had an extraordinary pastoral gift to speak God's word to others. Even when he was wrapped up in such internal anguish, his generous spirit and his gift remained intact.

22. The Way Home

IN 1990, a number of priests and friends involved with L'Arche, including Jean Vanier, came to help Nouwen discern whether Daybreak was still an appropriate long-term home for him. The process culminated in an evening to which Anglican and Catholic bishops, along with friends from many churches, were invited to the community for a formal affirmation of the pastor and renewal of his mandate. Members suggested areas in which he could grow, and he accepted their critical acclaim. Afterwards, he was not so much sent out as sent up, when talented mimics from the community presented a host of skits based on his life among them, evidence to the assembled clergy of just how loved Henri was by the community. For all his sensitivity, Nouwen could usually laugh at himself. On that occasion he was both touched and amused by the affectionate sketches: 'I didn't know you knew me so well', was his delighted response.

The spiritual life of the Daybreak community was transformed by Nouwen's energy and vision – he called people to worship together more often than they would in a church. There was a morning Eucharist five days a week, several evening services and community worship on Fridays. On Sundays people went off to their own churches. Under Henri's leadership, core members and assistants took their own spiritual journeys much more seriously than they ever had before, and received guidance from him on how best to live that out.

The Eucharist had gradually became a daily event, celebrated at 8.30 a.m. before the working day began. With his sensitivity for an appropriate liturgical setting, Nouwen decided he would prefer to have a low altar, like a long coffee-table, which would be large enough for lots of glass chalices and flowers but low enough for all the people sitting on the floor to see. With characteristic skill for bringing out the gifts of others, he invited Joe Child at the Daybreak Woodery to design and build the table – though he grew impatient because the Woodery made it slowly, fitting it in between their more pressing business contracts. When the beautiful cherrywood altar was finally completed, it exceeded the pastor's wildest hopes and he asked Joe to talk about the process of creating it from damaged wood which had been rejected and dumped in the corner of a timber yard.

After Christmas Eve Mass and the Easter Vigil he held parties in the Dayspring centre, gathering everyone for food and drink, presents and conversations until the early hours. People from all over the world sent him gifts and he delighted in sharing them with his friends. These were special occasions, because he kept the fasts of Advent and Lent earnestly. When the feast days came, therefore, they were celebrated in style.

The prophetic aspects of his leadership came not from his being on the edge of the Church but from being deeply rooted in its spirituality and traditions. Like all of his theological understanding, his views on eucharistic inclusivity grew over time and were confirmed by particular experiences, often among the oppressed and marginalised, including his life among people with developmental disabilities at L'Arche. His eucharistic theology was connected with his identity as a pastoral, rather than a systematic, Catholic theologian. His theology was always incarnational: the Church was God's body on earth and its members made God's love, justice and peace visible in the world by following the teachings of Jesus. Informing all this was his habit of mystical prayer, in which he seemed to sink deeply into the presence of God. His inclusion of people came out of this depth of contemplative prayer and connection with God's love, and out of his own integrity.

As a Catholic priest, whose mind and heart had been transformed by Vatican II, Nouwen was ecumenical in word and sacrament, reaching out to the modern world, across and within all denominations and faith traditions. Wendy Lywood, an Anglican priest and house assistant, arrived at Daybreak feeling burnt out by her parish work – she had even started to doubt her priesthood. A few months later, during Holy Week, Henri asked her to preach the homily on Maundy Thursday, 'so the community knows that you and I are both priests here'. Wendy was terrified – she still felt emotionally drained from her parish experience:

> But Henri was very encouraging and, from that time on, he was always very affirming of me as a priest. Even when I went through my own time of depression and struggle, Henri was there to encourage me that it was all part of the spiritual journey, and he drew on his own experience. When I, too, had to leave the community for a few months, he continued the support by writing and sending flowers.

Henri Nouwen had a devoted following among churches of the Anglican communion in the United States and Canada, for whom he would often lead retreats. 'I suspect he was something of a prophet for the interior unity of the Christian family, looking for the true things and the good things to come', said Henry Hill, former Anglican bishop of Ontario. 'He wasn't deeply troubled by differences in denominations because he knew we were all Christ's children.'

Nouwen believed, however, that it was important for people to make a definite choice about which branch of the Christian family they belonged to. Some at Daybreak did not have any clear affiliation, so he encouraged them to join the denomination in which they felt most rooted. Moreover, if they decided to make or renew any commitment publicly, he was there to support them.

When Carol, a woman in her late thirties who cannot talk, came from an institution to live at Daybreak as one of its least able core members, it transpired that she had never made her first communion. Henri began to help Carol prepare, but at the same time he spoke frequently to the rest of the community about the importance of the occasion for everyone. He led people in praying for Carol at community worship, awakening their sensitivity and enthusiasm for the celebration. In the end, so many attended the service that it had to be held in the meeting hall instead of the chapel. Henri made sure that Carol, in her best dress and smiling broadly, was at the very centre of it. It was an experience both of welcoming her into the communion of the

Church and at the same time into the very heart of her new community. The marginal person had moved to the centre.

Participating in the liturgy was at the heart of faithfulness and, as time went on, Henri arranged for people to exercise their own leadership in the community – for example, training core members to serve at the altar, a service they continue to carry out with a sense of respect and duty. It is their gift to the community. He also organised courses to enable others to develop their spirituality, especially during Advent and Lent, opening up the opportunity for people to live the seasons of the Church's year in more meaningful and passionate ways.

One of his first plans after the renewal of his mandate was to set up a pastoral team, enabling other members of Daybreak to develop their own ministries while at the same time supporting his. Bringing out other people's gifts and offering them for the good of the community was fundamental to his ministry. He chose 15 people to give homilies, and taught them how to present them. (When he first came, he had found it difficult to let anybody else preach.) All these people grew up to proclaim the word of God – and, even in his absence, their ministry continues: there are now 30 people, named and mandated, who give homilies at Daybreak.

Nouwen continued to be an impassioned preacher both in the context of the Mass and at other community celebrations. An assistant at the Woodery, Lorenzo Sforza-Cesarini, recalled how the homilies defined something of his mystical presence in community:

> He had a very strong way of delivering the message of Jesus from his own knowledge, and somehow by his enthusiasm he was able to capture people's minds and hearts. You might not remember his words – but the Spirit was visible in what happened between him and individuals, or a group of people.

His relationship with those with developmental disabilities tended to deepen in personal encounters as they opened up to him and he to them: 'He was like a brother to me', (David); 'He sent me a plant when my nephew died' (Peggy); 'He talked to me about my temptations; He made tapes for me so he could talk to me about my life and I know it's good for me to go into my rooms and listen to them' (Gord).

As well as answering every letter he was sent – and he received hundreds every month – Henri also wrote to the core members at Daybreak affirming their gifts and their unique place in the community. The letters form part of what are known as 'Lifebooks', a compilation of reminiscences and photographs of core members' lives. The following is part of a letter he wrote to Annie:

> Ever since I came to Daybreak you have had a very special place in my heart because of the way you look at me, and the way you call my name. You have a wonderful, loving, and endearing way of calling me by my name, and you make me feel quite special when you say, 'Yes, Henri, yes Henri'.

In a letter to Roy, he commented that 'every time I walk into the New House, where you live now, you welcome me with a big smile and say "Henri you are a good man", and that always makes me feel really good'. Henri's bonds with the core members were established not only by the warmth he showed them but also by the affirmation they gave him.

Nouwen was both gifted and prophetic in showing the community how to befriend death. At the time of the death of Maurice Gould ('Moe'), a core member with Down's syndrome who had struggled with Alzheimer's disease in his last years, Nouwen was in Freiburg working on *Our Greatest Gift*, a book about dying and caring. He flew back to Toronto to be with Moe's family and friends. As he subsequently wrote:

> Of all the days that I have lived at Daybreak, those after Moe's death belong to the most intimate, the most uniting, and, in a strange way, the most sacred. A man who, through his fragility and weakness, has helped us create community during his life did so even more through his death. As we came together in our chapel, visited the funeral home, sang and spoke in gratitude in the Anglican Church of Richmond Hill, and carried the coffin to the grave in King's City cemetery, we shared a deep sense that not only does life lead to death, but death leads to new life.[1]

Paul Tuck, a Baptist minister whose wife, Remi, worked alongside Nouwen in the Dayspring centre, also found Nouwen a spiritual strength when their daughter died suddenly in the Philippines. Nouwen was on sabbatical in New York at the time but within an hour and a half of their getting the news, they had a call from Henri in New York: 'He was right there on the phone to comfort us. We were so impressed by this because we're not Catholics. On top of that he wrote us a cheque for a very substantial amount to help pay our air ticket to the Philippines. That was Henri.'

Nouwen's generosity was legendary at Daybreak. If assistants married or had children, they often received pieces of art from him as gifts. If somebody was in a particular place of pain or joy, a basket of flowers would arrive at the door. This was not a substitute for his personal caring, but an extension and expression of it.

Nouwen was particularly keen to encourage the development of the community's interfaith outreach. Beth Porter, a long-term assistant at Daybreak, was closely involved in this work which had begun with an interest in Judaism and a desire to support Jewish members, especially in strengthening their connections with the synagogues:

> Henri started to see that this was a gift for all of us in a community with people of other faiths. When Ellen was preparing for her Bat Mitzvah, he came down and met the Jewish folks who were supporting us in the synagogue. Henri was at the Bat Mitzvah along with many other Jewish people from Daybreak. He spoke at it and wrote a beautiful little note in her Bat Mitzvah album about how meaningful the event was for all of us and how it had brought the gift of her Jewish tradition into the community. He had a great many Jewish friends. He also helped me in supporting Alia, a Muslim core member unable to speak. He invited her Muslim father to come to Daybreak during Lent, and to speak to us about Ramadan. Henri listened, and responded in a very interesting homily the next day about what he had learnt about Lent from listening to Alia's father.

Although he worked hard at developing relationships at Daybreak, there were times when the art of diplomacy was lacking. Nouwen was often unaware of his behaviour and, when people had the courage to tell him that he had overstepped the mark, he was always apologetic. Nor did his physical clumsiness lessen. Some members of the community remember being in Montreal for a meeting and inviting Henri to come the night before to settle in. But he said he did not have the time. The next morning they received a message from him saying that he would be late for the meeting. The schedule was rearranged and began without him. At 11.30 a.m. Henri came running in with a large bandage on his arm and a nasty cut on his head: 'I was hurrying into the airport this morning', he told them, 'and I realised that, when I crashed through the door, it was a window'.

Henri Nouwen had his melancholic side, but he was also a man of mirth. When Daybreak was arranging its twenty-fifth anniversary gala, he was asked to take part. He was under the impression that he was being invited to give a lecture to mark the milestone – but that was not what the organisers had in mind: they wanted him to take part in a one-minute cameo for which he had to dress as a cowboy, ride a fake horse and sing a song called 'Bound to fail, but not bound by failure'. As he commented afterwards, 'I thought they wanted me to give a lecture about spiritual things in the middle of the play, but all they wanted me to do was to make a fool of myself!'

Nouwen's energy and passion brought great joy to the community, and he loved the vitality of the place. He allowed others to tease him and to make fun of him in some ways, but this was all part of the community's appeal. He loved going out to movies with colleagues, then coming back and analysing the plot and characterisation over a bottle of wine, discussions which sometimes went on for several hours. He also enjoyed taking core members out to breakfast and talking intently with them, making them feel understood.

For six years, Henri Nouwen worked closely at Daybreak with his secretary Connie Ellis. At the end of each working day, when the office closed, they had their own routine of shutting the door, lighting cigarettes, and, over a mug of coffee or a glass of wine, sharing personal memories. Some likened it to a mother–son relationship. Henri liked to discuss his family, especially his relationship with his own mother who had died by then. Connie was always concerned about Henri driving himself too hard and would often yell at him, 'You're going to die of a heart attack if you keep up this pace!' Laughing, Henri would reply, 'I'm too slim to die of a heart attack'. Connie rejoined, 'Well, you'll give me a heart attack'. Henri never changed.

But during Holy Week in 1992, it was Connie who was taken ill. Diagnosed as having a brain tumour, she underwent surgery in St

Michael's Hospital, Toronto, on Good Friday. Henri later turned up at the hospital and unhesitatingly made his way into the intensive care unit. The family sensed that something profound had happened when they were informed that Connie was much improved and in good spirits since Henri's visit: 'We don't know what went on between Henri and Mum during those ten minutes but it was clear that she had made the decision to fight the disease and go on living', said Connie's son Steve. She left intensive care on Easter Monday, and was moved to a regular room. Henri wanted to lead the family in prayer for Connie and proceeded to light a candle at her bedside. No one realised that another patient in the same room was on oxygen – before they knew it, a nurse rushed in and blew out the candle. At first Henri was quite offended; then the incompatibility of oxygen and fire was explained to him.

Connie became stable enough to leave hospital but, in January 1994, lapsed into a coma while Henri was in Germany. The family phoned him but insisted there was no need for him to return. The following day they phoned again with the news that she was deteriorating, but discovered that Henri had already left in the middle of the night. He arrived at the hospital later that evening, as Steve remembers:

> Visiting hours were nearly over when Henri rushed in to be at Mum's side. She embraced him with all the strength she had in her one good arm, kissed him and asked, 'Why are you here?' Henri said, 'I think it's time, Connie'. Mum seemed to let go from that moment and we supported her, and let go ourselves. The brief time before Mum's death was one of the rare times when Henri was totally free and available, with no commitments or time constraints. He spent his time just being with her, caring and praying. Henri's devoted friendship is perhaps the gift we treasure most.

Henri Nouwen brought the world to Daybreak, and his presence there was by all accounts a gift. People continue to talk about him as a prophet who revealed God to them, especially in personal encounters. He seems to have been at his best with individuals, as he called forth the spiritual life of the community through each one of them. As he had done at many other stages of his pilgrimage, he invited the community to live in the struggle, talking about their lives there as being 'a home on the way home'. There would be occasions when they felt rooted, comfortable and loved, but some of the time they would feel as though they were walking through the desert until God opened up new horizons. Each person in the community had to assume some responsibility for it. Nouwen journeyed with them, finding God in unexpected places, discovering core members as his own wounded prophets.

Henri Nouwen himself acknowledged that the experience of being pastor at L'Arche touched him profoundly:

> I'm a very restless person but L'Arche became for me the place where I really came home. There's nothing in me that desires to go anywhere else. I'm still a restless person but in the deeper places of myself I really feel I've found home. In many ways the little ones, the people with limited gifts, have become for me those who have called me home. In their simplicity they reveal for me God's love.[2]

The community had taught him the meaning of gratitude: it meant to receive the gift of others. The people with developmental disabilities and the assistants allowed him to see life as a gift, especially when it seemed so fragile. But he had to keep on making the movement towards gratitude and away from resentment – the cold anger caused by not being given what he thought he needed. He had to let go of that and to discover, through the community, that there were many gifts to be given. The core members brought him in touch with his own handicaps because they were so direct:

> Once, I came home after a trip to the community house where I live, and I brought gifts home for everybody. One guy who was very direct said, 'I don't care for your gifts. I don't need more gifts. You cover me with too many gifts. I don't even have a place on the wall to put it.' And I was very, very hurt – but suddenly I realised that he was touching me in the right place, in a very painful place . . . that I'd used the gifts as a substitute for an intimacy with him that he really wanted. He opened up that place

and I realised my handicap which was that I wasn't always willing to enter into a relationship with people who asked me for it.[3]

Yet it was Nouwen's ability to bring out the gifts of each individual at L'Arche which made him such a companion 'on the way home'. Although he was often away from the community for long periods, Daybreak had enabled him to live out the role of the father in the prodigal son painting: 'At Daybreak, you have to discover your own woundedness, your own brokenness, your own limitations. You can't go home and hide. You're so open and visible. Everybody knows you in all your smallness and bigness, weaknesses and strengths, but they also love you deeply.'

23. New Directions

THROUGH HIS priesthood, his writings and his preaching, Nouwen continued to put people in touch with God, with each other and with themselves, but he seemed completely out of touch with the degree to which his unrelenting schedule was taxing his own health. A desire never to let people down created more pressure. He always took time to write meaningful inscriptions in books he sent people, and he answered every letter in a personal way. He encouraged responses from people and was always eager to know what was happening in their inner lives. But when some wrote long, detailed letters back to him, only to receive brief replies, they felt cheated. Nouwen had appeared to invite intimacy through correspondence but was not able to deal with it at the depth they expected. Clearly Nouwen could not cope with being a spiritual director on an international scale – but there were some who felt disappointed, almost betrayed, by him. On top of this was the constant telephone contact he maintained with friends around the world, through which he offered long-distance counselling.

By 1995 it had all started to conspire against him. Trying to be all things to all people, however well intentioned, became a formula for mental and physical exhaustion. He was perpetually tired and in need of sleep, started to experience chest pains and shortness of breath, and had a couple of spells in hospital after two health scares. Warned by the family doctor in Holland that, unless he changed his lifestyle, he would lose his life, he told friends that he had been examined by a doctor and that everything was fine – which it was not.

When he visited The Netherlands, he stayed in Rotterdam with his brother, Laurent, and his family. They became concerned when they realised he was not looking after himself. In a jacket which was too short for him and old shoes, Henri always looked as though he was in need of a good meal. He would arrive in Holland with at least five suitcases, loaded down with books and records. Once he fell down the escalator with all his luggage tumbling on top of him. Laurent saw at first hand his exhaustion and restlessness:

> When he came here he generally slept for three or four days – or more. He was totally exhausted. But as soon as he'd rested, he was active again and started contacting everyone by phone. We had to have a second telephone line put in just for him, otherwise our house would have been isolated for weeks.
>
> No matter how late he had been up or how many people had called him from the States in the middle of the night, he would still be up early in the morning, pacing around, praying from his breviary before going to church. He was very disciplined. He would never miss that. But he would never look after himself; he gave himself to everyone else. The only rest I think he got was writing. He needed it for his own reflections, and then realised that what he wrote could be helpful to others.

It was part of the paradox of the man that as he became physically weaker, his passion for a new spirituality of the body became stronger. His association with Rodleigh Stevens and his fellow trapeze artists became both joyful and obsessive as he flew off to Germany in search of a new world of art, community and friendship. According to Stevens, 'Henri felt the handicapped communicating a very strong message to his heart through their broken bodies and silence. We, on the other hand, were the total opposite, yet still, without mentioning a word, we were giving him a very vibrant message through our healthy, strong bodies.'

Nouwen was getting in touch with the body as never before, and realising that it told a spiritual story. It was not mere flesh but an expression of self-identity:

The real spiritual life is an enfleshed life. That's why I believe in the incarnation – that God becomes flesh, God enters into the flesh, into the body, so if you touch a body, in a way you touch the divine life. There is no divine life outside the body because God decided to dress himself in a body or to become body.[1]

It was a far cry from the teaching in the seminary where the body had been kept strictly in check. In the last years of his life there was clearly a significant development in his own understanding of the body, as illustrated in one conference speech he gave to the National Catholic AIDS Network:

I want to talk about the body, sort of a scary thing for me to talk about. What I have learned here is that the body is indeed not just a metaphor; yet I have lived the body very much as a metaphor and I'm increasingly afraid to live it as a reality, as a real place of being. I know that I have to discover what it really means to be a body, to be in the body, to be incarnate. I need to learn to be at home in myself, a temple of the Spirit, and therefore fully intimate with God, at home in my home where God dwells. At this conference I've become aware of the incredible beauty of the body. This whole pandemic has asked us to look into the innermost and most intimate places of our bodies, all the way into the cell structures, and really see this incredible, mysterious work of God.

At the same time, he became more at ease with his own sexual identity, cultivating friendships with gay men both inside and outside the Church, discovering that there were a great many more than he had ever suspected, not all of them single but many of them spiritually minded. What distressed him was that some were on the point of leaving institutional religion for good – or already had. There was still pressure on him at times to be open about his sexuality, and equal insistence from other friends to keep quiet about it. For the man who liked to be on good terms with everyone, this cannot have been easy for him. It was important for Nouwen to have friends with whom he felt secure enough to talk through his dilemmas. A former Catholic priest, Maurice Monette, and his partner, Jeff Jackson, who live in California, were concerned about his sense of inner integrity and peace.

Monette had gone to Nouwen as a friend when he himself was agonising about whether or not to leave the priesthood:

> When, in August 1984, I told Henri that I was gay, he was very
> kind, very understanding but very un-self-revealing about his own
> struggle. Within a year, however, he was seeking my help with
> his struggle over the same issue. In this process, Henri didn't
> misbehave, nor was he 'scandalous'. He was an honest searcher
> who tried to operate out of a deep integrity as he explored this
> part of himself which terrified him.

Nouwen once asked Monette to go with him to see the film *Maurice*,
based on E. M. Forster's novel about homosexuality between the classes
of English society:

> I guess he felt shy about going himself. I think he knew the
> emotional impact that it would have on him. After the movie, as
> we were driving back to L'Arche, he had to stop on the highway
> because he was sobbing uncontrollably. He was just terrified. His
> whole body was shaking. He was so caught up with the story and
> the dilemma the two main characters were living, because it was
> his. All I could do was hold him and let him cry. He was really in
> pieces.

Nouwen loved the priesthood but, at some level, felt trapped by his
obligations and responsibilities, both to the Church and to the many
people who admired and looked up to him. And yet new possibilities
and friendships, affirming the truth of his sexual identity, lay open
before him and seemed attractive and liberating. These dilemmas must
have been disorientating. There were, however, other times when he
talked humorously about what seemed like a set of impossible options
which he discussed regularly with Maurice and Jeff: the first was for
him to stay a celibate priest and 'come out' as a gay man; the second
was for him to leave the priesthood and be open to a loving non-
celibate relationship; the third was for him to remain a publicly closeted
gay priest and be open to developing a relationship – not really an
option, they thought, for a man of such integrity. But the larger weight
of society, priesthood and his persona were such that he couldn't move

on the options, even though he could see them clearly. It was a time of confusion, inner pain and joy.

At times, Nouwen wondered if some of his gay friends were trying to force him out into the open to justify their own decisions. There were private – and occasionally more open – heated exchanges with gay people who wanted him to take more of a public stance on gay issues. But, as he told a close friend, 'If I came out I would be labelled as just another gay priest writing from my sexuality and not my spirituality'.

He was acutely aware of the dangers that labels could bring, and realised that some people were so frightened by homosexuality that they would dismiss the most talented of gay people out of hand, possibly as a way of protecting themselves from realities they would rather not face. Chris Glaser, a former student of Nouwen's and a prominent gay activist, asked to dedicate to him a book of prayers, *Coming Out to God* – but Henri refused. 'He was driven by his passion for communion and he felt called by his vocation not to express that sexually but to direct it spiritually', said Glaser. 'If you read his writings about Jesus, they are a lover's conversation with Jesus, which is typical of a lot of Christian mysticism.'

In Toronto, Henri Nouwen became a close friend of a gay Roman Catholic couple, Joseph Stellpflug and David Martin, who offered him their home as a sanctuary from the public demands of his priesthood. 'He recognised our relationship as life-giving and we became a safe haven for him where he could just be himself', said David. When the couple's relationship was formalised at a Metropolitan Community Church ceremony, Henri sent them a van Gogh print with 'an incredibly beautiful letter' affirming that they were making a very solemn and holy commitment.

From 1994, Nouwen visited the couple once a month. Joseph Stellpflug – who was later dismissed as a religion teacher and lay chaplain at a Catholic high school when details of the ceremony were leaked to the archdiocese of Toronto – explained:

> He needed a place where he could let his guard down and be himself. He was so afraid that if he was outed or came out himself, it would affect his work and the number of people who would

read him. He really felt that in his professional writing he was touching liberals, conservatives, Catholics, non-Catholics – and he didn't want to jeopardise that.

With so much going on in Nouwen at so many different levels, he needed a long spell away from Daybreak to relax his body and direct his mind to his forthcoming books. In September 1995, the community sent him off on a year's sabbatical with a mandate to write, but also to cut back on the public speaking which had spiralled again since his breakdown. He was to be accountable for how he spent his time. His friends hoped that, away from Toronto, he would both rest and find the energy to write the book he had in mind on the circus. He did neither. He seemed to be in the air more than he was on the ground and he had five manuscripts on the go, but none was about the Flying Rodleighs. In a prolific burst of writing, he ended up producing *Can You Drink the Cup?*, *Bread for the Journey* and *Adam*, edited *The Inner Voice of Love* and kept a detailed journal which was published as *Sabbatical Journey*.

In the autumn of 1995, Nouwen began a three-month stay in Watertown, Massachusetts, at the home of his friends, Robert Jonas, Margaret Bullitt-Jonas and her mother Sarah Doering. Henri looked forward to having time to rest and to write. He immediately set to work on three manuscripts. 'Henri was rushing around as much as ever and, as his friend, I was very concerned about his health', explained Robert Jonas. 'He and I, along with Sue [Mosteller] and Nathan [Ball] of Daybreak, had agreed together that his stay with us should be very low profile. So I did everything I could to shield him from the relentless demands that usually plagued him. It was all with his blessing, but he found it difficult to do himself.'

For the first two months, very few people knew he was there. He had hundreds of friends in the Boston area but almost no one visited. Except for the flurry of faxes back and forth to his publishers, and the almost daily visit of the Federal Express trucks to collect manuscripts or deliver proofs, Nouwen joined the relatively quiet cycle of family life. He wrote long-hand in the mornings, spent time on the telephone and took naps in the afternoon, and had dinner with the family each evening.

But the protective barrier around him did not last. He gave out his telephone number to a few friends and they quickly passed it on to other friends. People began phoning for some word of consolation and visiting for counselling and chats. Soon his writing time in the morning became shorter and shorter. This change concerned him, but he could see no way out of the dilemma. After all, his deepest identity lay in being a priest, someone for God, for others. But he was becoming nervous and exhausted.

Jonas often reminded him about the rest that he needed and about their contract with Daybreak. Recognising also that Nouwen was not in good physical shape, Jonas enrolled him in a local health club and, for a while, Nouwen joined Jonas there to exercise three days a week. They rode stationary bicycles, jogged, swam and had saunas, but none of it really appealed to Henri. Even on the treadmill he sometimes wore earphones, absorbed in a tape by Matthew Fox on creation spirituality. Nouwen had never cared much about his physical fitness. He joked with Jonas that the health club was 'a torture room' where men and women groaned their way around a circuit.

At Christmas Nouwen spent time with his father and stayed on in Europe to celebrate Mr Nouwen's ninety-third birthday. It was the best time they had spent together, and one in which he started to reflect in both old and new ways about their relationship. In Henri's eyes, his father had been a virtuous, righteous man, a real European of the old school, but not someone with whom he had felt intimate. When his mother died, Nouwen had suddenly become aware that he hardly knew the family patriarch whom he both respected and feared. But as they grew older and became less defensive, Nouwen came to see how similar they were in terms of their style of talking, their inclination to control and their impatience. After one conflict, his father had said to him, 'As a psychologist you know everything about authoritarian fathers. Try to be happy that you have one, but don't try to change him.'

Nouwen returned to Toronto in February, on hearing that Adam Arnett had suffered a severe setback in his health. He wanted to be with the person he had cared for during his first year at Daybreak and to anoint him for his eternal journey. When Adam died, he could not stop himself gazing at his face:

Here is the man who, more than anyone else, connected me with my inner self, my community, and my God. Here is the man I was asked to care for, but who took me into his life and into his heart in such an incredibly deep way. Yes, I had cared for him during my first year at Daybreak and had come to love him so much, but he has been such an invaluable gift to me. Here is my counsellor, my teacher, and my guide, who could never say a word to me but taught me more than any book, professor, or spiritual director. Here is Adam, my friend, my beloved friend, the most vulnerable person I have ever known and at the same time the most powerful. He is dead now. His life is over. His task is accomplished. He has returned to the heart of God from which he came.[2]

Adam's unexpected death and Nouwen's own grief was a stimulus for him to write a book about the sacred person who had become for him an image of God, a severely disabled human being who had been loved by God from all eternity and sent into the world with a unique mission of healing, which was now fulfilled.

Peggy McDonnell, another close friend, offered him her converted Red Barn on her extensive farmland property at Peapack, New Jersey, where he was able to write – but also started drawing the crowds. He celebrated the Eucharist every day, at first just for Peggy and himself. But as Peggy's friends got to learn of his daily Mass, so they would join him until there were 30 people from different denominations re-examining their faith-life in the light of his liturgies and homilies. Everybody wanted to meet him personally and he would visit them in their homes.

But as Nouwen entertained people by the score and moved between communities of friendship during that last year, he became more tired and worn out by the day. Robert Jonas visited him in Peapack:

I could see he was recreating a community and a ministry there, with all that that meant. The ministry was healing for many people, but it was quietly taking its toll. Again, his sacred morning writing-time had disappeared into liturgies, conversation and counselling. Sue and Nathan were concerned too. We all knew that it was no longer a real sabbatical. Henri was working and that was destructive to him. As a friend I felt angry, and then helpless, until I realised that, really, this was his choice. If he worked himself to death doing 18-hour days, we had to accept that this was how he wanted to live his life. And perhaps how he wanted to die.

Working harder than ever on what was supposed to be a sabbatical, and travelling far to visit as many friends as he could, Nouwen seemed always to be in departure lounges that year. One of his trips took him to Santa Fe where he found a deep affinity with the work of the celebrated American artist Georgia O'Keeffe. Her struggles in relationships and in developing her own art form spoke to him of a person who had great needs for love, affection and personal support, but also for independence, freedom, solitude, space and creativity. He could also see the parallels with Vincent van Gogh and with himself. As he carried on his marathon across the States, scheduling as many reunions as possible between writing another chapter or two, his own inner questions about the future were starting to revolve around the nature of his responsibilities – what did he owe to the world and what to himself? Friends he stayed with during the spring agreed that they had never seen Nouwen so relaxed about his sexuality. It was no longer the handicap it had once seemed.

In June Nouwen spent a ten-day holiday with his father in Belgium, when he managed to get long hours of rest in the hotel – and they made the most of their time together. He travelled through Europe, visiting friends in Berlin, Frankfurt and Holland. Some commented on how quickly he became exhausted, and on his breathlessness which they attributed to the North American lifestyle of driving everywhere – but he could not walk very fast or very far. He talked a lot about Daybreak and how happy he was to have got out of the academic establishment.

Returning to Canada he learned of a remarkable discovery by his friend Diana Chambers, who had recently visited Bosnia with a group of North Americans. One Sunday morning, in a very remote rural and mainly Muslim area, the group arrived in a village just in time to participate in the church service which was held in the garage of a house. Later, they were driven further up the hillside to the old village church which had been destroyed by the Mudjaheddin. Attached to the church was a little house where the priest had lived, and inside, in the midst of the filth, mess and rubble, a familiar name jumped out at Diana from a grubby book-jacket – it was a book of Henri's: 'We couldn't work out which book it was. It was in Croatian but when we translated the title into English, it wasn't anything that we recognised. We later discovered it was an edition of *Letters to Marc about Jesus.*'

Nouwen was intrigued by the discovery. He was unaware that any of his books had been translated into Croatian. It was one of the few texts which Nouwen had originally written in Dutch for his Belgian publishers, and it coincided with the growth of secularisation in the Netherlands. 'Marc, my nephew, was never touched by the book, but now I wonder if wrote it for someone suffering in Bosnia', he commented.

Before ending his sabbatical, Nouwen returned to New Jersey and his new-found 'Red Barn Community'. During that time he gave what was to be his last interview. The journalist was Rebecca Laird, editor of *Sacred Journey: The Journal of Fellowship in Prayer.* Speaking to her about the core elements of the spiritual life, prayer, community and ministry, he summarised so much of what his own life and message had been about. He talked about prayer as the discipline of going back to the place of solitude with God and claiming your spiritual identity as the beloved of God. Its larger mystery is greater than can be grasped with emotional senses and intellectual gifts. It is necessary first to know God in order to know other people and form community with them. Community is characterised by forgiveness and celebration; it does not mean emotional harmony because we are a pilgrim people, always on the move. If people are in communion with God and in community with one another, then ministry is the natural overflow of their love:

> Ministry happens. I have done nothing here while on sabbatical to do ministry. I didn't come here to get people who mostly don't go to church to join me in prayer and the Eucharist. I just started to pray, and invited one person to join me, and these others – neighbours and friends – simply came. I'm not concerned with fixing the marriage of the one who is considering divorce or

convincing the woman who doesn't believe in Jesus. I'm here to say this is who I am, and to be there for others.[3]

During one of his last Eucharists at the Red Barn, Nouwen and his friends spoke about the courage to listen to the heart, speak from the heart and act from the heart. As he writes in *Sabbatical Journey*: 'Often we praise prophets after they are dead. Are we willing to be prophets while we are alive?'[4]

Returning to a warm welcome at Daybreak after his year away, he looked far from refreshed. Gaunt and grey, he continued to complain about fatigue. He told colleagues that he needed to change his lifestyle, and desired just to write – but it was impossible for him to change. He knew that, as soon as he went into the office, it would start all over again. The burden of resuming his public life again began to weigh heavily. That weekend he phoned his Toronto friends, Joseph Stellpflug and David Martin, in a panic, desperate to see them:

When he arrived, we started to catch up with all that had been happening, and then Henri suddenly said, 'I have to say something. I am feeling really vulnerable right now and I can't even hear what you're saying. I just need to be held.' He sat between us on the couch and we wrapped our arms round him and just held him for ten minutes. He was just so anxious and agitated, but felt safe. We later wondered if he knew he was going to die and just had to see us.

24. The Mystery of Love

In SEPTEMBER 1996, during one of Henri Nouwen's last services at Daybreak, he gave a special blessing to Joe Vorstermans whom he had appointed lay pastor to work alongside him. It was the first such appointment in the entire L'Arche movement. Joe, a Roman Catholic, had worked in the community for many years, but this appointment was directly connected to Henri's nurturing of his spiritual life:

> He was very close to me when I was struggling in my marriage, and discovering reconciliation really catapulted me forward into understanding that my life was more of a spiritual journey and less of a psychological one. Henri was also very supportive of lay ministry – it just made sense to him to have a lay pastor. Henri gave me his final blessing in the chapel in front of the community two days before he left to go back to Europe.

That same weekend Nouwen was preparing for another trip to St Petersburg where he was due to make a film version of *The Return of the Prodigal Son* for Dutch National Television. He told some friends that he felt too exhausted to go but, despite experiencing pains in his shoulders and down his arm, he ruled out a visit to the doctor's in favour of packing his bags for the night-flight from Toronto to Amsterdam. He was to meet up with the production team including executive producer Jan van den Bosch, whom he had known for some years, and they would travel to Russia later in the week. The flight arrived at Schipol on the morning of Monday 16 September and Nouwen was met by one of the team and taken to his hotel in Hilversum, where he asked to go to his room for a sleep before a meeting at the TV centre that afternoon. At about noon, he called the front desk and said he wasn't well. The manager, on seeing just how ill he looked, called for an ambulance. Nouwen talked about having pain over his heart – the emergency services told the hotel staff to keep him talking and make sure he did not lose consciousness.

Nouwen had very low blood-pressure, so the ambulance crew summoned the fire brigade, so that he could be taken out of his room horizontally and not tipped vertically. The firemen hoisted him down over the fire stairs at the side of the hotel on a hydraulic lift. Despite the gravity of the situation, it was a chaotic scene which bore all the hallmarks of the drama of Henri's extraordinary life. Specialists in intensive care confirmed that he had suffered a heart attack. His brother Paul drove straight to the hospital:

> When I saw him I thought he wasn't going to make it. He was in such a lot of pain and couldn't speak. I slept by him the first night. He said some words, but not much. But then over the next couple of days he suddenly got better, asked for a telephone and started phoning all around the world. I don't know what the bill was but it must have been enormous. I didn't see him writing, but he was reading the Bible and praying. He was sure he was getting better.

As soon as Daybreak heard the news, they agreed to send Nathan Ball to Holland to be with Henri. Meanwhile a number of his Dutch friends came to visit, among them TV producer Jan van den Bosch:

> We set a new date, two months on, for filming in Russia. He wanted to do the project desperately, and so did I. He asked me to send letters to staff at the Hermitage in St Petersburg apologising for the inconvenience of his illness. On the Thursday a psychologist visited him to explain what had happened to his heart and how he must behave in the future. Nathan and I told her jokingly, 'Well, ma'am, you don't know Henri Nouwen'. But she made him promise he would change his lifestyle. It was a

happy occasion – there was no way in the world I thought we were going to lose Henri.

His seminary friend, Louis ter Steeg, remembered him talking about the pain he had suffered. He realised that he had been in danger of dying but thought he had come through:

> He told me with a certain discontent that it had been very difficult to get a priest at his bedside. There was a non-ordained pastor, but Henri wanted a priest to administer the last sacraments. He finally got hold of a priest and made his confession. It struck me as an expression of his deep appreciation of the sacraments of the Church. If there had been an Anglican priest I think it would have been all right, man or woman, but it had to be an ordained priest.

That same Thursday Henri told Nathan, 'I don't think I will die, but if I do, please tell everyone that I'm grateful'. By the Friday Henri had been moved out of intensive care and appeared to be recovering. That evening Nathan and Jan said Night Prayer with him, from his Liturgy of the Hours office book; together they read from Psalm 91:

> He who dwells in the shadow of the Most High,
> and abides in the shade of the Almighty
> says to the Lord, 'My refuge, my stronghold,
> my God in whom I trust!'
> It is he who will free you
> from the snare of the fowler who seeks to destroy you;
> he will conceal you with his pinions
> and under his wings you will find refuge.
> You will not fear the terror of the night,
> nor the arrow that flies by day,
> nor the plague that prowls in the darkness,
> nor the scourge that lays waste at noon.[1]

As Nouwen walked with Jan van den Bosch to the hospital doors, they talked about the psalm and Henri's last words to him were, 'My God in whom I trust'. He waved goodbye from the door, went back to talk further with Nathan and then rested. But in the early hours of the morning he suffered another heart attack and was rushed back into intensive care where, despite the best efforts of a medical team, he lost consciousness and died at about 6 a.m. on Saturday 21 September 1996. Paul and Laurent Nouwen were summoned, but arrived at the hospital too late. When Henri's father arrived, he bent over to his son, kissed him and said, 'I should have been there, not you'.

Never one for half-measures, Henri had two funerals. The first took place the following Wednesday, 25 September, in the cathedral at Utrecht. Cardinal Simonis presided; sunflowers surrounded the coffin by the very steps where he had been ordained 39 years before. There were representatives from many spheres of Nouwen's life, people who had known Henri for many years – and, appropriately, there were mourners who had never met him. One woman in her thirties, for example, who had never met Nouwen, was clearly going through a deep grieving process. She had read two of his books, and they had transformed her life. It felt as though her best friend had died. In a mysterious way, and without knowing it, she represented many thousands of people the world over who thought they knew Henri Nouwen, and that he knew their struggles too. Such was the power of his writing that they felt understood and affirmed, and had established a relationship with him.

In his eulogy, Jean Vanier spoke of 'a mystery in Henri'. He had been a man of great energy, vision and insight, but also a man of great pain. Anguish had fuelled his activities and his movement. Even though in some ways he ran away from pain, at the same time he had chosen to walk through it:

> Sometimes I sensed in Henri the wounded heart of Christ, the anguish of Christ. For God is not a secure God up there telling everybody what to do, but a God in anguish, yearning for love; a God who is not understood, a God on whom people have put labels. Our God is a lover, a wounded lover. This is the mystery of Christ, the wounded lover. And somewhere that is Henri, a wounded lover, yearning to be loved, yearning to announce love.

Vanier described how Nouwen had chosen to go to L'Arche, whose ethos was to welcome people in pain because they had been rejected and abandoned: 'Was there not some mysterious relationship between Henri's own cry for love and the cry of those in L'Arche who had been rejected?' Vanier asked. L'Arche had been a gift for Henri, but Henri had been an incredible gift of Jesus to L'Arche, the gift of a priest, a compassionate friend:

> He announced something very important: that unity in our Churches will spring from the poor . . . Many will weep at his leaving because he was a sign of hope, a sign of meaning in a divided world with divided Christians. Henri brought the word which brought meaning to many . . .
>
> Many people will weep because there was something prophetic in Henri. He accepted pain, he chose to walk through pain because it is the road of all of us. To choose the cross, to walk through the cross, because never will we discover resurrection unless we walk through the cross, unless somewhere we are stripped.

The funeral brought together many people who were not comfortable in each other's presence. Healing and reconciliation were happening in the open space which Henri had left behind. It was a powerful testimony to Nouwen's life and the challenge which lay ahead to 'fill this empty space'. After the Requiem Mass, members of the L'Arche community went over to the banks of huge sunflowers and each picked one of the large stems. Then, following the coffin into the street, they began singing songs as their way of bidding farewell to their priest and friend. Outside the cathedral there was such a mixture of life, energy, people, music, grieving and flowers that stunned passers-by could only stop and look in amazement: 'It was like a circus', said one mourner, 'and so very Henri'.

The body was flown to Toronto where it was transferred to a coffin made by the Daybreak Woodery. On Friday it lay open at St Mary Immaculate Church, Richmond Hill, where Henri had often preached and where many came to pay their respects. The body was dressed in a suit and an off-white cassock. Rosary beads were in his hands and a lavender-coloured altar cloth from Latin America was draped below his waist. Photos and drawings by his handicapped friends were placed alongside him. Henri Nouwen believed strongly in the availability of the body after death so that grief could be felt and expressed. Mourners cried and prayed over a friend they had never seen so still. In gentle acts of touching, caressing and kissing, they reverenced a man who had yearned for such affection in life and who, in death, was only perhaps beginning to realise just how much he was loved. The coffin was then taken to Daybreak where a Mass was offered before an all-night vigil.

The following morning, Saturday 28 September, more than 1200 people, including Henri's family from Holland, packed into the Slovak Catholic Cathedral of the Transfiguration in Markham, Ontario. Nouwen had always been attracted to the Orthodox architectural style of the church with its grey and gold onion domes. His body lay in an open coffin at the entrance, greeting friends who had travelled from all over North America for the three-hour service. Jewish friends quietly prayed the Kaddish as the coffin was brought up the central aisle by the family and on to the rotunda. Children carried vases of sunflowers and irises. As the presiding bishop sprinkled water over the coffin, one of the core members gave out a great cry of anguish. The emotions were soothed by Taizé chants, Latin American music and the flute playing of Henri's niece, Sara. There were opening speeches and readings from members of the family and from Nathan Ball. United in sorrow and love, people from every category of life grieved for a person who had touched their lives in so many different ways. Only Henri could have managed to get them together under the same roof – so wide was his embrace. Each intercession illumined a sphere of his concern and influence. And there were many of them.

In a tribute, Sue Mosteller described Nouwen as a man of com-passion, a man of the word and a man of the Eucharist:

> We have only to look around this church to see the ways in which he built bridges between us and brought us together: rich and poor, from north and south, from family in Holland to family in Canada, from differing backgrounds, cultures and religious denominations. Henri brought us together. Each of us met him, or heard him, and we said, 'It is good. Give us more.' We read his books and we said 'It is good. Give us more.' Now he has left us and it is the time for us to take responsibility for the spirituality he gave us. If we enter into the privileged and very sacred centre of our hearts and listen to God's Spirit who is living there, we will hear the message that Henri was sent to teach us: don't be afraid

of your pain, choose to love when relationships are difficult, choose to believe when hope is flagging, help each other, step through wounded and bitter feelings to be in union with one another, forgive each other from your hearts because God is near, calling each one of us, 'Beloved'. This call to step out of our spiritual adolescence is Henri's legacy.

The gospel reading was the parable of the prodigal son. The church hierarchy had stressed privately that only Roman Catholics should receive the sacraments but nobody was refused. A Presbyterian friend observed:

> When I received the body and blood of Christ, I happened to be in the line that drank from the golden chalice passed down to Henri from his Uncle Anton. After I returned to my seat, I noticed a male celebrant and a female acolyte walk over to two Anglican bishops – a man and a woman – join hands with them and pray for the unity of the Church. I was able to receive Communion because my being a Protestant was unknown; they were there in their official capacities and could not. This moved me deeply and then I looked up and realised those gathered around Henri represented many groups the Church failed to include adequately.

Henri's coffin was taken from the cathedral to its resting-place in land belonging to the Sacred Heart Catholic Church at King City, Ontario, surrounded by Canadian hemlocks and close to the graves of an order of 'restless' Augustinians. The burial plot was decorated with sunflowers, flowering plants, a sheltered candle, an angelic statue draped in green rosary beads and a double white cross. In a traditional custom, Jewish friends placed small stones on the grave.

Friends observed that the Catholic Church wanted to own Henri more in death than it had in life, trying to insist that he was buried on Catholic-owned land. But in the end some kind of compromise had to be reached because Henri had wanted to be laid to rest where non-Catholic members of the community could later join him. They were given a plot on the edge of the cemetery, and there is the possibility of buying some land behind where other members of the Daybreak community may one day be buried.

That same month, copies of Henri Nouwen's latest book, *The Inner Voice of Love*, arrived at the Daybreak office. As colleagues turned the pages, one entry sprang out. He had entitled it 'Bring Your Body Home', and that was exactly what had happened:

You have never felt completely safe in your body. But God wants to love you in all that you are, spirit and body. Increasingly, you have come to see your body as an enemy that has to be conquered. But God wants you to befriend your body so that it can be made ready for the Resurrection. When you do not fully own your body, you cannot claim it for an everlasting life.

How then do you bring your body home? By letting it participate in your deepest desire to receive and offer love. Your body needs to be held and to hold, to be touched and to touch. None of these needs is to be despised, denied, or repressed. But you have to keep searching for your body's deeper need, the need for genuine love. Every time you are able to go beyond the body's superficial desires for love, you are bringing your body home and moving toward integration and unity.

In Jesus, God took on human flesh. The Spirit of God overshadowed Mary, and in her all enmity between spirit and body was overcome. Thus God's spirit was united with the human spirit, and the human body became the temple destined to be lifted up into the intimacy of God through the Resurrection. Every human body has been given a new hope, of belonging eternally to the God who created it. Thanks to the Incarnation, you can bring your body home.[2]

Epilogue

IN HIS BOOK *Our Greatest Gift*, Henri Nouwen wrote that, in our dying, we become parents of generations to come. This was particularly true of many holy people who, even through weakness, had given us a view of God's grace. Their lives and deaths were still 'bearing fruit in our lives. Their joy, hope, courage, confidence, and trust haven't died with them but continue to blossom in our hearts and the hearts of the many who are connected with us in love.'[1]

In the time since Nouwen's own death, there has been an upsurge of interest in his books which are selling around the world in greater numbers than ever before. The Henri Nouwen Literary Centre, set up in his memory at Daybreak, deals daily with enquiries from people in many countries, and is clearly witnessing the fruits of his lifelong endeavours. Henri Nouwen Societies have been formed in North America and Holland, while retreats and conferences are doing much to evaluate his work and legacy. In early 1999 the first doctoral seminar on the life and work of Henri Nouwen began at Drew University, New Jersey. Focusing on Nouwen's mystical theology, it is believed to be the first of its kind. Meanwhile, students, notably from Protestant backgrounds, still write theses about his work. His influence is set to continue well into the twenty-first century, but it is still too early to define his place in the history of Christian spirituality.

Undoubtedly Henri Nouwen was one of the most remarkable spiritual figures of his generation, above all a charismatic priest who powerfully mediated the presence of God both through his life and through his writings. But he was also a man with wounds, which became a source of healing for many people. He lived the spiritual life through his struggles and encouraged other people to live it through theirs. He was not a harmonious person who had everything in perfect balance. He lived with tensions.

As an author, he had words for the age, enabling others to find – and be found by – God. He recognised the spiritual thirst of the times and could offer reassurance where there seemed only disillusionment. He managed to communicate highly complex theological ideas and concepts in ways which were effectively structured and simply stated, but none the less profound. He was a theologian who prayed, his words coming from both heart and mind. He called people to a living theology of encounter and community, where relationships with God and one another could be empowered and built up. His books describe the ways in which readers can begin to embrace that vision. Nouwen himself was someone through whom people encountered the mystery of God and the mystery of love. He described this 'prophetic vision' as 'looking at people and this world through the eyes of God'.[2]

'Spiritual' is the most important word in Henri Nouwen's vocabulary, and one with which he will always be associated. Part of his particular genius was that he not only transcended religious divisions, appealing to all Christians, but that he also drew people from other faith traditions – as well as those who did not follow any spiritual path at all. He was a faithful priest from a traditional Roman Catholic background who broke through the denominational barriers. People of whatever religious persuasion discovered through him a way to the heart of God. While careful not to be seen making public gestures which might embarrass the Church, his understanding of the Eucharist as a gift to the whole of humanity was ecumenically prophetic. His entire life and ministry were shaped by the Mass which he celebrated as an experience of reconciliation and transformation. That he could happily receive the sacrament from an Anglican woman priest in certain pastoral contexts said much about both his eucharistic theology and his ecclesiology.

He had his flaws and shortcomings but was essentially a person of intelligence, integrity and compassion. An inner intensity drove him, resulting at times in behaviour which was dramatic, demanding and temperamental. Some people found him manipulative, obsessive and egocentric, traits which cannot be denied. At times he seemed oblivious to his behaviour, perhaps because, at a fundamental level, it arose from the part of him that needed to be loved and admired. As one person put it, 'He got more affirmation than anyone I know' – but it was never enough. The truth that he was loved, not only by his many and most critical of friends, but by the scores of readers who wrote to him every week, seemed to make little difference.

This deep-seated anxiety had surfaced early in childhood and was heightened by his relationship with his father. It also accounted for much of the loneliness which accompanied his pioneering work in such places as Nijmegen, Menninger, Notre Dame, Yale and Harvard, as well as in Central and Latin America. This wound of love was both the root of his creativity and the source of his despair. It was only after he had made the audacious move from high-profile academia to the hiddenness of L'Arche that he could finally confront the truth about himself as a deeply wounded healer. For the first time in his life he started to consider the nature of his own vulnerability, and began to accept it fully as a reality. But this happened in response to a distinct sense of calling and it came about primarily because he wanted to find a place where he could live the spiritual life more radically and with more integrity. His faithfulness to God through those difficult years, and his own desire to change, gradually resulted in a more integrated individual, less inhibited and more at one with himself. The poor in spirit became his teachers: from them he learnt most about God's love and the presence of God in his heart.

It would nevertheless have been difficult for any one community – or any one person – to have contained the ever-restless Henri Nouwen, who was not a man to be controlled at any time of his life, even though there were those along the way who tried it. He was a priest restlessly searching for love and liberty.

During his final years, he discovered a joyful freedom with a travelling circus troupe, where he could forget about people's expectations of him; the experience engaged both his child-like wonder and his theological wisdom in creative new ways. The trapeze was a simple, yet powerful metaphor for the spiritual life: it was about letting go and being caught. At one level Nouwen was obviously the flyer who needed to be caught and held – but at another he was very much the catcher, in the way in which he received people unconditionally and non-judgementally, being present to them with a spirit which gave them security and confidence and pointed them to something beyond. They were born in the heart of God and would be held in the arms of God for eternity. Their lifespan was an opportunity to express gratitude for the love which had caught them. The image of the catcher was also one he used when he was ministering to the bereaved. Death was not the last word, and resurrection not merely a theological concept, but a conviction that God had caught the person who had died. He could communicate all of this in ways which consoled and uplifted those who were grieving. As he himself put it:

> Dying is trusting in the catcher. To care for the dying is to say, 'Don't be afraid. Remember that you are the beloved child of God. He will be there when you make your long jump. Don't try to grab him; he will grab you. Just stretch out your arms and hands and trust, trust, trust'.[3]

Such captivating insights also opened up a new appreciation of the incarnation: the spiritual life as the enfleshed life. There was a beauty in it which helped him feel more comfortable with his own body and, in turn, to be more relaxed about his own sexual identity. Just as intellectual formation could not be separated from spiritual formation, so he came to see that spirituality and sexuality were not rival forces, but gifts from the same source. In his BBC interview in 1992, he said that he wanted to write more explicitly about sexuality, but in order to do that well he had to speak about it with language which came from the place of mysticism and not just the place of morality. The whole issue of sexuality was about communion, involving bodies, minds and hearts:

> Every human being lives a sexual life, whether you're celibate, married or whatever. Sexual life is life, and it has to be lived as a life that deepens our communion with God and with our fellow human beings. If it doesn't, then it can be harmful. I haven't found the right language for it yet but I hope I will one day.

Had he lived, Henri Nouwen's next major work may well have been a study of homosexuality, a story of the heart, the mind and the body.

He read about the matter voraciously and questioned many people, even alerting publishers to his plans. He told friends that he wanted to write about it thoroughly and when he was emotionally free to do so. Some wanted him to avoid writing about homosexuality, suggesting that it could have far too many repercussions. It would have indubitably brought him close to his own personal struggles, and he would probably have wanted to be more open about himself than some of his friends would have advised. Emerging from his own pen, in his own lifetime, such self-disclosure would clearly have been a risk – though the nature of his sexuality is implicit in a number of his books, especially those written in the last decade of his life. He did, however, leave unpublished writings on sexuality and spirituality which a number of academics are now hoping will be edited and published.

The sabbatical in the last year of his life was a time for weighing up the options about his future and he may well have been on the verge of making radical changes. He had planned to retire to an apartment, which would have been built on to the Dayspring centre at L'Arche, so he could enjoy the privacy of his own home within the community – but he probably wouldn't have been found there that often. His final year, while relentless in terms of travelling, writing and supporting other people, gave him some time to reflect on his worldwide reputation which was starting to stifle him. He appreciated the esteem in which he was held as a Catholic priest, a spiritual writer and the pastor of a community of people with developmental disabilities. But he began to feel restricted and pressurised to live up to the many different expectations of him, including those of the Church, L'Arche, his family and friends, and his readers. He felt caught because he believed there was some kind of agenda that he had to follow in order to be faithful. As he writes in his last book, *Sabbatical Journey*:

> Since I am in my sixties, new thoughts, feelings, emotions, and passions have arisen within me that are not all in line with my previous thoughts, feelings, emotions, and passions. So I find myself asking, 'What is my responsibility to the world around me, and what is my responsibility to myself? What does it mean to be faithful to my vocation? Does it require that I be consistent with my earlier way of living or thinking, or does it ask for the courage

to move in new directions, even when doing so may be disappointing for some people?"⁴

Henri Nouwen was always torn between the meaning of his spiritual calling and his own psychological needs and longings. He could not integrate them, except in his books – and then not with complete openness. He knew that he taught best those things which he needed to learn most – which is one reason why so many people thought he was accompanying them on their spiritual journeys. He had an extraordinary skill, both in literary and pastoral terms, of making people feel he was connecting with them personally. This was always authentic, but it may also have been part of his great hunger for intimacy, even though intimacy scared him. He was a man with a multitude of friendships, some of which became for him experiments of trust as he tried to get close and test the waters of reciprocation. His demands proved too overwhelming for a number of people, yet at the same time he seems to have kept hidden from some of his closest friends episodes of his life which he would share with strangers. This might have been another reason why his writings seemed so personal: he preferred to be intimate at a distance.

Despite this well of inner conflict and confusion (and probably because of it), he was an outstandingly inspiring spiritual guide for the Church and for the world, who not only transformed people's lives but brought God into them. His message focused on God's reaching out to embrace the belovedness, uniqueness and vulnerability of each individual person, and hoping for an intimate relationship in return. Because of his wounds he was able to be a prophet – in his priesthood, his writing, his teaching, his public speaking alongside the disabled, his work for justice and peace, his ministry to those with HIV and AIDS and, towards the end of his life, his clear support of faithful gay relationships, especially among Roman Catholics. As a priest who was also a clinical psychologist, he understood Carl Jung's view that homosexual people are often endowed with an abundance of religious feelings, creating a spirituality which makes them responsive to revelation; while as a mystic he empathised with St Teresa of Avila who said that the journey to God was also a journey to the self, a movement into self-knowledge. Like many mystics, Henri Nouwen was in tune with the energy of divine life, passionate about Jesus and committed to speaking words of hope from his own mysterious anguish. It was a vocation for connecting the spiritual with the earthbound.

While something of a boundary figure in the world of contemporary spirituality, he remained a faithful priest of the Church and it is true that he never really put himself on the line in the manner of biblical or even modern-day prophets, fearlessly proclaiming what he believed without considering the consequences: he was too cautious and anxious for that. But in the sense that prophets are people who cannot be controlled or assimilated by human ideologies and systems, who judge and love the world by divine standards of justice and compassion, Nouwen was a prophet. The fact that he was often overlooked and criticised by his fellow Dutch priests, and at times experienced the indifference of his own family, meant that he could vow to the truth of Jesus' words that 'prophets are not without honour except in their own country and in their own house' (Matt. 13:5). However, towards the end of his life, there was more of an appreciation of him in Holland, and his family are now reading his books with greater conviction. His brothers in Rotterdam say that, since his death, they have been challenged and changed by his words.

It was in Holland that it all began and in Holland, too, that it ended – a life which had all the swirl, colour, contradiction and transcendent mystery of Vincent van Gogh's *The Starry Night*. There were always countervailing forces of brightness and darkness but, as with the painting, the spiritual remained at the centre: 'Through his oils and pastels he was able to unite the visible world with the world of his heart' – a description of van Gogh which could so easily apply to Nouwen in his own unique way.[5]

Both were highly sensitive mystics of great creativity and great suffering who revealed God in new ways. It was Nouwen himself who remarked of the artist, 'This deeply wounded and immensely gifted Dutchman brought me in touch with my own brokenness and talents in ways nobody else could.'[6] There are many across the world who feel the same way about Henri.

Blessing

May the face
of Our Lord
Jesus shine
upon you
and bring you
joy and peace

Henri Nouwen

Notes

Prologue

1. Henri J. M. Nouwen, Foreword to Cliff Edwards, *Van Gogh and God* (Chicago, Loyola University Press, 1989), p. x.
2. ibid. pp. ix and x.
3. From an interview with Brian Stiller, included in *A Tribute to Henri Nouwen*, a video compilation from the Cross Currents Vision TV series, Windbourne Productions.
4. Carolyn Whitney-Brown, Introduction to the memorial edition of Henri J. M. Nouwen, *The Road to Daybreak* (London, Darton, Longman and Todd, 1997), p. xii.

Encounter

1. Michael Hollings, Preface to Henri J. M. Nouwen, *Reaching Out* (London, Fount, 1980), p. 12.
2. ibid.
3. *Seeds of Faith* (interview by Michael Ford for BBC Radio 4, transmitted Sunday 11 July 1993; producer, Norman Winter).

1. Mystical Path

1. Henri J. M. Nouwen, *In the Name of Jesus* (London, Darton, Longman and Todd, 1989), pp. 30–31.
2. Henri J. M. Nouwen, *With Burning Hearts* (London, Geoffrey Chapman, 1994), pp. 93–4.
3. *In the Name of Jesus*, p. 46.
4. Henri J. M. Nouwen, *Here and Now* (London, Darton, Longman and Todd, 1994), p. 8.
5. Henri J. M. Nouwen, *The Return of the Prodigal Son* (London, Darton, Longman and Todd, 1994), p. 17.
6. *Here and Now*, p. 75.

7. ibid.

8. ibid.

9. Fred Bratman and Scott Lewis, *The Reader's Companion* (New York, Hyperion, 1994), p. 74.

10. ibid.

11. Henri J. M. Nouwen, *Clowning in Rome* (New York, Image, 1979), p. 88.

12. As described in Henri J. M. Nouwen, 'Pilgrimage to the Christian East, Ukrainian Diary Part 1', *New Oxford Review* (April 1994), p. 14.

2. Deep Wells

1. Henri J. M. Nouwen, *Bread for the Journey* (London, Darton, Longman and Todd, 1996), p. 136.

2. ibid. p. 137.

3. Todd Brennan 'A Visit with Henri Nouwen', *The Critic* (Summer 1978), pp. 43–4.

3. High Wires

1. *Angels over the Net* (The Company, Spark Productions, 1995).

2. *Clowning in Rome*, p. 2.

3. ibid. pp. 2–3.

4. Yale Divinity School archives.

5. *In the Name of Jesus*, p. 37.

6. Henri J. M. Nouwen, 'Circus Diary Part 1', *New Oxford Review* (June 1993), pp. 11 and 12.

7. Henri J. M. Nouwen, 'Circus Diary Part 2', *New Oxford Review* (July–August 1993), p. 7.

8. ibid. p. 10.

9. *Angels over the Net*.

4. The Dance

1. Henri J. M. Nouwen, *Creative Ministry* (New York, Image, 1991), p. 34.

2. ibid.

3. ibid. p. 35.

4. ibid. p. 40.

5. Henri J. M. Nouwen, *A Cry for Mercy* (New York, Orbis, 1994), p. 85.

5. Backstage

1. Henri J. M. Nouwen, *The Inner Voice of Love* (London, Darton, Longman and Todd, 1997), p. 67.

6. The Wounded Healer

1. Carl Jung, *Memories, Dreams, Reflections* (London, Fontana Press, 1995 edition), p. 156.
2. Quoted in Henri J. M. Nouwen, *The Wounded Healer* (London, Darton, Longman and Todd, 1994), pp. 81–2.
3. *The Wounded Healer*, p. 84.
4. ibid. p. 84.
5. ibid. pp. 84–5.
6. ibid. p. 87.
7. ibid. p. 88.
8. John McFarland, 'The Minister as Narrator', *The Christian Ministry* (January 1987), p. 20.
9. Henri J. M. Nouwen, *The Road to Daybreak* (London, Darton, Longman and Todd, 1989), p. 53.
10. *The Inner Voice of Love*, p. 91.
11. 1 Peter 2:24, The Holy Bible, New Revised Standard Version (Oxford, Oxford University Press).
12. Vera Phillips and Edwin Robertson, *The Wounded Healer* (London, SPCK, 1984), from the Introduction, pp. vii and viii.
13. ibid. pp. 103–4.

7. Visions of Justice and Peace

1. Henri J. M. Nouwen, 'A Pilgrimage to Selma', Yale Divinity School Archives.
2. ibid.

8. The Gift of Friendship

1. *Bread for the Journey*, p. 98.

9. A Priest is Born

1. Henri J. M. Nouwen, *In Memoriam* (Notre Dame, Indiana, Ave Maria Press, 1984), pp. 15–16.
2. Henri J. M. Nouwen, *A Letter of Consolation* (Dublin, Gill and Macmillan, 1983), p. 20.
3. ibid. pp. 45–7.

10. Holy Ground

1. Henri J. M. Nouwen, *Can You Drink the Cup?* (Notre Dame, Indiana, Ave Maria Press, 1996), p. 15.
2. Henri J. M. Nouwen, *The Genesee Diary* (London, Darton, Longman and Todd, 1995), pp. 95–6.

3. *Can You Drink the Cup?*, pp. 16–17.
4. ibid. pp. 109–10.

11. A Meeting of Minds

1. Henri J. M. Nouwen, *Beyond the Mirror* (New York, Crossroad, 1992), pp. 41–2.
2. Henri J. M. Nouwen, *Notes on Anton Boisen* (Yale Divinity School archives).
3. ibid.
4. *The Genesee Diary*, p. 15.
5. Seward Hiltner, 'Pastoral Theologian of the Year', *Pastoral Psychology* 27 (Fall 1978), pp. 4–7.

12. Connections

1. Henri J. M. Nouwen, Donald P. McNeill and Douglas A. Morrison, *Compassion* (London, Darton, Longman and Todd, 1982), pp. 19–20.
2. *The Genesee Diary*, p. 68.

13. The Art of the Teacher

1. Roland H. Bainton, *Yale and the Ministry* (San Francisco, Harper & Row, 1957), p. xi.
2. John Mogabgab, 'The Spiritual Pedagogy of Henri Nouwen', *Reflection*, (vol. 78, no. 2, January 1981).
3. ibid.
4. ibid.
5. ibid.
6. Henri J. M. Nouwen, Introduction to Yushi Nomura, *Desert Wisdom* (New York, Doubleday, 1982), p. ix.
7. *In Memoriam*, p. 61.

14. Silent Cloisters

1. *The Genesee Diary*, p. 14.
2. ibid. p. 52.
3. ibid. pp. 65–6.
4. ibid. p. 131.
5. Thomas Merton, *Learning to Love*, vol. 6 of *The Journals of Thomas Merton* (HarperSanFrancisco, 1997), p. 232.
6. *The Genesee Diary*, p. 184.

15. The Mission

1. Henri J. M. Nouwen, *¡Gracias!* (New York, Orbis, 1993), p. 1.
2. ibid. pp. 2–3.

3. ibid. p. 17.
4. ibid. p. 110.
5. Henri J. M. Nouwen, Foreword to Gustavo Gutiérrez, *We Drink from Our Own Wells* (London, SCM, 1984), p. xvi.
6. ibid. p. xx.
7. ibid. p. xxi.

16. Brainstorms

1. 'Faces of Faith: Henri Nouwen', interview by Arthur Boers, *The Other Side* (September/October 1989).
2. Henri J. M. Nouwen, *Love in a Fearful Land* (Notre Dame, Indiana, Ave Maria Press, 1985), p. 107.
3. *The Other Side* (interview – see note 1 above).

17. Icons

1. Henri J. M. Nouwen, *Behold the Beauty of the Lord* (Notre Dame, Indiana, Ave Maria Press, 1987), p.14.

18. Slowly Through the Forest

1. Henri J. M. Nouwen, Foreword to Thomas Philippe, *The Contemplative Life* (New York, Crossroad, 1991), pp. vii and viii.
2. ibid.
3. *The Road to Daybreak*, p. 222.
4. ibid. p. 99.
5. ibid. p. 99.
6. ibid. p. 216.
7. *Seeds of Faith* (interview by Michael Ford for BBC Radio 4).

19. Rite of Passage

1. Henri J. M. Nouwen, *Adam* (London, Darton, Longman and Todd, 1997), pp. 34–5.
2. ibid. p. 36.
3. ibid. p. 38.
4. ibid. p. 65.

20. Inner Darkness

1. *The Inner Voice of Love*, pp. x and xi.
2. *The Road to Daybreak*, p. 223.
3. *The Inner Voice of Love*, p. ix.
4. ibid. p. 84.

21. The Father

1. *The Return of the Prodigal Son*, p. 21.
2. ibid. p. 137.
3. ibid. pp. 123–4.
4. *Beyond the Mirror*, p. 55.

22. The Way Home

1. Henri J. M. Nouwen, *Our Greatest Gift* (New York, HarperCollins, 1994), pp. xv and xvi.
2. *Seeds of Faith* (interview by Michael Ford for BBC Radio 4).
3. ibid.

23. New Directions

1. *Angels Over the Net* (film).
2. *Adam*, p. 87.
3. Rebecca Laird, Interview with Henri Nouwen, *Sacred Journey, The Journal of Fellowship and Prayer* (vol. 47, no. 6, December 1996), p. 14.
4. Henri J. M. Nouwen, *Sabbatical Journey* (London, Darton, Longman and Todd, 1998), p. 221.

25. The Mystery of Love

1. From *The Psalms: A New Translation* (England, The Grail, 1963); as quoted in *Christian Prayer, The Liturgy of the Hours* (The Daughters of St Paul, 1976).
2. *The Inner Voice of Love*, p. 17.

Epilogue

1. *Our Greatest Gift*, p. 98.
2. *The Return of the Prodigal Son*, p. 17.
3. *Our Greatest Gift*, p. 67.
4. *Sabbatical Journey*, p. 168.
5. Dennis Billy, *Under the Starry Night* (Notre Dame, Indiana, Ave Maria Press, 1997), p. 13.
6. *Van Gogh and God*, p. x.

Bibliography

Intimacy: Pastoral Psychological Essays (Fides, 1969; Harper & Row, 1981)

Creative Ministry: Beyond Professionalism in Teaching, Preaching, Counseling, Organizing and Celebrating (Doubleday, 1971)

With Open Hands (Ave Maria, 1972, new revised edition, 1995)

Thomas Merton: Contemplative Critic (Fides, 1972; Harper & Row, 1981)

The Wounded Healer: Ministry in Contemporary Society (Darton, Longman and Todd, new edition, 1994)

Aging: Fulfillment of Life, co-authored with Walter Gaffney (Doubleday, 1974)

Out of Solitude: Three Meditations on the Christian Life (Ave Maria, 1974)

Reaching Out: The Three Movements of the Spiritual Life (Fount, new edition, 1996)

The Genesee Diary: Report from a Trappist Monastery (Darton, Longman and Todd, new edition, 1995)

The Living Reminder: Service and Prayer in Memory of Jesus Christ (Seabury, 1977; Harper & Row, 1983)

Clowning in Rome: Reflections on Solitude, Celibacy, Prayer and Contemplation (Doubleday Image, 1979)

In Memoriam (Ave Maria, 1980)

The Way of the Heart: Desert Spirituality and Contemporary Ministry (Darton, Longman and Todd, third edition, 1999)

Making All Things New: An Invitation to the Spiritual Life (Harper & Row, 1981)

A Cry for Mercy: Prayers from the Genesee (Doubleday, 1981)

Compassion: A Reflection on the Christian Life, co-authored with Donald P. McNeill and Douglas A. Morrison (Darton, Longman and Todd, 1982)

A Letter of Consolation (Harper & Row, 1982)

¡Gracias!: A Latin American Journal (Harper & Row, 1983; Orbis, 1992)

Love in a Fearful Land: A Guatemalan Story (Ave Maria, 1985)

In the House of the Lord: The Journey from Fear to Love (Darton, Longman and Todd, 1986)

Behold the Beauty of the Lord: Praying with Icons (Ave Maria, 1987)

Letters to Marc About Jesus (Darton, Longman and Todd, 1988)

The Road to Daybreak: A Spiritual Journey (Darton, Longman and Todd, 1989; memorial edition, 1997)

Circles of Love: Daily Readings with Henri J. M. Nouwen, edited by John Garvey (Darton, Longman and Todd, 1988)

The Primacy of the Heart: Cuttings from a Journal, edited by Lewy Olfson (St Benedict Center, 1988)

Seeds of Hope: A Henri Nouwen Reader, edited by Robert Durback (Darton, Longman and Todd, 1989, new edition, 1998)

In the Name of Jesus: Reflections on Christian Leadership (Darton, Longman and Todd, 1989)

Heart Speaks to Heart: Three Prayers to Jesus (Ave Maria, 1989)

Beyond the Mirror: Reflections on Death and Life (Crossroad, 1990)

Walk with Jesus: Stations of the Cross (Illustrations by Sr Helen David; Orbis, 1990)

Show Me the Way: Readings for Each Day of Lent, edited by Franz Johna (Darton, Longman and Todd, 1993)

The Return of the Prodigal Son: A Story of Homecoming (Darton, Longman and Todd, 1994)

Life of the Beloved: Spiritual Living in a Secular World (Hodder and Stoughton, 1993)

Jesus and Mary: Finding Our Sacred Center (St Anthony Messenger Press, 1993)

Our Greatest Gift: A Meditation on Dying and Caring (Hodder and Stoughton, 1994)

With Burning Hearts: A Meditation on the Eucharistic Life (Geoffrey Chapman, 1994)

Here and Now: Living in the Spirit (Darton, Longman and Todd, 1994)

Path Series: *The Path of Waiting / The Path of Power / The Path of Peace* (Darton, Longman and Todd, 1995); *The Path of Freedom* (Crossroad, 1995)

Ministry and Spirituality: Three Books in One (Continuum, 1996)

Can You Drink the Cup? The Challenge of the Spiritual Life (Ave Maria, 1996)

The Inner Voice of Love: A Journey Through Anguish to Freedom (Darton, Longman and Todd, 1997)

Bread for the Journey: Thoughts for Every Day of the Year (Darton, Longman and Todd, 1997)

Spiritual Journals: Three Books in One (Continuum, 1997)

Adam: God's Beloved (Darton, Longman and Todd, 1997)

The Road to Peace: Writings on Peace and Justice, edited by John Dear (Orbis, 1998)

Sabbatical Journey (Darton, Longman and Todd, 1998)

Index